GREEN
POLITICS
IN AUSTRALIA

GREEN POLITICS
IN AUSTRALIA

EDITED BY DREW HUTTON • WITH A FOREWORD BY JAMES MCCLELLAND

A collection of essays by DREW HUTTON • BOB BROWN • JO VALLENTINE
• ARIEL SALLEH • BURNAM BURNAM • JACK MUNDEY • MERV PARTRIDGE
• NOEL GOUGH • JOHN CRIBB • DUDLEY LEGGETT

ANGUS
& ROBERTSON
PUBLISHERS

ANGUS & ROBERTSON PUBLISHERS

Unit 4, Eden Park, 31 Waterloo Road,
North Ryde, NSW, Australia 2113, and
16 Golden Square, London W1R 4BN,
United Kingdom

First published in Australia
by Angus & Robertson Publishers in 1987

National Library of Australia
Cataloguing-in-publication data.

Green politics in Australia.

ISBN 0 207 15624 7.

1. Conservationists—Australia. 2. Conservationists—
Australia—Political activity. 3. Conservation of
natural resources—Political aspects—Australia. I.
Hutton, Drew, 1947-   .

333.7'2'0994

Typeset in 12 pt Bembo by Midland Typesetters
Printed in Australia by Australian Print Group

CONTENTS

FOREWORD

Recently an earth-shattering announcement was made by Senator Graham Richardson: he had become a conservationist convert.

This born-again Greenie, who would have trouble distinguishing a melaleuca from a marguerite and who is widely regarded as one of the most cynical of "Labor" politicians, often referred to as the "numbers man" of the Hawke government, was really signalling nothing more than that the message of the environmentalists had at last got through to the pragmatists of the Labor Party. Not to put too fine a point on it, there are a lot of votes in a pro-environmentalist stance.

We can rest assured that, under its present minders, the Labor Party will never carry its new-found environmentalism too far. Beneath the veneer of its pro-conservation stance the traditional developmentalists fight a rearguard action. Tensions persist, manifested by the determination of some powerful figures in the Party to permit mining in the Kakadu National Park or to work out some compromise with the woodchip industry on New South Wales' south coast.

In the past there have been many great contests, in which the heroic figure of Jack Mundey has been the shining light, directed against the despoliation of the urban environment: Kellys Bush, the Rocks, Woolloomooloo, Victoria Street, Kings Cross were merely some of the battles won by the Green movement.

But despite its good record in the expansion of national parks and the preservation of rainforests, the Labor Party, especially in New South Wales, has sold the pass in the cities. The shape of Sydney especially is being determined by greedy, philistine developers rather than by enlightened Labor policies. Emblazoned on the banner of the Wran government when it came to office in 1976 was the intention, in the Premier's own words, "to make provision for maximum feasible participation by the community in a wide range of areas". In particular, he stated, there were clear demands for community participation in planning and environment.

True to his word, Wran introduced the Environmental Planning and Assessment Act, which came into effect in September 1980. The Act included in its objects: "to provide increased opportunity for public involvement and participation in environmental planning and assessment". It was justifiably touted as the most enlightened piece of environmental legislation in Australia.

But almost from the outset there has been a steady retreat from the promised land and it has become increasingly clear that the Act was always intended to have a mainly cosmetic significance. From the outset the New South Wales Labor government reserved to itself an important escape route from the controls imposed by the Act. This is to be found in Section 101, which gives the Minister, if he "considers it expedient in the public interest to do so, having regard to matters of significance for State or regional environmental planning" the right to "call in" a development application—that is, to take the decision as to whether it should be granted or refused out of the hands of the local council and decide the matter himself. In such a case the Minister can ignore all the elaborate, democratic provisions for public participation contained in the Act.

Of late the New South Wales government has gone even further along the road of arbitrary developmental decisions by introducing special Acts of Parliament to put major developments outside the reach of its own environmental legislation and to oust any participation by concerned citizens whose lives will be affected by such developments. Members of that government have fallen victims to some sort of Edifice Complex which propels them into the erection of large, ugly structures by which they hope to be remembered. The process started with Wran himself.

Thus the "conversion" to environmentalism of a Graham Richardson will not blind the Australian people to the fact that so-called Labor governments are allowing developers to call the tune everywhere. In this, as in so much else, the prevailing ethos of the Labor Party is philistine, sensitive to the interests of the greedy and indifferent to the needs of the ordinary man and women.

It is high time that voices from the Green movement be heard. This book, I hope, will bring a significantly new direction to Australia's political agenda.

JAMES MCCLELLAND
Sydney, 1987

1:
WHAT IS
GREEN POLITICS?

Drew Hutton

DREW HUTTON often finds himself on the top side of a soap box and the wrong side of the law in Queensland where he has been active in social movements since the early seventies. Drew was born in the small Queensland country town of Chinchilla in 1947. During the mid-sixties the humanitarian values instilled in him by his parents were combined with an anti-authoritarianism engendered by four years in a boarding school. Consequently, he was attracted to the New Left philosophies which were a part of university life during the late sixties and early seventies. Since then, he has been active in the peace and civil liberties movements in Queensland and was a foundation member of the Green Party which was established there in late 1984. In March 1985 he stood as the Green Party's Lord Mayoral candidate in the Brisbane City Council elections. Drew has been a teacher for nearly 20 years and, for the last ten years, has lectured in history at the Brisbane College of Advanced Education. He has been very active in recent years in curriculum development for peace and human rights education. He is currently committed to the development of a national Green movement.

It is difficult to pinpoint the beginning of Green politics in Australia. Perhaps it was the campaign by Jack Mundey and the New South Wales Builders' Labourers Federation in the early seventies to save Kellys Bush in Sydney, which led to the implementation of the famous

Green bans;[1] or perhaps it was the campaign in the late sixties and early seventies to save Lake Pedder in Tasmania's south-west wilderness and the setting up of the United Tasmania Group. Others might place it later in the seventies, with the anti-uranium campaigns; or perhaps even later, with the campaign by the Tasmanian Wilderness Society to prevent the damming of the Franklin River. No doubt, some well-meaning historian in a future time will pinpoint it with great accuracy and describe its "inevitable" emergence as a force in Australian political life. For those of us, however, who have had too many meetings, too few co-workers, too many deadlines and too little money, there has been little time to think about where we came from or the "inevitability" or otherwise of our emergence.

Yet it is essential for even the most active among us to pause every now and then, to reflect on our actions, and to reassess our positions. The last five years have been enormously important for people involved in alternative and social movements—and this book reflects much of the creative turmoil of the period. Each of the contributors has been very active in one field or another and each, after much reflection, has arrived at a political position which can be called "Green". This does not mean that they are inexperienced or naive, and it does not mean that they are concerned only with the protection of nature. It does mean that, although each has tended to focus his or her energies on one particular concern such as rainforest protection, women's issues or Aboriginal land rights, they see the interconnectedness of all issues, they appreciate the link between one's personal values and political beliefs, and they seek for root causes of the problems faced. The solutions found reflect an entirely "new way of doing politics" as well as the resurrection of some minority political traditions such as ecological anarchism and utopian socialism, and also some very old wisdom characterised in Australian society by Aboriginal modes of thinking.

For me, the odyssey to Green politics began in the late sixties when, along with thousands of my generation, I was caught up in the anti-Vietnam War struggle. Although only a marginal member of this movement, I was very influenced by the New Left philosophies of the time with their trenchant criticisms of Western capitalism and their rejection of the old left (which was often no better than their capitalist enemy, and sometimes a whole lot worse). The feeling of the time — the commitment to grassroots democracy, the anti-militarism, the counterculture — had a big impact on me; and when I became a teacher in 1968, I felt the contradiction between these values and those of the education system of which I had become a part. Influenced by such libertarian educators as Ivan Illich and Paulo Freire, I joined the Self-Management Group in Brisbane. For the next 12 years I was involved with it and various other groups in campaigns for more democratic schooling, for civil liberties (always an issue in Queensland), for nuclear disarmament and against uranium mining. I never lost my loathing for militarism and it seemed natural in the early eighties, especially given my job as a teacher, to become involved in peace education. Since I always accepted that peace had to be a concept with positive connotations (justice, environmental sensitivity, global awareness) and should not just have the negative connotations of opposition to war, the path to Green politics had become quite clear to me by this stage.

However, the path was different for many others. The rise of the women's and anti-racist movements in the early seventies added a welcome personal element into alternative politics, and forced many of us to come to terms with our entrenched sexist and racist attitudes. At the same time, the development of the conservation movement added a whole new dimension to alternative politics. As well as adding new issues to the political agenda, it also challenged the exclusively humanist frameworks within which most people operated.

Still others left the cities and went into areas like northern New South Wales to set up alternative communities. For some time there was only sporadic contact between these rural counterculturists and other social movements. However, many of these have been operating for well over a decade now and they have developed lifestyles and methods of community living which place them in the forefront of the social experimentation which is so important to the development of Green alternatives. Many of these activists — especially in more recent times — have been directly involved in peace and environmental campaigns and the influence of this movement now extends into all the major cities of Australia where alternative households, embryonic alternative communities and permaculture projects have established footholds.

Despite the herculean efforts of its adherents, Marxism generally failed to impose a unified philosophical framework on the alternative movement: many people joined single-issue campaigns rather than Marxist groups. Many, of course, joined the Labor Party because they felt it was the right thing to do and, since 1984, many have been leaving it—also because they feel it is the right thing to do. The heady days of Whitlam have long gone, to be replaced by the heavy doses of pragmatism and numbers-gathering which characterise all factions of the ALP today. There is the need for a new synthesis— both philosophically and organisationally—which Marxism and traditional Left groups are unable to provide. The emergence of Green politics has begun.

❖

Soon after the atomic bomb had been tested on many live targets at Hiroshima and Nagasaki and on (mostly) uninhabited Pacific targets in the aftermath of World War II, the famous scientist Albert Einstein declared: "The unleashed power of the atom has changed everything save our modes of thinking and thus we drift toward unparallelled catastrophe." For Einstein, this was a cry of anguish as he observed the same combinations of national chauvinism, paranoia, megalomania and vested interests (which had plunged the world into two monstrous wars this century) entering the international arena of the postwar world. This time, however, the contestants possessed weapons with a destructive potential which hitherto could not have been imagined. In Einstein's view it was not enough for governments merely to adopt different policies; the state of the art of nuclear technology had made it essential for all of humanity to adopt a whole new way of looking at life so that war—and especially nuclear war—would become unthinkable.

The irony of Einstein's position was, of course, that, in many ways, he helped lay the foundations for the nuclear age. Firstly, in an immediate sense, he had counselled US President Roosevelt, in the early years of World War II, to begin the project which was to develop the first atomic bomb. Although Einstein was later to regret this move, he was motivated by the fear that Nazi Germany would develop the bomb first. He believed, understandably, that such a development would be catastrophic—and as a Jew he had no reason to place any faith in the good sense or humanity of the Nazis.

However, if Einstein's work helped to usher in the nuclear age with all its attendant terrors, it also helped lay the basis for much of what has come to be called "new paradigm" or "ecological" thinking. This is "the new mode of thinking" to which Einstein refers and which he believed is the only hope for our planet. However, it has taken much more than Einstein's brilliant intellectual achievements to begin changing people's consciousness. Before we look at this new paradigm (or world view), therefore, it is necessary to look at the old paradigm, which Einstein and many others believed has brought us to the brink of destruction.

THE OLD MODES OF THINKING

If you want to find the best examples of the dominant modes of thinking in our society, I believe the best places to look at are those media by which the power wielders in our society are attempting to teach children what the world is *really* like, such as children's TV cartoons, video games and school textbooks. Any trip to a leisure centre will reveal a world where reality is presented as black and white, where good is versus evil, where paranoia about "enemies" reigns supreme and where quick responses (with no time for reflective pauses) are all that can ensure survival. Computer games give young people, who are too young to remember the Vietnam War, such instructions as: "Fly over the jungle villages. Points are gained by scoring direct hits on the village huts. You have to avoid the fire coming at you from the villages." Another game advises young people: "Steer your fighter-bomber through the difficult terrain, avoiding the mountains. Launch your rockets at the military installations. Points are scored by direct hits on the military installations." TV cartoons contain similar messages. The main theme is, inevitably, combat. If "freedom" is the goal of this combat, then this is invariably defined as occurring in a society characterised by wise (but always powerful) rulers, loyal followers (who display initiative, however), high technology and a consumerist lifestyle.

Australian school textbooks are often more explicit. They usually define "freedom" or "democracy" in the same way as the cartoons, they usually stress citizens' responsibilities far more than their rights, they are often sexist and Eurocentric and they usually portray our society as one that is "progressing" (with the occasional hiccup of a world war, imperial conquest or economic depression). This view of progress is sometimes expressed in quaint ways — witness one geography textbook used in Australian schools prior to World War II:

> [Man] is limited by the forces of nature; but he controls and directs those forces so that they become ever more obedient to his will. We still see the contest between man and nature in those regions where tropical heat and abundant moisture bear . . . dense forests. There, for a long time, vegetation seemed to win; man was checked in growth of body and mind, his faculties are but little higher than those of the apes that share or contest the forest domain with him.
>
> Gradually, however, the conflict between the giant plants and man is being decided in favour of man . . . trees . . . are being hewn down ultimately to become tables and chairs in distant lands. The forest gives place to grass that more readily answers man's purposes . . . man's control over vegetation is so complete that he preserves in his parks . . . remnants of the plant life that once dominated him. [2]

I have, at times, shown this passage to my students at college in order to generate a discussion on how world views are reflected in school texts, and each time they characterise it as "quaint" and, certainly, "anachronistic". However, further questioning usually reveals that the students are reacting primarily to some of the writer's terminology: when presented with a more contemporary statement of the same ilk, they are by no means as certain of their ground. One such passage is from James Christian's *Philosophy*:

In the life/death struggle between Man and Nature . . . the question has been . . . who would win: Man or Nature? Man has won—or is winning . . . Man has loved his earth; it nourished him. But he has also hated it for its relentless attempts to annihilate him . . . Man is on the threshold of setting controls over ever larger forces of nature—climate and earthquakes, for instance. The control of life and evolution is near . . . Man may eventually establish control on a cosmological scale. We might alter the orbit or tilt of the earth . . . Man is now in process of taking control of his own evolutionary destiny and, by default, of all other living creatures on this planet . . .[3]

If progress is often equated, under the old paradigm, with the increasing domination of human beings over nature, it is also seen as being consistent with the domination of some human beings over others. The achievements of any particular epoch are usually attributed to a handful of leaders while industrial societies have had to destroy less technologically developed societies in Africa, Asia and Latin America in order to bring "progress" to these parts of the world. This is often seen as unfortunate but inevitable. One Australian history textbook used in the sixties and early seventies devotes a paragraph to the destruction of Aboriginal society by the European invaders. The author sees white Australian society emerging from this period of conflict smelling like roses. The blacks, he asserts, were harmless, but "they refused to change their values and customs. Consequently, the settlers' approach changed to one of intolerance." His analysis of the continuing problems faced by Aborigines in white society reflects the kind of racism which makes anyone with a social conscience despair:

Their old way of life is gone; and with it has gone most of their dignity. Entry into their adopted community is blocked by two serious obstacles, (a) their own unwillingness to lift themselves out of the substandard life they have chosen to follow and (b) an unwillingness by the white community to extend them a welcome hand—not because of racial prejudice but because of that very

*substandard behaviour which seems to be part of most fringe
dwellers' manner of living.*[4]

A history textbook used in the United States in the sixties described
the destruction of the Pequot Indians in the same way:

> *[The] little army attacked in the morning before it was light and
> took the Pequots by surprise. The soldiers broke down the stockade
> with their axes, rushed inside, and set fire to the wigwams. They
> killed nearly all the braves, squaws and children, and burned their
> corn and other food. There were no Pequots left to make more
> trouble. When the other tribes saw what good fighters the white
> men were, they kept the peace for many years.*
>
> *'I wish I were a man and had been there,' thought Robert.*[5]

It is quite possible that many little Roberts, when they were sent
to the Vietnam War and found themselves carrying out "search and
destroy" operations against villagers in that country, found themselves in very similar circumstances to those white Americans who
massacred the Pequots. It is also very possible that another generation
of young Americans (and Australians) could find themselves in a
similar unjust imperialistic war if, for example, trouble breaks out
in the Philippines and the US buys in on the side of the military.
If so, such cartoons, textbooks and *Rambo*-type movies will have
helped to develop the very attitudes which make such criminal
ventures palatable to the general public.

THE DANGERS TO THE PLANET

However, the old paradigm is under challenge not only because it
provides rationalisations for unjust practices or because it presents
an unreal view of the world. It is also under challenge because it
is the sort of thinking which has brought us to the brink of
destruction. Zbigniew Brzezinski, US President Carter's National
Security Adviser in the seventies, is typical of the new breed of
technocrats who best reflect this old form of thinking in positions
of political power. Brzezinski spelt out his apocalyptic views in an

interview with the *New York Sunday Times* in March 1980:

> Brzezinski: *All of these reviews are designed to enhance our ability to bargain in the context of severe crisis, to avoid a situation in which the President would be put under irresistible pressure to pre-empt, to avoid leaving the United States only the options of yielding or engaging in a spasmodic and apocalyptic nuclear exchange.*
> Question: *Are you saying that you want the United States to be able to fight a "limited" nuclear war?*
> Brzezinski: *I am saying that the United States, in order to maintain effective deterrence, has to have choices which give us a wider range of options than either a spasmodic nuclear exchange or a limited conventional war.* [6]

The development of the Strategic Defense Initiative (or Star Wars as it is commonly known) has added a new dimension to the nuclear threat. Under the guise of building a defensive umbrella against Soviet missiles, the United States is building a system of laser weapons and killer satellites which would give that country unrivalled first-strike capacity and which could, quite conceivably, force the Soviet Union to attempt a pre-emptive strike of its own before the US gets Star Wars operational.

It is difficult to gauge the extent of the madness of this sort of mentality. It is not simply that we might have enough nuclear explosives to create a "nuclear winter" which could obliterate most organic life from this planet; nor that the arms industry is receiving billions of dollars which might, otherwise, be used for sensible purposes. It is also possible, as historian E. P. Thompson asserts, that society has gone beyond capitalism, beyond state capitalism or "late" capitalism or great power imperialisms—and that these concepts are no longer adequate for understanding the nature of modern industrial societies. To quote Thompson:

> *There is an internal dynamic and reciprocal logic here which requires a new category for its analysis. If the hand-mill gives you society with the feudal lord; the steam mill, society with the*

industrial capitalist, what are we given by those Satanic mills which are now at work, grinding out the means of human extinction? I have reached this point of thought more than once before, but have turned my head away in despair. Now, when I look at it directly, I know the category which we need is that of "exterminism". [7]

The technocratic (or exterminist) mentality is not merely obsessed with possessing bigger and more sophisticated weapons of mass destruction. Such a mentality is generally obsessed with the notion of control, or of domination—the domination of nature and of other human beings. If a nuclear explosion can be regarded, by those who measure human progress in terms of our ability as a species to dominate nature, as orgasmic (as it obviously was by many of the people who first developed and tested the atomic bomb), then the act of controlling the process of nuclear fission and harnessing it for nuclear power can be seen as a gigantic feat. The possession of such knowledge and such technology is beguiling. In the meantime, Chernobyl has already spewed its deadly emissions across Europe, and researchers are continually discovering new dangers associated with long-term exposure to low levels of radiation. In Australia, we salve our consciences by saying "If we don't sell uranium, others will" while, inevitably, the stage is being set for the extension of the nuclear industry in this country. This may not be in the form of nuclear power stations but could certainly take other forms. In my home town of Brisbane, for example, plans are being drawn up for a food irradiation plant which will subject such things as fruit, fish and nuts to radioactive exposure from Cobalt–60 gamma rays to give them longer shelf-life. Apart from the possible threats to health from the process, our area will have to provide a site for the quite large amounts of radioactive waste created. We are constantly told how "safe" and "efficient" such processes are—but those scientists who have not been seduced by such technology (and the highly paid jobs which so often come their way) constantly warn that there is no adequate research base for such confident reassurances. Ordinary common sense should also teach caution. In the words of Jonathan Porritt:

. . . as we contemplate the dangers of carting spent nuclear fuel around all over the country, or of the disposal of nuclear waste through sea-dumping or in deep burial sites on land, one might well ask who exactly gives them permission to say what's permissible?[8]

There have been human voices warning us about these developments for many years. But it was not until, in the words of a friend of mine from the German Greens, "nature began trying to tell us something" that people began to listen. There has been much publicity about the destruction of the Black Forest in West Germany through the acid rain which is caused by industrial pollution. In fact, over 50 per cent of *all* the forests of Europe are dead or dying. As well, the major waterways of Western Europe are little better than fetid sewers: the November 1986 chemical discharges into the Rhine were merely an extreme example of what has been occurring at an ever-increasing rate over the last few decades. Industrial society has also created new child-killing respiratory diseases whose causes are directly linked with industrial pollution in Europe.

If anything, the situation is even worse in Eastern Europe. Due to the authoritarianism of the regimes there it is often difficult for the public to get adequate information about these problems. However, the Soviet Union's nuclear problems — from the enormous radioactive waste explosion in the Urals in 1957 to the recent Chernobyl disaster — are quite well known. Also, the mammoth tinkering with nature associated with the proposed $100 billion water diversion schemes in that country are sending shock waves through the European conservationist community, given the possibility of resultant climatic changes in the entire northern hemisphere due to the alteration of the Arctic ice cover.

During periods of liberalisation in Eastern Europe there have often been protests about the state of the environment. During the rise of Solidarity in Poland, for example, people along the Baltic coast protested about the pollution in Gdansk Bay by oil and chemical industries which, according to the Governor of the Gdansk district at the time, had "all the symptoms of an ecological catastrophe". The *New Internationalist* journalist reporting these events quoted the prophetic words of the great Russian novelist and Christian anarchist, Leo Tolstoy:

> *They want to flatten the whole world*
> *And thus introduce equality.*
> *They want to spoil everything*
> *For the common good.* [9]

The holy grail of corporate profit is often the only argument used for the enormous destruction of nature that occurs in the West. However, the "common good" is sometimes used as a justification, usually in such terms as "it will provide jobs". What underlies such arguments is unqualified adherence to the goal of economic growth. This growth is usually measured by the increased levels of Gross National Product (GNP). The idea is that, as the economy grows and as the benefits obviously go to those who own the means of production, other benefits will "trickle down" to workers in the form of increased wages, to governments in the form of extra taxes paid to them, and even to those on welfare since there is a larger economic "cake" to divide amongst everyone. Therefore, all political parties, whether of the left, right or centre, are committed to economic growth.

In recent years, however, the goal of economic growth has come under some sustained criticism. This came first from a number of *Limits to Growth*-type reports (the most recent of which was US President Carter's *Global 2000* Report) which forecast that current rates of growth would soon exhaust the planet's resources. While these reports appear to have been overly pessimistic, their basic logic remains valid — the planet is quite evidently incapable of providing resources at the rate which industrial systems are currently demanding.

However, criticisms of growth-oriented economies go much further than this. Growth economies — with their penchant for huge consumption rates and therefore massive problems with pollution and waste disposal; with their identification with large urban complexes instead of smaller, close-knit communities; and with their desire for "development" and the alienation of natural areas — are creating a spiritual and aesthetic wasteland. According to Hazel

Henderson, a well-known critic of economic growth, "the social costs of a polluted environment, disrupted communities and disrupted family life may be the only part of GNP that is growing."[10]

Attempts to achieve rapid industrial growth in the developing world have also been disappointing. Where benefits have accrued, they have usually gone to small élites while the vast majority of the populations live in poverty. At the same time, in an attempt to produce goods for a world market, these countries have laid the basis for ecological catastrophe. This occurs where the best agricultural land is given over to cash crops (which go to the industrialised world), forcing subsistence farmers into marginal—and environmentally vulnerable—lands where natural resources, such as forests and minerals, are depleted at ferocious rates.

And yet, it seems inevitable that societies which intensively use the world's resources will continue in their extravagant ways for some time to come. Most of us live in cities which are constructed as urban sprawls—a direct result of the fact that, as car owners, we can afford to live far away from our workplaces and drive to work. We have developed lifestyles in which not only cars but also refrigerators, washing machines, motor mowers and other high-energy users are essential, and significant sections of our population own power boats, second homes and so on. Any government which opposed such practices and introduced policies for more ecological lifestyles would undoubtedly be thrown out at the following elections. Just as important a factor in the retention of economic growth is the fact that, without it, the system which allocates wealth very unequally would be threatened. Economic growth, combined with the "trickle down effect", allows improvements in the lot of the poor without having to alter the power structures or the criteria for allocating wealth. This was stated quite succinctly by one of President Nixon's top advisers in 1970:

There is every reason to be concerned about the costs of economic growth and [the] need for a balanced national growth policy . . . But this is a quite different thing from proclaiming the immediate necessity to put an end to growth . . . In general terms, how much sense would this make for society, given the great stabilising role of economic growth which makes it possible to increase the incomes of less well-off groups in the population without having to decrease the incomes of others?[11]

Australia is as threatened by these developments as any other place. According to Bernd Schorn, a recent visitor to Australia from the German Greens, we are only ten years behind Europe with our environmental problems. We also have a number which are already well advanced. The degradation of our arable soils is a problem which most governments are aware of but are ideologically and structurally constrained from doing much about. At a time when farm incomes are down and rural Australia is militant, no government is going to insist on the adoption of ecological farming practices which would, at least in the short term, make life even harder. Nor are governments prepared to put in the hundreds of millions of dollars necessary to enact reasonable soil conservation measures during a recession. So the problem continues. Rainforests are disappearing or being degraded by logging at an alarming rate and for every Franklin-type victory for the conservation movement, there are many other defeats. According to the respected environmentalist Charles Birch, the entire east coast of Australia, which is such an ecologically vital area for the whole South Pacific region, should consist of long stretches of preserved nature with pockets of development. Instead, it contains long stretches of development with small pockets of preservation.[12]

It has become clear to many over the last decade that the threats to our planet do not come merely from misguided policies or ignorant politicians. Nor do they come simply from the particular dynamic of the capitalist system, a dynamic which will supposedly change when the capitalist class is overthrown. Instead, these threats to the planet are the logical outcome of a world view. It is a world view which sees the needs of the person and the needs of the planet as completely different, even contradictory; which sees the domination of some human beings over others as a necessary pre-condition for human progress; and which measures this "progress" as the degree to which human beings are dominating nature and harnessing it for their own benefit. It is possible for people to ignore such threats for a long time—but rational self-interest dictates that people cannot ignore them forever. There is a saying in the Green movement which goes, "We do not inherit the earth from our ancestors, but hold it in trust for our children". It is clear that we will not have to wait for another generation before we begin to see massive ecological crises on a global scale. They have already begun. And the pursuit of an ecological society is the only sane course for society to take.

The Green alternative

When I was campaigning for the Green Party in the 1985 Brisbane City Council elections I was asked by a radio talkback host, "But you're not one of these Greenies who are against *all* development, are you?" The question was obviously guiding me towards some statement of moderate "rationality" and I responded accordingly. In retrospect, however, I would have answered this question quite differently, even at the expense of confusing many listeners. Instead of pointing out that Greens were opposed to development which was needlessly destructive of nature, my response should have explored the assumptions underlying the question. Greens, because they reject many of the assumptions of the old world view and so much of the system of industrialism, mean different things when they use words like "development" and "rational". The fact that so many people are beginning to think like this has prompted many observers to talk about a "paradigm shift". The "dominant paradigm", that of industrialism, is being challenged by the "new paradigm" which stresses an ecological way of looking at the world. The result is not merely that there is conflict in society over issues like disarmament, conservation and social justice. Significant sections of the population in modern industrial societies—perhaps as many as 10 per cent—see reality in a whole new way: they have a different system of ethics from mainstream society, and they organise themselves on principles which are different from what is usually held up as the norm. In many parts of the industrialised world, communities are being built in a way which is consistent with this new paradigm.

The Green movement has no set ideology from which has emerged certain strategies and forms of organisation. Instead, this movement has emerged in a somewhat incoherent fashion, responding to the various crises which the planet and its people have had to face over the last two decades. These single issues have been the basis of most of the social movements which have developed in industrial societies (especially in the West).

The first response of these movements was to organise themselves on the basis of combating the perceived threat, mobilising concerned people, and then using this pressure to lobby governments to change their policies. However, after a while, it became clear to many activists that these problems were largely incapable of solution through simple changes of government policy. Instead, substantial changes would be needed to social structures and decision-making — even to people's values and lifestyles. For example, the anti-nuclear power movement was forced to do more than argue against the erection of nuclear power plants. It had to come to terms with the argument that if we don't have nuclear power and if coal- or oil-based power stations create serious environmental problems anyway, then our society simply has to *consume less energy*. Resorting to renewable energy systems like solar power assumes the necessity for small-scale systems and more decentralised social structures and human communities. If people are going to use less energy, then they will need to feel recompensed for this reduced consumption by the achievement of goals other than consumerism. Logically, wealth would have to be shared more evenly even if only to avoid the social disruption which would be caused if people were asked to consume less but maintain the same unequal income levels.

It is very difficult for those who are working flat out on a crucial issue like rainforest protection, Aboriginal land rights or nuclear disarmament to pause long enough to reflect on the common interests which the social movements share. Another campaign is always around the corner waiting to be waged. The contributors to this book, however, are typical of an increasing number of activists who have reflected on this problem and have reached the decision that a holistic approach to their particular problem is the only one capable of achieving a satisfactory solution to it. Slowly, root causes of our problems are being identified, creative strategies are being developed, visionary alternatives are being articulated, and organisational principles are being developed. A new self-consciousness is emerging and this is represented by the term "Green politics".

According to Jonathon Porritt, Director of Friends of the Earth in the UK and a leading member of their Ecology (now Green) Party, there are certain common elements to this "Green" consciousness. These are:

- *a reverence for the earth and all its creatures;*
- *a willingness to share the world's weath among all its peoples;*
- *prosperity to be achieved through sustainable alternatives to the rat race of economic growth;*
- *lasting security to be achieved through non-nuclear defence strategies and considerably reducing arms spending;*
- *a rejection of materialism and the destructive values of industrialism;*
- *a recognition of the rights of future generations in our use of all resources;*
- *an emphasis on socially useful, personally rewarding work, enhanced by human-scale technology;*
- *protection of the environment as a pre-condition of a healthy society;*
- *an emphasis on personal growth and spiritual development;*
- *respect for the gentler side of human nature;*
- *open, participatory democracy at every level of society;*
- *recognition of the crucial importance of significant reductions in population levels;*
- *harmony between people of every race, colour and creed;*
- *a non-nuclear, low-energy strategy, based on conservation, greater efficiency and renewable resources;*
- *an emphasis on self-reliance and decentralised communities.* [13]

However, more is required of the Green activist than a shift of loyalties and a new set of policies. We need to make substantial changes to our personal values if we are to lead lives which are consistent with the ethics of Green politics. The norms of such a system of ethics would include the following:

- *a rejection of humanity/environment dualism in favour of a holistic perspective which emphasises the relationship between the two (and the connections between all things) and the need for humans to see themselves as part of nature;*

- *adherence to the notion of sustainability. We need to develop an anti-consumer ethic which allows us to appreciate the finite resources of the planet and to live in harmony with nature. We also need to lead sustainable lifestyles so that working, learning and loving all help to unfold our full potential as persons. The compulsiveness, destructiveness and boredom which characterise so much of these activities in this society must be changed;*

- *a valuing of diversity in many areas but also valuing the need for equality in social terms, including between developed and developing nations, men and women, highly educated and less educated;*

- *maintaining the value of personhood against the person-annihilating forces of the state, the company, the school and the mind-numbing egoism of consumerism. This norm does not contradict that of social equality outlined above but it is opposed to how state socialist societies define equality and to the selfishness, competition and egoism enshrined in capitalist notions of individualism;*

- *an emphasis on local autonomy and decentralisation in human affairs, an acceptance that social organisation is most compatible with nature when it is small-scale and based on principles of direct democracy. Besides, when a local community makes a decision about its environment, it then has to live with it.*

The absurdities inherent in such actions as arming for peace or developing class hatred as a vehicle for bringing about a harmonious, classless society have prompted Greens to make their means consistent with their ends. In this, they are in the tradition of such great activists as Gandhi and such great religious reformers as Jesus Christ and the Buddha. Greens reject the disjuncture between means and ends which characterises many of the movements based on Marxism. Of course, this does not mean that Greens reject the idea of struggling against oppression or of a dialectical process in human affairs. However, most would reject the purely materialist basis of this dialectic and the assumption that class struggle could, in itself, provide a motor for developing an ecological society.

However, to rephrase Marx, philosophy must do more than change the world; it must also understand it. A Green philosophy which consisted only of a series of ethical norms would soon degenerate into an inflexible moralism. The Green movement is developing a new way of looking at the world and understanding it. This has generally been described, as I mentioned before, as the "new paradigm". Since the "old paradigm" usually takes science as its model for understanding the world, it is ironic that this new way of looking at the world is being articulated most forcefully by men and women who are scientists. One of the most influential of these new writers has been Fritjof Capra.

Capra points out that with the decay of the medieval world view (which made scientific knowledge subservient to religious dogma) and with the rise of science since Isaac Newton nature has now come to be seen as a mechanical system composed of elementary building blocks, and scientific method has come to be regarded as the only valid approach to the accumulation of knowledge.[14] When this is added to the view that life is a competitive struggle for existence, then it is hardly surprising to find that science and technology have become the tools which humanity has used to dominate and exploit nature, and which some humans have used to dominate and exploit other humans. This approach, which is part of what is often called a "technocratic" world view, pervades the thinking of people in all modern industrial societies regardless of the dominant ideologies. This approach has transformed our planet. According to one writer:

The notion of an organic living and spiritual universe was replaced by that of the world as a machine and the world-machine became the dominant metaphor of the modern era. [15]

To this is added the belief in unlimited material progress to be achieved through economic and technological growth and the assumption that our planet is able to sustain ever-increasing levels of exploitation of its resources. Interestingly, the first indications that this last assumption might not be valid came from nature itself — in the form of dead fish in our streams, dying forests and deserts in the place of thriving agricultural land.

Intellectuals are obviously important in the maintenance of this technocratic world view. In general, they have accepted uncritically its assumptions and norms, carried out their research within its framework and then insisted that their work was "value free". Under this guise approximately half the world's scientists and engineers are engaged in military-related work. The giant corporations largely dictate what sort of scientific research and development will be carried out, and appointments and promotions in higher education are usually reserved for "safe" academics rather than dissenters. A rather candid description of this process came from Zbigniew Brzezinski:

. . . the largely humanist-oriented, occasionally ideologically-minded intellectual dissenter, who sees his role largely in terms of proffering critiques, is rapidly being displaced either by experts and specialists who become involved in special government undertakings, or by the generalist-integrators who become in effect house ideologues for those in power, providing overall intellectual integration for disparate actions. [16]

Those intellectuals who are challenging the technocratic world view are coming from a variety of backgrounds and traditions. Scientists like Einstein, forced to come to terms with the realisation that sub-atomic physics made no sense if one accepted the "mechanical world" notion that nature consisted only of discrete material particles, opened the way for the new paradigm. For these scientists, the sub-atomic world made sense only if it was seen as a constant flow and flux of energy transformations with, say, an electron sometimes acting like a particle and sometimes like a wave — so that its movements can only make sense when seen *in relation to* all other things. According to Capra, physicists had to accept that

> ... *the universe is no longer seen as a machine, made up of a multitude of objects, but has to be pictured as one indivisible dynamic whole whose parts are essentially interrelated and can be understood only as patterns of a cosmic process.* [17]

Finally, atomic physicists had to realise that their own consciousness was a vital factor in the process of scientific observation. The types of answers they received about this world depended on the types of questions they asked so that, when they asked a particle-type question of electromagnetic radiation, they received a particle-type answer; and when they asked a wave-type question, they received a wave-type answer. [18]

These three aspects of the "new physics" — the view of nature as a constant series of transformations, the interrelatedness of all things, and the importance of the consciousness of the observer — are all important in the new ways of thinking. The relatively new discipline of ecology is explicitly based on these three features. And in such humanities areas as art, literature, psychology, healing, and even the staid discipline of history, the complex and organic relationship between human beings and their natural environment is more and more being seen as a vital factor.

Finally, Green perspectives are often influenced by mysticism. For some, the reverence for nature becomes a form of pantheism, while for others, the insights of such non-European mystical traditions as Buddhism and Taoism are important. As John Cribb shows in his chapter of this book, various activities and traditions within Christianity also have much to offer Green politics.

Greens, then, see the world in a different light from people in the mainstream of society. For Stephen Cotgrove, as for numerous other writers, the differences are clear enough to warrant being described as different paradigms. Cotgrove has attempted to sum up the major points of clear differentiation in Table 1. [19]

Table 1

	Dominant Paradigm	Alternative Environmental Paradigm
Core values	Material (economic growth)	Non-material (self-actualisation)
	Natural environment valued as a resource	Natural environment intrinsically valued
	Domination over nature	Harmony with nature
Economy	Market forces	Public interest
	Risk and reward	Safety
	Differentials	Egalitarian
	Individual self-help	Collective/social provision
Polity	Authoritative structures: experts influential	Participative structures: citizen/worker involvement
	Hierarchical	Non-hierarchical
	Law and order	Liberation
Society	Centralised	Decentralised
	Large-scale	Small-scale
	Associational	Communal
	Ordered	Flexible
Nature	Ample reserves	Earth's resources limited
	Nature hostile/neutral	Nature benign
	Environment controllable	Nature delicately balanced
Knowledge	Confidence in science & technology	Limits to science & technology
	Rationality of means	Rationality of ends
	Separation of fact/value, thought/feeling	Integration of fact/value, thought/feeling

As Cotgrove points out, the first and major difference centres on the core values — the creation of material wealth. For most people in our society the creation of material "wealth" is a moral imperative, while for those in what Cotgrove calls the "alternative environmental paradigm" the earth's resources are finite, the pursuit of economic growth is exhausting those resources, and so the planet's capacity to absorb the wastes from this pursuit is fast reaching its limit— beyond which eco-catastrophe looms. Consequently, they stress the importance of non-material values, which include such things as the quality of family and community life. They also believe in the development of a close relationship with nature as well as the realisation of the various capacities within each of us for meaningful work, leisure, learning and decision-making.

For a recent seminar I attempted to extend these points of clarification still further by looking at various areas where there seemed to me to be clear differences. This is outlined in Table 2.

Table 2

	Dominant Paradigm	Ecological Paradigm
Decision making in workplace	Hierarchical organisation, rule by managerial experts, corporations free to set working conditions.	Industries controlled by workers, emphasis on holistic understanding of enterprise by all involved.
Economic growth	Favoured, also high technology, "trickle down" effect, production for manufactured needs.	Production for needs, selective or no growth, use of more small-scale technologies, redistribution of wealth.
Economic institutions	Market forces, differentials in income, entrepreneurial, public sector support for private sector.	Work cooperatives, self-management in industry.
Private ownership of property	Supports this as a necessary pre-requisite for democracy and for a stable society and personal fulfilment.	Limited private ownership, more community ownership and control.

Table 2 continued

	Dominant Paradigm	Ecological Paradigm
Role of centralised decision-making	Favours economic & political centralisation, except where this favours wealth redistribution.	Limited role for centralised authority, used to provide services which cannot be assured at regional or local levels.
Role of regional decision-making	Supports & extends central power.	A more developed role, bio-regions rather than states to encourage human identification with natural environment.
Role of local community	Anachronistic, undermined by economic & political forces eg supermarkets, freeways, big government.	Seen as basic for a caring demo-cratic society; mutual aid mechanisms at this level replace many services of welfare state.
Attitude to social action	Must be "up the right channels".	Representation seen as a limited principle; people should exercise the right to act in defence of legitimate interests.
Support for parliamentary democracy	Favours this where a democratic tradition & favourable political culture exist. Favours more authoritarian forms of govern-ment where exploitation is more blatant.	Support for parliamentary demo-cracy as a forum for Green ideas; electoralism seen as only one of a number of activities undertaken by the movement & not necessarily the most important.
Attitude to building alternative social structures	Opposed; support for nuclear family (with all its implications for urban life).	Communal lifestyles, viable local communities, cooperatives & mutual aid programs all outside the sphere of state organisation—all vital parts of Green strategy.

Table 2 continued

	Dominant Paradigm	Ecological Paradigm
Identification of main social change agents	Entrepreneurs, scientists, "experts".	Activists in social movements, community development projects, permaculture, cooperatives, progressive teachers, health workers, trade unionists.
Attitude to state violence	Support for deterrence, usually pro-nuclear, military blocs. Usually supports rule of law but no recognition of structural violence.	Rule of law (with emphasis on civil liberties), protection of minorities. Anti-nuclear, usually in favour of alternative defence strategies; supports nonviolent social resistance.

Of course, there have been forms of opposition. Radical liberalism and socialism (and, less extensively, anarchism) have all challenged elements of the dominant paradigm. Liberals, for example, have often attempted to mitigate the most destructive effects of hierarchy, centralisation and exploitation which are inevitable consequences of industrialism and they have often defended the rights of the individual when the industrial dynamic has threatened to overwhelm it completely. Socialists have long fought for a more just distribution of wealth and, often, they have argued for more participative social structures.

However, both liberalism and traditional leftism are human-centred to the point where they believe that we can achieve our full potential as human beings in a society which does not concern itself with the relationship between humanity and the rest of the natural world. Greens differ not only from the old paradigm but also from traditional humanists. Humanists tend to accept the human/nature dualism, they believe that social and cultural environments are the only important contexts for human affairs, and they hold that all social problems are ultimately soluble and that social and technological progress can continue indefinitely. They, therefore, are prepared to accept levels of economic growth, industrial technology, centralisation and hierarchy which would be disastrous for the planet and for the person. For people with Green politics, a far more appropriate starting point is that of Theodore Roszak's:

> My purpose is to suggest that the environmental anguish of the earth has entered our lives as a radical transformation of human identity. The needs of the planet and the needs of the person have become one, and together they have begun to act upon the central institutions of our society with a force that is profoundly subversive, but which carries within it the promise of cultural renewal.[20]

Green politics, then, attempts to redefine both individual freedom and social responsibility and to achieve compatibility between the two. Individual freedom, as redefined by Greens, involves achieving a sense of harmony—with nature and with those around us. Most importantly, we need to achieve a sense of harmony with ourselves— what might be called our "inner ecology". Roszak, in writing on education, says:

> Bad enough that Johnny can't read or write. But why do we stop worrying there? Why are we not every bit as concerned that Johnny is such a stranger to his organism and emotions that he will (like most of the rest of us) spend the rest of his life struggling under the burden of his ignorance? Why do we not worry that Johnny's body is gripped by thwarted anger and desire, that his metabolism is tormented by a diet of junk food and nervous tension, that his dream life is barren, his imagination moribund, his social conscience darkened by competitive egoism? Why not worry that Johnny can't dance, can't paint, can't breathe, can't meditate, can't relax, can't cope with anxiety, aggression, envy, can't express trust and tenderness? Why do we not spare some concern that Johnny does not know who he is, or even that he has a self to find? If the basic skills have nothing to do with all this, then let's admit that they have nothing to do with Johnny's health, happiness, sanity or survival, but only with his employability. Whose interest, then, is Johnny's education serving?[21]

Socialists tend only to ask the last question in this passage and are largely uninterested in questions of the individual's emotional or spiritual development. Liberals, while they may often address the sterility and authoritarianism of much that poses as education, are largely incapable of addressing Roszak's last question.

Greens also attempt to redefine the goal of social responsibility which socialists have so often raised and acted upon. Socialists have mainly attempted to mitigate or eradicate the excesses of capitalism through state control, state intervention or state regulation. In the West this has mainly taken the form of the welfare state. For Greens, social responsibility takes on the added dimensions of acting responsibly with regard to the natural environment, the Third World and future generations.

However, there should be no reason to prevent both liberals and socialists from being involved in Green politics. The British Liberal Party and the Australian Democrats (both coming from "small l" liberal positions) have adopted sound policies on nuclear issues and the environment, as well as having reasonable stances on welfare and social justice issues. They both tend to believe that issues can be resolved piecemeal rather than by tackling fundamental social questions, although the "Green" tendencies in the Democrats have strengthened their position of late. Similarly, there is a growing body of people calling themselves "eco-socialists" (some of whom have contributed to this book). They are concerned that a Green movement might concentrate only on environmental and peace issues and not give sufficient attention to questions of economic and social justice. They also stress that a Green movement should take working-class concerns into account in their programs. These are legitimate concerns and there should be little reason for the Greens to have a social base only in the professional and middle classes as the movement grows to maturity in the next few years. The challenge for socialists then will be to remove environmental issues from the bottom of the list of priorities, make them central to their world view, and ensure that socialism is redefined so that it is compatible with an environmentally sustainable society and personal freedom.

THE FUTURE OF GREEN POLITICS

Green politics has had a short history in this country and it is a brave person who would predict with any certainty its future directions. However, there are some things which, I believe, can be stated with some degree of confidence. Firstly, there will be attempts to put forward electoral coalitions at all levels around Australia. This will not necessarily be an Australian Green Party but, if discussions and movement building are conducted with sensitivity and intelligence, then a new political formation should emerge which could radically alter the shape of politics in this country. The Australian Labor Party under Bob Hawke has so alienated the social movements and their supporters that it is difficult to believe that the most sophisticated public relations exercises would ever win them back. The ALP is so enmeshed in industrialism, in power plays, in hierarchical politics, in the US global nuclear network and the intricacies of international capital that it is difficult to see it ever reverting to its traditional role of the party of mild reform—let alone occupying a crucial role in challenging the destructiveness of many aspects of the system of industrialism.

Despite Hawke's constant sneering question "Where else could they go?" it seems clear to me that Greens, people from social movements, disenchanted ALP supporters and—hopefully—a revamped Australian Democrats could come together in an alliance which might win as much as 20 per cent of the vote in a federal election, as well as representation in both State parliaments and local government. I should imagine that this new formation would have three major groupings (I won't call them factions). Firstly, there would be those whose main emphasis is the development of sound, realistic alternative policies; secondly, there would be a tendency which would stress that part of the program which dealt with questions of social and economic justice and the redistribution of wealth; and thirdly, there would be the radical ecologists whose main emphasis would be on urging fundamental changes in social structures and in people's values in order to establish a more harmonious relationship with nature. Despite these differences in emphasis they should all be held together by a common vision, by tolerance of differing views, and by a commitment to certain ways of working together.

There is one other thing that I can assert with confidence about Green politics. This is that it will fail with a miserable whimper if it consists only of an electoral strategy. The most important part of Green politics is the Green movement—organisations for Aboriginal land rights, nuclear disarmament, progressive education, environmental protection, self-managed community development, industrial democracy, issues concerning women, anti-imperialism, Third World support, animal rights and, of course, those elements of these movements which are constantly expanding their focus so that they cease to become single-issue. Without an organic link between an electoral organisation and the social movements, the electoral strategy will degenerate into a race to see how quickly its proponents can become integrated into the existing structures of parliamentarianism with their radical message dulled. The adoption of such principles as limited terms for parliamentary representatives is some sort of brake on this process but, in the long run, integration can only be prevented by the constant reassertion of the supremacy of grassroots organisations and the maintenance of a viable alternative culture and economic institutions.

The activities of Green politics, then, include the following:

1. *Networking*: Building up communication and trust among the various social change groups and movements (regular meetings and forums, newsletters and so on).

2. *Imagining the future*: Using our knowledge and understanding of the current crisis and building on the utopian aspirations which are so demeaned by the utilitarians of this world, we can develop a more sophisticated vision of an ecological society.

3. *Modelling the future*: Various projects have been under way for some time and others are in train. These attempts to "grow the new within the old" include such things as ethical banking, work cooperatives, recycling experiments, alternative communities (both urban and rural), appropriate technology

and permaculture projects. These also provide activists with experience in living and working in such a new environment as well as having a working model of the sorts of things which can replace present methods.

4. *Direct action*: Concentrating on the most destructive aspects of modern industrial society, confronting those who have made the decisions which have brought this about and challenging popular attitudes which endorse such activities will all remain vital elements in a Green strategy.

5. *Communicating our message*: The Green alternative has to be communicated throughout society. It has to reach beyond the relatively narrow forums it currently occupies to fire the imaginations (or at least alert the curiosity) of ordinary people. Newspapers and radio and television presentations can do this but I would argue that Greens need to participate in elections where they can communicate a political and social alternative in the context of a dramatic event in which most people are thinking politically.

An electoral strategy, used in conjunction with the Green movement's efforts to revitalise democratic community life, should reduce the potential for violence in the struggle for an ecological and socially just society. A Green strategy of social change would be aimed at strengthening civil society against the state and does not simply aim to use the state to force through reforms against the wishes of many people (which is the strategy of the Labor Left and the rest of the traditional left). Green politics does not accept the philosophical dualism which underpins modern industrial society (mind/body, humanity/nature, boss/worker, male/female) nor that of the traditional left (class struggle and class war leading to a classless society). Instead, it presents the goal of a society where people live in harmony with each other and with nature and, where oppression and destructiveness exist, they are resisted by the Green movement with nonviolent means. In this dialectical process the humanity of one's opponents is respected, conflictual situations are humanised as much as possible, and the possibilities for principled compromise are left open. In this way "the means become the ends" as Gandhi pointed out, and at the same time the potential for violence is minimised. Once we accept that the strengthening of civil society and nonviolence are the main elements of a Green strategy, then the role of electoral activities is put into perspective. Various reforms would be introduced by Green governments *along with* the handing back of power to the grassroots community organisations.

CONCLUSION

There are positive and negative aspects behind every great movement for social change. Liberals of the eighteenth and nineteenth centuries were inspired by their vision of a democratic society where individual rights would be protected. However, much of their support came from those who saw such an individualistic creed as providing the most appropriate political framework for capital accumulation and rapid social mobility. Socialists of the nineteenth and twentieth centuries were inspired by the dream of an egalitarian society and a cooperative commonwealth. However, much of their support came from the class hatred which workers developed as a result of the exploitation inherent in capitalism. The Green movement, likewise, has its positive and negative elements. Green activists are driven by their vision of an ecological society, where people live in harmony with nature and with each other, and where a sense of oneness and wholeness pervades. However, much of the support for such a development will come from those who fear what will happen to the earth if such a movement does not prevail. This fear is not irrational and is not necessarily a bad thing. It becomes destructive only if the fear becomes so intense that it overwhelms the altruistic and utopian elements of Green philosophy. In such a situation people begin saying such things as "the means justify the ends", the vision becomes blurred and compromise becomes the order of the day. If a Green consciousness has not penetrated deeply enough into society and the ecological crises seem overwhelming, then the only political alternative will be eco-fascism — totalitarian governments which impose ecological practices on powerless populations.

Still, I remain optimistic. While the sickness of domination pervades political life, together with our closest relationships and even our very musculature, and while many people remain trapped in an exterminist logic, there is still a life-affirming force in most people and they will be open to the message of Green politics. As the situation gets worse, these people will be able to break out of the circle of domination and will begin to face up to the hard decisions which need to be taken to maintain the rich diversity of life on this planet. And, of course, the Green message is not that people have to become ascetic. Once the obsession with consumerism and domination is ended, then the possibilities for a rich and satisfying lifestyle are endless. Then, what we shall discover is not something completely new but an old wisdom known to aboriginal societies around the world, including Australian Aborigines. One of the most poignant and best-known expressions of this view comes in a letter from Chief Seattle, chief of the six allied tribes of Puget Sound, to US President Pierce in 1854. Chief Seattle's people were faced with annihilation by the whites if they refused to sell their traditional lands:

The Great Chief in Washington sends word that he wishes to buy our land. The Great Chief also sends us words of friendship and goodwill. This is kind of him, since we know he has little need of our friendship in return. But we will consider your offer. For we know that if we do not sell, the white man may come with guns and take our land. How can you buy or sell the sky, the warmth of the land? The idea is strange to us. If we do not own the freshness of the air and the sparkle of the water, how can you buy them? Every part of this earth is sacred to my people.

Every shining pine needle, every sandy shore, every mist in the dark woods, every clearing and humming insect is holy in the memory and experience of my people. The sap which courses through the trees carries the memory of the red man. The white man's dead forget the country of their birth when they go to walk among the stars. Our dead never forget this beautiful earth for it is the mother of the red man. We are part of the earth and it is part of us. [22]

I shall know that the ecological vision of the Greens is near at hand when I can walk into any school classroom and have as many of the children find President Pierce's actions as ludicrous and unjust as today they find Chief Seattle's words anachronistic.

2:
GREENING
THE CONSERVATION
MOVEMENT

Bob Brown

BOB BROWN grew up in bush towns of New South Wales and became a medical practitioner at Launceston in 1972. He was Director of the Wilderness Society during the campaign to save the Franklin River in Tasmania and is now, along with Gerry Bates, a Green independent in the Tasmanian Parliament.

The afternoon was warm and still. An alabaster light through the high clouds lit up the shadowless landscape. I sat in a meadow looking west from the ridge which runs from Projection Bluff to Quamby Bluff in northern Tasmania. Looking miles and miles.

Around the meadow the forest, recovering from long-passed farmers' fires, gathered in young greens, stepping, slowly, bit by bit, back across the grass it had left a century ago. Here and there, a great old eucalypt grew out of the meadow, which fell away from my feet—down to the valley, down, down, to Jackeys Marsh. To the north a short spur ran west from the ridge, rainforests hugging its sides: a myriad of greens, celery-tops, blackwoods, sassafras and myrtles. Above the ridge towered the rocky turrets of Quamby Bluff.

To my south, the drier, sunnier slopes carried more gums,

including some more of the great old giants who saw the white settlers come and struggle, who saw the farmhouse and shingled sheds cut from the peppermint grove. They saw the horses work the meadow; the comings and goings of occasional visitors down the decades; then the departure, the crumble, the collapse. Now the roof of the stables lies skewed and rotting on the ground.

Those giant gums—with their own scramble of nesting birds and possums, the upward-downward rush of ants, the bark-entwined webs of spiders which arrived on the wind—held the ridge, way back. Before us. They grew by the Aboriginal Tasmanians' track down off Projection Bluff and along this ridge, the track down to the ochre pits of the Mersey River which is beyond Jackeys Marsh.

On the south rim of the steep meadow, in a sandstone outcrop, there's a cave. It is as big as my kitchen but rounded out and echoing. Its northwards entrance (away from the west which brings in the weather) is just wide enough to have two dozen bodies lie alongside one another, snug and dry on the most turbulent night, while the Roaring Forties blow and snow. The cave has been badly roughed in recent times. In fact I think it has been a bullock corral; the rotten, fallen fence nearby adds up to a corral. There are no historic signs on the stones—except some charcoal-drawn farm—together with some initials and the dates "1927" and "1940" on one wall. But the cave gave me its self and I knew about its original occupiers: the ancestors—the people who walked, who lived, who felt this place aeons before the farmers.

I sat for a long while on the ridgetop meadow. Thinking about the forests, the cave, the people. Staring out over the Jackeys Marsh to the sharp-edged, lofty peaks of the Great Western Tiers. Despite the hot spell, Mt Ironstone is still streaked with snow. And Mother Cummings Peak cuts up, with its deep blue spire pointing northwards against the sky, towards the distant ocean. Eighty kilometres away, far beyond Mother Cummings, the bluffs of the tiers merged with that alabaster sky. The first showers of a squall from the west washed out the dolerite horizon.

That ridge gives one of the island's most pleasant, open and refreshing spectacles. The meadow is small. But it affords a wonderful view of Tasmania's forested country: only a few patches of farmland and a glimpse of gravel road in the valley floor mark two centuries of European pressure on the island.

I wandered for a while down the meadow. Across from the cave is a small pond, with reed-clumps and surface-running insects. I came upon the pond suddenly, stepping up the mound which holds it against the slope (the hold will be brief—the pond will not be there a hundred years from now); and I stood, instinctively, stock-still. Four tiny black chicks were wading in the shallows under a drooping reed-patch. Their incessant "cheeping" was as soft as their downy coats. After a minute or so the mother native-hen emerged, saw me, and raced off across the meadow. These speedsters cannot fly. She screamed and screamed as she fled—hoping I would chase. The chicks froze, then gathered in beneath the reeds. Then the father appeared from the brush at the meadowside, 50 metres away, took one look and let out a challenging staccato—strangely enough, it is like the sound we make when clicking our tongue at babies. With that the chicks disappeared deeper into the reed-clump. Decency forbade me to stay longer. I stole quietly back to my lookout on the ridge, smiling as the parent birds moved warily—running, stopping, weaving—back to find the chicks safe and snug, though doubtless terrified, in their reedy fastness.

I never spend time in such a place without wishing that everyone else was there too. Not all together, of course. But one by one, with me. Everyone in the world. Just to sit. A whisper now and then. A tap on the shoulder and hand pointing to the wedgetail eagle rising on the thermals. An inrush of breath as the sun breaks the clouds and lights up a patch of forest in the valley. A whisper to explain the cry from the tea-tree grove or the babble in the marsh.

Such moments, such wild places, connect us with the universe. There are no answers written on stone. But in the stones, the trees, the skies, is a fulfilment for humanity, a contentment, without which no life can be satisfied or rested in the deepest sense.

Alas. This wild world is being torn to bits. As the human population grows, now to five billion, in ten years' time to six billion, the crush of the cities threatens to crush the heart from us—from humanity as a whole.

We cannot speak for other things. But we know that we, at least, need natural beauty and that our human beings resonate with nature, its forests, seashores and mountain grandeur. We may not say it well—or at all—except by the pictures we hang on our walls, the books on our shelves, the gardens we eke out of suburban confines or grow upon window sills and bathroom ledges.

Our bodies and minds are made for wildness. Through millions of years, every human cell has been created and made ready for the Earth's terrain. The spread of our toes, the grip of our hands, the curl of our ears to catch the faintest movement of air molecules by fur or feather or fin; billions of wilderness cells making us up.

Now, in the last blink of history, the universe is quaking at its own invention. Through us, through humanity, it has become aware of itself, it is sensing its existence and magnificence and it is itching to alter things. And it is frightened.

The problem is the same as with any baby. We haven't yet learnt. We don't know how close to the edge, or the fire, or the water, is safe. We are not patient or knowing enough to wait till we can read the labels on the bottles.

We have no "parent" in this "infancy"—we are a birthling of the universe with, so far as all can tell, no precedent, no example or guidebook.

Yet, because we are nature, the laws of nature are ours from the start. The earth is finite and fragile. Its substance, its living cover, its creatures, plants, its weather, oceans, icecaps and clouds are all interrelated: to tinker with one is to tinker with every other.

That's what we are doing. Tinkering. Interfering. At an accelerating rate.

Of course, this can seem very good—for now. But it is also problem-ridden. We have emerged from being part of Earth's nature to dominate the natural process. Nothing is changing Earth as much as twentieth-century humanity. It would take a meteor to crash into us to have as much impact. Though, I suspect, a meteor coming towards us would unite our efforts at least as much as the scramble for riches on Earth has set people at each other's throats.

Earth's environment is being degraded at the fastest rate ever. The world's oceans have become dumping grounds for poisons—sewage, oil, nuclear wastes and pesticides. Trawlers along Australia's coast trail 40-kilometre-long lines with a hook every metre. A search party went looking for blue whales (the world's largest mobile creature of all time) off Antarctica two summers back—and they found only six!

The air darkens and smells from the pollution of millions of chimneys and billions of spraycans. Scientists are predicting a warm-up because the sun's heat is trapped as the Earth's atmosphere thickens. The result, they say, will be the melting of the polar icecaps, the rising of the seas by up to nine metres within a century. Look at our cities, look at the maps to see what that means. But who is stopping the pollution process for the future's sake? Who?

On our islands and continents, six million tonnes of pesticides are sprayed into the greenery every day. Fifty thousand or more nuclear bombs are aimed, ready to cause a fiery cataclysm for the sake of foolish argument. The Earth's forests are being cut down at something like 15 hectares every minute. That's nearly a football field of trees chainsawed down every second—morning, noon and night.

By the end of the century most of the world's forests will be gone. Whereas in 1900 one species of wildlife was becoming extinct each year, it is now one species every day; and in the year 2000 it will be 100 species every day.

Sitting there on the ridge, that afternoon, these troubles all seemed far away.

I heard a ruckus in the tea-tree thicket. Now you would expect tea-tree thickets down in the swamps. Well, this one is up on the ridgetop; in fact, on the flat sandstone top of the top. I climbed up. But not before slipping on some moss and crashing down into some little trees growing on the rockside. Scratches on my shins, a bleeding little finger and a dilemma about whether to curse myself or the slippery slope. Then I grinned to myself and snorted at the thought of getting upset about a slip and a scratch: people have been slipping and scratching for ever. In two seconds I learned about moss on sandstone, the saving grace of little trees which scratch (without them I'd have fallen a bone-breaking distance extra) and how, with a little more knowledge and forethought, I could have saved myself much trouble.

I applied the forethought, found an easier way up and, almost immediately, the cause of the ruckus took off. A falcon. It had been perched in the bush, no doubt eyeing off the ruckus-raisers' nesteggs or nestlings. Now with the falcon gone they had new cause for ruckus-making.

Me.

I moved on, drawn by a patch of brilliant green. It turned out to be a tiny, round, room-sized sphagnum bog. Bogs aren't what we think they are. This one, at least, wasn't. It was simply beautiful. A carpet of luminous green, moist and, though I don't know exactly what, hosting a myriad of tiny creatures all busy eating, fighting, reproducing, resting, yearning in a universe which has no concept or experience of existence outside that thicket. The tea-trees crowded to the bogside like schoolboys around a marble pit. They are the bog's view of infinity.

Sphagnum bogs are finite. It's not that the tea-trees are being cut down to make attractive, brushy, suburban fences. The sphagnum is such a wonder at holding moisture that it is wanted by plant nurseries everywhere. And so the licences are being handed out by governments of all kinds to cut furrows round the bogs, drain them, ship off the sphagnum for once-only nursery use and cut out the peat beneath for fires in houses far away. I am told that Tasmania's biggest bog has just had a 12-kilometre trench dug around it and is, right now, dying of thirst.

The little sphagnum bog is safe for the time being at least. And, though I got lost in the tea-tree thicket on the way out (the guiding sun was lost in its alabaster sky), I emerged back at the meadow well pleased with the visit.

I left the ridgetop renewed. The hours had lifted the weighty weeks of parliament, microphones, meetings, and Budget discussions. The mountains looked so splendid. All around, and in the valley below, the forests made life feel buffered and welcome and unlimited.

Then the crunch. The new despairing. The horror of global destruction in our times, at our hands. It came in the form of an item on the evening's national news. Before I made my late-afternoon visit to the highland meadows, the bulldozers and chainsaws had moved into the Jackeys Marsh–Quamby Bluff national estate forests. Those forests in the valley far below. The loggers had cut down the first two hectares, the first 200 trees, the first 2000 possums, owls, pigmy bats and daddy-long-legs.

The news made my heart sink. I felt frustrated. Because I know that in 50 years' time logging of primal forests — those that are left — will be banned worldwide.

Then, the bright side. Fifty years ago no-one here would have raised an eyebrow. That's the difference. Certainly, it would have been no national news item. Nor would there have been the swift response from the conservation movement. As I drove down from the mountains I smiled to myself again, thinking about people like Alec and Martin, the erstwhile truck-and-bulldozer drivers who have become mainstays of Wilderness Society strategy. That night they and the dozens of other "forest folk" would be busy in our city offices using the best of modern technology — telephones, telexes, videofilm — to help ward off the misguided modern machinery which is destroying Australia's national heritage forests.

That's what's so good about being alive today. We are in the midst of a revolution in environmental awareness. I think it is a most exciting time in history. And here we are in this rich, secure, democratic country, better placed than anyone else on Earth to shove the revolution along.

There have been environmentalists in Australia forever. The Australians of the millennia before 1788 were part of the environment, the same as all of our forebears were — no matter where those forebears lived.

There have been active, eloquent conservationists at work in the post-colonial epoch, at least since a Mr Meredith looked with disgust at the bush, out Redfern way near Sydney Town in 1839 and noted "the system of clearing, by the total destruction of every native tree and shrub gives a most bare, raw and ugly appearance . . . the trees are frequently cut down within a yard of the ground, which remains thickly encumbered with the ugly, blackened and burned stumps, giving the appearance at a little distance of a large and closely occupied graveyard."

In 1874 Australia gained the world's second national park—simply called the "Royal National Park", south of Sydney. And by 1908 James Watt Beattie was engaged in a successful tussle to stop BHP mining the limestone Marble Cliffs, beside Tasmania's wild Gordon River. Between the world wars, bushwalking and native plant appreciation clubs were springing up in our capitals and Myles Dunphy and friends in New South Wales were campaigning for primitive areas or wilderness to be set aside for these areas' own intrinsic value.

Artists have captured, for the public imagination in this highly urbanised nation, the romance and peril of Australia's bush. Poets like Henry Kendall, Dorothea MacKellar and Judith Wright have helped mould a special appreciation for the environment.

Somehow, in the sixties, the world stirred as never before. Maybe it was the Cuban missile crisis. Or the destruction and cruelty caused by the Middle East and Vietnam wars. Or Rachel Carson's book, *Silent Spring*.

The Green bans, starting with the protest by local residents and union action which saved Kellys Bush from the bulldozers in suburban Sydney, were a milestone in Australia. The tragic destruction of Lake Pedder, one of the world's most gently beautiful places in the heart of Tasmania's south-west wilderness, was another milestone in 1972. There had been conservation milestones before. But now for the first time the nation as a whole was being drawn in. And the starched, blinkered, dollar-oriented thinking that is tearing our heritage apart was held up so that none of us could ignore it.

Modern education, leisure time and mass communications mean the issues of the day challenge us in our own living rooms. We can't ignore them. Nor can we, alone, solve them. But the answer to the challenge is rewarding. It lies in each of us doing what we can, as soon as we can.

I have been too Calvinistic and obsessive–compulsive for my own good. Which means for anyone else's good too. In 1967 I was (gulp) strangely annoyed when university students so disrupted and hurried President LBJ's motorcade in Sydney that none of us million street-liners got a good view. I went on to write "500 peaks in Tasmania", a definitive, ordered classification of mountain heights, resulting from weeks on the floor with maps. Such order and precision is easy and comforting and the stuff of modern industry and militarism. It is also the asphalt on the meadow, the cement wall to shut out nature's chaos.

This pillar of the work-and-order community crumbled and was set free. I saw and could not ignore the relentless destruction of the natural world by the sheer force of modern mechanised power.

I came to Tasmania, flew over Lake Pedder, signed a petition and made a donation.

Then I wrote a letter-to-the-editor, and went to a public meeting—disaster: I rose to ask a question and was so nervous I couldn't end it. Somehow, I stood for federal parliament, for the United Tasmania Group (UTG), and scored 172 votes.

The UTG was the world's first Greens party. It was instigated by the people fighting to save Lake Pedder—including founding President Dr Richard Jones—at a time when both the Labor and Liberal parties in Tasmania backed the lake's flooding by the Hydro-Electric Commission. The UTG came within 200 votes of winning a seat in Hobart in the 1972 State elections.

But it was a little UTG pamphlet which caught my breath. There in black and white was the party's ethic—a broad-ranging, inter-locked concern for nature, people and peace on planet Earth. The Greens' philosophy. A concern based on the understanding that as we treat the Earth so, ultimately, we treat ourselves. The obvious but long-disregarded truth that we do not own the planet, that we are part of it—a passing part. We have inherited the Earth from all life before us. We are its brief custodians. We must pass it on to future generations the better, not the worse, for our passing.

I had spent many years wanting to help the planet. Now, here was a group of people doing something. I joined them late, and watched their agony as the lake was destroyed and as their aspirations were trodden over by the powers that be—most of the industrialists, engineers, and unions and all of the newspapers and political parties.

Yet, in an indirect way, the Pedder people saved the Franklin River in the years that followed. They gave us such a headstart. We had the view from their shoulders. We began the campaign years before the HEC planned to pour its first load of cement. With such a headstart there was time to meet the "experts" on their own ground— to argue economics and employment as well as environment.

In 1976 people floated down the Franklin, Gordon and Jane Rivers and, for the first time, got a broad picture of the enormity of destruction the dams would bring. The Wilderness Society was formed. From people younger than myself I heard discussed and articulated what I knew but couldn't yet say: the value of wilderness; the need for large areas of wild Earth to be kept intact; the very concept of wilderness as a place with no roads, fences, factories or kiosks; the wisdom that we have no right to send other species to extinction; nor to fell a forest without asking whether people, ten generations from now, would give that act their warrant.

Add to that a healthy handling of the disdain for authority which Green groups often have. Private humour, caricaturing and mock bluster—these are such a gain over public anger, dread and hate. When all is said and done, the authorities and vandals of nature are people like us, born in different beds.

By 1982 when the heavy machines rolled south down the Franklin Valley and were barged up the Gordon to Warners Landing, the nation knew what was at stake. Thanks again to modern communications. Thanks to a warmhearted group of wilderness workers: to the thousand arrested or jailed, to the donors, the letter-writers, the stall-holders, shop volunteers and voters. Thanks most of all to the wild river's wilderness and its articulate self-advocacy: through television, books and newspapers the river had found a transformed Australian audience. The nation, now aware of this heritage, demanded a stop to the destruction.

Yet the destruction does go on. Witness Jackeys Marsh and Tasmania's south-west forests. Witness the karri forests, East

Gippsland's wilderness, the wet tropics of Queensland, the miners' targets in Kakadu, the vast despoliation of Australia's deserts by mining company seismic lines and squalor.

The vandals (from those other beds) have a headstart. Their companies are often multinational. They dine with our dignitaries. Their money buys such advertising power that they can swamp the right of people to be fairly informed. In short, they have an access to money, information and the ears of power which drains the decency from democracy.

They have managed to have the world, communist and capitalist, kept under the foot of the consumerist idol. Their standards of money, gross national product and consumption of nature, have been used as the very measure of human success. So far.

The Greening of Australia is growing faster than the gross national product. There are more than 300,000 members of conservation groups alone. The "them–later" concern is reaching out to overtake the "us–now" ethic of traditional politics. Many more people are becoming involved, crossing the barrier from the silent majority to join the activists who are changing the political agenda and reshaping the world's future.

There are pitfalls and failures and the process seems too slow. But the Green revolution is a change of awareness, not a taking up of guns. There will be horrible things yet done and the world's peace, environment, and people face a series of catastrophes.

But no change for human betterment has come overnight. The fights for the abolition of slavery, for universal education and for the women's vote took many long years. The arguments against those revolutions were based on economics. The people seeking change were being vilified, tarred-and-feathered or hanged.

Now the Green revolution is on. There is no turning it back. There are crosscurrents and back-eddies, but the tide is against those who see the Earth's resources as infinite, profitable and theirs.

The revolution is for a peaceful future, for a fair go for everyone on the planet, for care of our environment and fellow creatures. These things are all interlinked. What benefit is there in a wild Franklin River, running free to the sea, if a nuclear war leaves no-one to know it? What chance is there of peace if, while some folk struggle to find grain in the dust, others fill restaurant bins with leftover opulent tucker? What good will the world be for the survivors of our age if the Earth is barren of forests or wild creatures? How will we live with the history of Australia, so rich amongst all the poorer nations, if we have shown no restraint, forbearance or generosity to our own country or its neighbours?

The banner over the Franklin blockade river camp in 1982 distilled the essence of the Greening for us all: "Think globally, act locally."

And for those who still shudder at Earth's problems, feel helpless— and worse, useless—here is a little philosophy to help ward off the chaos. If it doesn't matter, and you live as if it does, it won't matter. But if it does matter and you live assuming it doesn't, then it does matter, greatly. This much is self-evident: the future is in our hands. The purpose of our lives is what we make it.

We have high hurdles to cross: a planetary reorganisation, no less. We must have a united, global effort to police and defuse technological horrors like nuclear weapons, genetic mismanipulation and chemical armaments. And we must have a global vision—to ensure that instead of fighting ourselves across artificial boundaries, we join together to undertake the monumental challenge to keep humanity going. To keep this astonishing universal awareness (us) evolving, flowering, finding out more: to halt the destruction of the Earth's environment which cradles humanity.

That is the environmentalists' task in Australia. The popular feeling for Australia's natural heritage is vigorous and growing. Yet, faced with the power of the cut-loose miners, loggers, dammers and developers, it needs accelerating.

The boundaries we set on national parks and the human-made heritage we save now mark out the most we shall ever have. We must have far stronger national, State and local laws to protect this heritage and the air, the land and the waters we enjoy. The foundations of this environmental protection, which we are setting, must go deep: predicated on the maxim that each environmental battle lost is lost forever, and that each battle won is won to be fought again.

Ah but it's good to be in this melee. Good to be a Greenie. Good to have future generations as our inexhaustible cheersquad. Good to mix with such generous, thoughtful people. No wonder everyone—I've found no exception to this rule—says that she or he is, whatever else, an environmentalist at heart.

And it's good to be gunless. We have no future except by peaceful means. The violence of the age will not be humbled with violence. The dilemmas are there: is it violent to put sugar in the tank of a bulldozer which is destroying a living scrub? No, it is not. It only is if the appeal to reason has not been made first. Or where the avenues in our political process, if open, have not been tried. Or if anyone, by such action, is brought to personal harm.

Our other Australian task is to lead in linkups with the world. It's a burgeoning business. Environmental groups are trading ideas, experiences, problems and support around the world.

At the Franklin blockade we were bolstered to hear of spontaneous support on the streets of Dublin, London and Paris. Messages poured in from people in dozens of countries. David Bellamy came from England, saw the primeval Franklin forests and, though he had never so much as cast a vote before, came back to the blockade, was arrested and jailed. On returning to Britain he declared he would chain himself to the railings of Westminster until the British government agreed to sign the World Heritage Convention. The government signed. So Durham Cathedral, for one, because of the Franklin River, is now a World Heritage Site.

We have a special onus to help beleaguered neighbours: the West Papuans, whose culture and rainforests are being desecrated by the Indonesian generals; the Solomon Islanders, whose forests face the ravages of multinational companies; Antarctica, the last wild continent, facing a scramble of dollar-vision mercenaries; the peoples of South East Asia, facing all manner of inappropriate development including dams, woodchip mills and trade in endangered species.

As I write this, at home by the fire, I think of the trip to Sydney tomorrow to talk with friends about whether a new Greens Party should emerge or not. Whatever happens, the future of Australia is with the people, not the passing parade of politicians. Political parties reflect the popular mood, they do not engender change: the basis for the future remains with the grassroots groups.

Insofar as parties and political organisations can divert our energies from campaigning, they are better avoided. Australia's archaic, undemocratic single-member electoral system makes party politics even less valuable. Britain's Ecology (now Greens) Party, though older than the German Greens, has never won a seat because of Britain's similar single-member electorate system.

But in Tasmania, with seven members elected in each House of Assembly seat, there are now two independent Greens. Next elections there could be more. In West Germany there are 27 Greens in the Bundestag. The European Parliament has eight. Around the world these numbers are growing. But they reflect, and in no way replace or emulate, the importance of community peace, social justice and environment groups.

The Greening of Australia is to me just like the progress of the labour movement a century ago: awkward, sometimes badly organised and divided, yet with its tide coming in. Who, amongst those strugglers of the last century, could have foreseen their gains which we now so take for granted?

Next century people will take Green ideas for granted. Trees will not be chopped down on a whim. Scientists will get no accolades for death-machines. Species will not be driven to extinction unsung and even unknown. Babies will not starve by the million while, as now, the world's leaders spend one trillion dollars each year on armaments.

The future beckons. The mind of humanity is capable of leaping to freedom. People, just like us, will be grateful if each of us, in our own way, does what each of us can to pass on life and the Earth's bounty to their future times.

That afternoon on the ridgetop meadow, I wished everyone else could have been there too. Not just to take in the view. But to be entertained by the forests, the mountains and wildlife and to come home eager to help hasten the day, the day when all the world will think Green.

3:
A GREEN PEACE: BEYOND DISARMAMENT

Jo Vallentine

JO VALLENTINE's election to the Australian Senate in December 1984 on the single issue of nuclear disarmament heralded not only her entrance into Australian politics, but also into the history books. She had become Australia's first "peace politician". Jo was born in the wheat and sheep farming community of Beverley, about 100 km north-east of Perth, Western Australia. As the fourth of five daughters, there was no shirking the hard work of running a farm. She attended a boarding school in Perth and at 16 she was awarded an American Field Service scholarship and for 12 months lived and schooled with a farming family in Illinois. The year was a truly internationalising experience for Jo, as she not only gained some insight into her hosts' way of life, but also met with many foreign students who were participating in the AFS. The experience left many indelible impressions on her, the fruits of which were to manifest themselves in her work for peace. On her return to Perth, she trained to become a teacher at Graylands Teachers' College and the University of WA. She married Peter Fry in 1972 and they have two children. The decision to have children motivated Jo to work even harder to make the world a better place for her two daughters and for other children in a tattered world. From a background of community work, where she was involved in Community Aid Abroad, the WA Council of Civil Liberties and the Aboriginal Treaty Support Group, she was asked to run as a candidate in WA for the fledgling Nuclear Disarmament Party. Her campaign slogan, "Take Heart", continues to embody her hope and enthusiasm for a true and sustainable peace.

The struggle for peace is as much a process as it is a destination. For those who clutch the vision of a peaceful sustainable world, as I do, the process becomes a daily awakening to the horrific symptoms of an apparently terminal society. And it would be a terminal society, if we ignored the enormous power of people to alter the course of history.

Poverty, environmental rape and pillage, racism, violence, oppression, exploitation, militarism and domination all face this generation of earth dwellers. They affect us all, and sadden many of us. Despite the apparent enormity of these complex problems, I have an overriding sense of hope.

It has been said many times that hope springs eternal in the human heart. Thankfully, yes. I think hope emerges from many sources: an appreciation of the world's natural beauties, so much more wonderful than any goods which money can buy; a sense of awe at the joy of new life, the wondrous on-goingness of our existence; a feeling of belonging to an intangible spiritual network which is an amazing source of strength; a longing just to *be*. So often, as I fly over Australia, I find affirmation for the hard struggle towards peace and justice. I feel strongly that the enormous effort we need to sustain our struggle for survival is worth every bit of pain along the way.

I started out in my activist life striving for civil liberties and Third World development. Then I came face to face with 50,000 nuclear weapons and the political–military institutions sick enough to use them. I felt then, as I do now, that the removal of these weapons must be the priority on my activist agenda.

We are a world already at war, both with each other and with the earth. All weapons of mass destruction are a deadly byproduct of a world system sustained on the principles of individual and structural violence, exploitation and domination. But without their removal, the world has no time for the holistic healing it so desperately needs. Disarmament of all these weapons must be an intrinsic part of a worldwide move towards a new, sustainable economic, social and political order. That's my vision . . . The hard work remains to be done.

We live in a world of militarism gone mad, but it shouldn't come as a surprise to anyone. The present world crisis is the result of 5000 years of domination by oppressive, exploitative, hierarchical and militaristic forces.[1] Since the first violent aggressive detonation of nuclear weapons in 1945 on Hiroshima and Nagasaki, and the worsening relations between the two superpowers, our planet's future has been hanging in the balance.

The world is horribly entrenched in "bloc thinking" — encouraged, of course, by those who stand to gain from the continuation of the spiralling arms race and all the political, economic, and social superstructures that go along with it. Both East and West are equally guilty of promoting the notion of threat. It serves those at the helm of these lurching monoliths to clearly identify an "us" and a "them". There is nothing so effective as threat — either on a large or a small scale — to extricate loyalty and discipline from those least likely to know the full truth . . . the people. The biblical injunction to "love one's neighbours" has become the global imperative.

Since the fifties, the world has lunged from one nuclear crisis to another; and we have been told, rather unconvincingly, that the world has been saved by the mutually held belief that no nation could win a nuclear war. The deterrence theory, or perhaps more accurately the deterrence myth, has now been exposed. Since the 1979 Presidential Directive 59, which uncomfortably moved us on from Mutually Assured Destruction (MAD) to Nuclear Use and Tactics strategy (NUTs), we cohabit a planet with mindless people who believe that a limited nuclear war is possible and winnable. And you can bet that such revolutionary changes in strategy are not unilateral.

So this decade, the world's people have been edged ever closer to the brink. The nuclear threshold has been deliberately lowered for the sake of bloc nationalism and the powerful industrial–military lobby on both sides of the Atlantic.

The arms race costs us and the earth too much.

In 1980, the United Nations estimated that the world expenditure on defence and armed services, including manpower, weapons, munitions research, and development cost $500 billion. The

Disarmament Commission in 1982 quoted $650 billion; and figures released in 1984 have shown this figure spiralling to between $800 and $820 billion annually. In the United States alone, the defence budget allocation for 1985 was $253 billion.

To put these figures into terrible perspective: while we, the "developed" world, spend such phenomenal amounts on bombs and guns, 15 million people are allowed to die of starvation each year. Five million children in Third World countries die each year from six contagious diseases; these diseases are preventable by immunisation. These are the symptoms of a system rotting on its foundation of global capitalism—economic and social exploitation by either the few, by the state, or by both.

The developing nations of the Third World are the pawns in this global Russian roulette. They are at the very core of the expanding arms race, as they are the central focus of those industrialised arms-producing nations. Not only are Third World nations the casualties of considerably reduced aid allocations due to the industrialised countries' defence commitments, but they are also the biggest potential and actual markets for much of the world's arms trade. Community Aid Abroad claims that 67% of arms exports from industrialised countries goes to Third World markets.[2] There are no scruples when it comes to big business, even though this insidious trade flourishes from the suffering of millions. Political instability in the Third World adds to the heightened militarisation of these countries—as do gross social injustices, which make up the very fabric of these societies. Appalling wages, shocking abuses of civil liberties, widespread corruption emanating from the very highest echelons, extraordinary economic mismanagement are but a few of the stumbling blocks in the way of progress on the human and national level. Thoroughly blended into this recipe of social, economic and political catastrophe is the contemptible self-interest of the major arms-producing countries.

According to the Stockholm International Peace Research Institute, the percentage of participation by the four leading arms producers is as follows:[3]

USSR .....*69.1% of its arms exports goes to Third World
countries. (It produces 37.2% of the total world arms
exports.)*
USA ......*50.3% (35.5%)*
France......*79.3% (9%)*
Britain......*77.3% (3.9%)*

To bring these figures a little closer to home, the Australian Department of Defence in 1982/83 allocated $44.1 million of military aid
to the Asian/South Pacific region, including $10.2 million to
Indonesia . . . supposedly the biggest bogey to Australia's national
security.

The arms trade puts an onerous burden on the economies of the
Third World, economies that are already susceptible to the cold winds
of global capitalism. Perhaps since the deregulation of the Australian
money market, and worsening rural crises in many of the major
industrialised countries, the plight of the Third World primary
producer is made painfully clear. In an attempt to boost flagging
foreign exchange, mostly to allow for more armaments purchases,
Third World producers are encouraged to grow exotic cash crops
for export instead of produce for consumption on the domestic
market. So while their coffee and exotic perishables do battle on the
open market, subject to disgraceful trade collusions, their people starve
for want of bread.

However, the overblown military budget is responsible for more
than the neglect of the developing world. In our own economies,
this expenditure robs the civil sector of valuable primary, secondary,
and tertiary resources. These scarce and finite resources are being
channelled into weapons and military regimes when they could—
and should—be made to produce more socially useful goods and
services, and also to ensure that there is money available to assist
developing countries. Our commitment to militarisation also denudes
government treasuries of the ability to allocate funds to areas such
as welfare, housing, health care and environmental protection.

Continuing this argument in the tongue of economists, countries with large military sectors suffer shortages of other goods and services because of the diversion of scarce resources towards defence requirements. And this in turn creates an inflationary pressure on general price levels and the costs of civil production. Also, wage rates in military-related industries are usually higher because of the high technological development, and this spills over to other industries leading to a general rise in wages in other sectors, such as service industries. Of course, the economic corollary to inflation is unemployment.

The increased military expenditure presents a complex mathematical problem which, in my opinion, just doesn't add up. The military domination of scarce resources not only seems ideologically unsound, but economically unsound as well. One economist, L. Aspin, has calculated that for every $1 billion spent on defence in the United States, the expenditure creates about 35,000 jobs. A similar amount spent on housing construction would create 66,455 jobs; in the area of public services, $1 billion would create 87,450 jobs; in labour deployment programmes, this amount would result in an extra 151,000 jobs.[4] Aspin's figures are backed up by the 1981 United Nations Report on Disarmament and Development, which says there is strong evidence to suggest that investment of capital in the civilian sector of industry would "create twice as many jobs as the same amount of money used in the military sector". One of the many arguments I encounter in my travels is the effect of disarmament on employment. The studies I have seen suggest that only ten per cent of those employed directly or indirectly on worldwide military activities would need to be retrained before being engaged in any job outside the military complex. The remaining 90 per cent would find employment as a result of stimulated economic activity resulting from the redirection of resources away from defence to civil use.

All that seems to remain is the political will to turn these hypotheses into realities.

In the charter of the European Greens the new political expression is "recognition that today's problems are not a 'crisis' that will pass, but a breakdown of the complex social, ecological and economic systems . . . attributed to the logic of industrial consumerism", of which the industrial–military complex comprises a sizable portion in both Eastern and Western blocs. The machismo that feeds and breeds from our society's obsession with aggression and violence has dispossessed many people of the ability and right to control their own lives and determine their own destinies.

Politically, we are a world disempowered by our own aggression. The Green view is to move towards a new order. This vision has my total support, yet I believe we must also work with the old order in the process of wreaking change. As Petra Kelly writes:

> There is a need for a new force, both in parliament and outside it . . . We (the peace movement) voice the needs of those no longer able to express their concern for a peaceful and environmentally conscious future through the established party system. However, a movement operating exclusively outside parliament does not have as many opportunities to implement demands . . . We have no option but to relate to the political system as it is.[6]

I made my decision to take the struggle for nuclear disarmament into the political mainstream after two significant events. The first took place in 1983 on the steps of Winthrop Hall on the campus of the University of Western Australia just after Bob Hawke delivered the 1983 Curtin Memorial Lecture. I went up to congratulate him on appointing an ambassador for Disarmament to the Conference on Disarmament in Geneva, but I also expressed my deep concern at the growing possibility of the ALP reneging on its anti-uranium position. I told Mr Hawke that it would make a lot of people very upset with the Party and may prompt them to show their displeasure in the ballot box. To which he replied with that famous sneer: "Who else are they going to vote for?"

The heavy irony of the last comment was not going to be made apparent to either of us till 12 months later.

The second event was the ALP's 1984 conference decision to allow the opening of Roxby Downs uranium mine. Within six months I was elected to the Senate.

The ALP uranium decision left a vacuum in the electorate. Many people—in fact more than 500,000 people—felt disenfranchised and looked to a new order. At the time of the 1984 election, the single-issue Nuclear Disarmament Party was perceived to be such an order. Though I was the only successful candidate of the campaign, the *issue* was the real winner. Not only did the election campaign and the NDP's relative success expose the flaws in the policies of the established political parties, but it also took the cause of nuclear disarmament in Australia to its widest possible audience.

I have never changed from my position as an activist rather than a politician and my first two years as an independent senator have only reinforced this belief. What this year has shown me, however, is that parliamentary representation is a valid way of working for nuclear disarmament and a "Green Peace". But nothing will be achieved in the parliamentary arena unless there is a strong and healthy grass roots movement to lead from behind.

Australia has sat back for too long in the comfortable, but false, sense of security gained by being an island continent on the edge of nowhere. The threat of nuclear weapons has made the world a very small place indeed and there will be no safe place to hide if the unthinkable occurs. The new political order, in its very infancy, has made significant gains in illustrating Australia's role in the immoral arms race. And Australia is involved . . . up to its eyeballs.

The uranium decision which galvanised me into political expression is the first insidious link in the chain. Proponents of "peaceful" nuclear energy are loud in their criticism of the nuclear disarmament movement because we will not allow them to get away with their misleading propaganda. Surely Chernobyl will silence the cynics. The nuclear technology is no nearer to being under control than it was in the early fifties with the "Atoms for Peace" project. There have been numerous serious accidents, widespread environmental contamination and deaths while this industry continues to shroud itself in secrecy. This is apparent for two very good reasons: in the first place, the experts are totally incapable of controlling this technology — so that the consequences of a serious accident such as Chernobyl can be neither promoted as "peaceful" nor safe; and of course, in the second place, the nuclear energy industry is a rapidly fading front for the nuclear weapons industry. This last factor makes it even more imperative that Australia, as one of the world's best future suppliers of uranium, stops the mining and the exporting of this mineral. There are no safeguards that can ensure that Australian uranium does not find its way into nuclear warheads. The nuclear weapons manufacturers and traders cannot be entrusted with moral responsibility when there is money to be made. It is outrageous to hear Liberal/NCP and ALP politicians constantly proclaiming that Australia has a moral obligation to fulfil its uranium contracts: Is it moral to supply uranium to an industry which clearly has no control over the energy it harnesses? Is it moral to be involved in an unnecessary technology that has proved that it causes great human and environmental suffering? Is it moral to provide the raw materials to an industry that, due to its growing complexities and secrecy, renders it impossible to keep those raw materials undefiled . . . in terms of where it ends up, be it in nuclear power plants, in nuclear weapons, or in the hands of terrorists? If morals are the point in question, I'm not sure that in any case there are many governments in the world which can argue from such a standpoint. It is crystal clear to me that we abdicate any moral position and all our responsibility to the international community each time a shipload of yellowcake leaves our shores.

The US bases, euphemistically referred to as joint facilities, are also high on my removalist list. As the evidence mounts daily, these bases, particularly Pine Gap and Nurrungar, serve the causes of peace perhaps little more than 0.3 per cent of their capacity.[7] Of Pine Gap we know it is a CIA-controlled base and part of the Rhyolite satellite system which has the ability to monitor the diplomatic, military and commercial communications from the Soviet Union and other countries . . . Greece for instance! Nurrungar is equally suspect and with the development of the Strategic Defense Initiative or Star Wars program it is likely to play a vital role. In 1983, it handed over a database to the Strategic Defense Initiative Organization, which has detailed some 6000 Soviet missile and satellite launches since it became operational in 1971. The Star Wars program will rely on quick reliable information on the launch of Soviet missiles . . . and it is exactly this information that is already being supplied by

Nurrungar and its twin station in Colorado.

Brian Toohey in the *National Times* (July 4–10, 1986) wrote that the government line — that "the main function of the bases in Central Australia is to assist arms control and early warning" — rings very hollow:

> *If this were really the case then there should be little objection to giving the Soviets similar facilities here, or at least to putting them under international control. The truth is of course that the bases are designed to benefit the United States. Of themselves, they neither help nor hinder arms control. How they are used depends on who is in the ascendancy in Washington.*[8]

The third major US facility is the North-West Cape Communications Base, which has no verification or monitoring role at all. In fact an article by William Pinwill in the same edition of the *National Times* described the operations of the base as having been scaled down: "Since the major upgrading of the VLF stations at Jim Creek (Washington State) in 1976 and the phase-out of the Polaris submarines from the Pacific after 1982, the role of the Australian station has diminished until it is now, at least in peacetime, redundant in its stated primary function."

The Labor government's rationale to legitimise the continued presence of foreign bases on Australian soil is that they serve verification and monitoring roles. Political manoeuverings have meant that North-West Cape is lumped in with two spy bases when it clearly does not fit. A healthy start to 1988, the year of the Great Embarrassment of 200 years of exploitative and bloody European domination of Australia, would be to exert our sovereign rights and give notice to the United States of termination of the bases' lease.

Pine Gap, Nurrungar, and North-West Cape are the Big Three. But there are many more installations serving foreign interests, the operations of which remain all too secret to the Australian people. Most Australians would have little first-hand knowledge of the bases or of uranium mining, but millions have witnessed the peacetime invasions of American nuclear warships. They are the tangible evidence of Australia's involvement in a nuclear nation's war-fighting strategies. It is a horrific sight.

The visits of nuclear warships have taken on a new perspective since the New Zealand government banned them in July 1984. The courageous and moral stand by New Zealand has given the Australian peace movement hope and vision . . . if Wellington can do it, so can Canberra. The warships ban has also put the spotlight on ANZUS and consequently on our actual and assumed obligations under this treaty. Since the Lange government's stand, the question of the alliance's cost–benefits ratio has been under study. The converted have simply had their convictions strengthened; but for many people in the wider community, the questions far outweigh the answers provided by those who allow, and by those who support, the frequent visits of nuclear-powered and nuclear-armed warships into ports which have no *actual* obligations to let them in, nor which have adequate safety procedures in the event of a nuclear accident. The question must be asked: what is more important to the Australian government . . . the safety and health of our people and our environment or the comfort of the US Navy?

Entangled as we are in the offensive defence strategies of the United States, Australia is in danger of becoming a poor subculture of our great friend and ally. Economically our "preferred position", because we say "yes" to just about every military request from the Pentagon, has done us no good at all. The rural crisis is a perfect example of just how much, or little, we can depend on our friends . . . and this scenario runs as true on military grounds as it does on the economic. There is no guarantee that the US will come to our aid. When it comes to self-interest, the free world and a free market come a very poor second and third when the US has a crisis at home or abroad.

For Australia as a player on the world stage, the dilemma is complex. There are no easy answers, but there is great hope because hundreds of groups of compassionate and concerned people are working hard for a real Green Peace.

I began this article by explaining my vision. I think it is pretty clear where we are now . . . firmly entrenched in one superpower's nuclear nightmare; globally corrupted by the old, outmoded order of power; motivated and fed by the driving force of self-interest.

But the process of getting from where we are, to where we want to be, is going to be step by step; in the words of Catholic peace worker Dorothy Day it is going to be "little by little and by little". The Green perspective is years ahead of the general mode of thinking, and it provides us with a model of peace through lifestyle. It is important for us to have this goal as a focus for the struggle at both the personal and global levels. The journey towards change is often lonely and always arduous. The examples of people who have put their philosophy into practice are signposts often obscured by the aggressive and violent world we inhabit. Many times I have been branded as "naive and idealistic" when I have talked about a world disarmed and at peace. It is as if I have contracted a highly contagious disease. Not that I mind—I am only concerned that the "disease" spread.

Disarmament can be so easily a reality in this war-torn world. I understand that we can't unlearn the technology; we can't overnight flip the switch on the nuclear energy industry or decommission all 60,000 weapons at noon on Hiroshima Day (although this sounds like a pretty wonderful idea to me). Disarmament is about political will.

Of course, it cannot take place in isolation from other Green aims . . . There will be no peace without social justice, participatory government and life in balance with the environment. But to only talk, and never to take the first step on this rocky road, only fuels and entrenches the old expansionary, sexist, militaristic and patriarchal society we hope to change.

The path to oblivion is lined with fence sitters, so the old proverb goes . . .

The hard work of building trust between the armed, aggressive nations of the world must begin before the threat of annihilation can be totally removed. Step by step we must move back from the brink. We know that peace is possible. And we know that arms control and disarmament agreements are also possible. It only took Kennedy and Kruschev four months in 1963 to negotiate the Partial Test Ban Treaty banning atmospheric testing of nuclear weapons. Obviously it was expedient for them to do so. According to

Australia's Ambassador for Disarmament, Richard Butler (who seems to work interminably on commas in the right places in arms control negotiations because that is all the superpowers are prepared to discuss) the technology exists for a Comprehensive Test Ban Treaty to be put in place tomorrow. What is lacking is the political will. The race in space has corroded world security to such an extent that even the threat of nuclear war seems not to deter the major protagonists.

I suppose there is a good argument for keeping the diplomatic wheels turning, but our future cannot rely on the Geneva talkfests. They need to be led by a strong groundswell of action and public opinion which will point out the human necessity of disarmament in political terms. Surely the day will come when the nuclear superpowers will run out of allies. They will run out of nations prepared to put their people at risk as pawns in the deadly game of nuclear terrorism.

That is why I believe the Green perspective of politics is one of the most powerful tools the peace movement has in achieving its goal. It is only by empowering the people that the work can be done. Individuals need to feel effective. The first step may be writing a letter, but in time the process of involvement will accumulate to action and then the enlightenment of self-determination.

One of the greatest stumbling blocks put in the way of broad acceptance of disarmament, apart from the bloc-induced scare mongering, is the hip pocket. What will the 50 million people employed worldwide in the military sector do if the toys are taken away from the boys?

The simple, but honest, answer is that they will find other jobs.

At present, with the struggle for ascendancy between the two superpowers, the United States and the Soviet Union, defence spending becomes progressively more capital intensive. The International Metalworkers Federation, which has undertaken a detailed study on the effect of disarmament on their members, cites the development of the MX missile system as exemplifying this tendency. While estimates of the system's cost vary from between $30 billion and $70 billion, the project will create only 38,000 jobs during its eight to ten year lifespan and half of these jobs will go to engineers

and professionals.[9] Dovetailing into this study is one conducted by
Marion Anderson for the Machinists Union, whose members work
in the most labour-intensive area of weapons construction. Her
evidence suggests that although disarmament would cause unemployment among members of this union the domination of resources by
the military at present is preventing about 118,000 jobs from being
created for machinists in civilian industry.[10]

There has been a lot of excellent work done worldwide on industrial
conversion from military to civilian production. Sweden leads the
way with a comprehensive report undertaken by the distinguished
politician Inga Thorsson. In 1981 Thorsson was chairperson of 27
experts who prepared a report for the United Nations on Disarmament and Development; and in 1984 Thorsson headed a Swedish
inquiry into conversion. What becomes apparent from the Swedish
inquiry, and indeed in any discussion of industrial conversion, is the
need for careful and long-term planning, essentially coupled with
the necessary political will. Conversion planning must include: trade
unions, the firms involved in the production of military equipment,
an education programme which would demonstrate that conversion
was feasible as well as desirable in industrialised countries without
severe disruption, and studies into new national developments and
job creation schemes.

It would be during the process of conversion that the Greens'
perspective of a new order could also emerge. What better time to
introduce new ideas than at times of great change? In the United
States, a report carried out by Robert De Grasse indicated that the
realities of conversion would affect only a small percentage of
companies producing munitions goods: "Only eight of the top 20
industries selling to the Pentagon depend on defence orders for more
than 10% of their sales."[11] De Grasse also pointed out that the
impact of shifting $62.9 billion in 1981 from military purchases to
personal consumption expenditures would have shown a net gain
or about 1.5 million jobs. However, any conversion programme
undertaken in the Soviet Union would need greater planning, with
the appropriate political climate being a top priority. The military
industry enjoys a privileged position in the Soviet Union, with

higher pay and better conditions being offered than in the civilian sector. It must be remembered that the military sector comprises one-fifth of all Soviet productions.

In the case of disarmament occurring over a long period of time, and production being channelled away from tools of war to socially useful goods, the level of global threat would be reduced considerably. With lowering threat perceptions, disarmament would be encouraged to continue. Inga Thorsson writes:

> *A precondition for disarmament is a considerable improvement in international relations. Disarmament will only occur if the super-powers display greater mutual consideration and increased trust. If NATO and the WTO were to cut their total military forces by half, including a sharper reduction of their clearly offensive units, I am of the opinion that Sweden could also reduce its defence effort by 50 per cent without renouncing its security policy goal of maintaining independence and security.* [12]

The lowering of international threat perceptions is good news for the developing world. With a world disarming, impoverished countries could stop their preoccupations with building up offensive–defensive forces and get on with the job of feeding, educating and keeping their people healthy. The impact of disarmament would be felt around the world. And on the way to this peaceful world, our whole way of thinking about our security would change. In Australia, we are so entrenched in a nuclear alliance that a whole new defence strategy for Australia must be considered. At the same time, a new way of dealing with conflict non-violently should be canvassed and brought before the people.

I have no hesitation in supporting and promoting the idea of social defence, whereby individuals and communities strive to solve conflict fairly and non-violently. Human conflict will not stop even in the face of general disarmament. We must learn non-violent conflict resolution techniques at the personal, national, and international levels. But for the majority of people right now, social defence would be seen as an open door to invaders. The process needs to be wound back to the position of an Australia independent and free of any alliance with either of the superpowers, and with defence capabilities able to defend itself . . . in short, to just (in every sense of the word) a *defence* position.

This must be seen as the first step in removing us from the debilitating nuclear alliance in which we are currently entangled. According to the 1981 report of the joint parliamentary foreign affairs and defence committee, the only serious threats posed to Australia's security, in military terms, comes from the Soviet Union and the United States. At this time, the report concluded that the Soviet Union probably didn't have the capabilities for launching a full-scale invasion; and that our great friend and ally would surely not have the desire to do so. I believe Australia's immediate defence needs should be modelled on a revitalised foreign policy that would take this country out of superpower alignment and place it in a regional interdependent network. Australia, for all our sakes, must learn to become a good neighbour in the Asia/Pacific region. It is a relationship which we have neglected for 200 years because of our Eurocentricism and, more recently, because of our servility to the United States. We have always been a colonial client state, merely swapping one master for another.

As the Bicentenary approaches, it would be a worthwhile project for all Australians to buy an atlas, and refer to it each day for a year — and perhaps that way it will dawn on many that the land was here long before a white person set foot on it and that its future lies in a region many thousands of kilometres away from the decaying old order. This embarrassing Bicentenary will be no joy for the Aboriginal people of Australia. There will be no peace in this country until the European invaders redress the injustices suffered by Aboriginal people during the continued occupation of their land.

The hope for our world lies in the hands of the people. For too long we have allowed the state to make our decisions for us. We must reclaim our rights. Perhaps one of the greatest reasons for accepting the challenge of working in the main political process is that it gives the people greater political expression by giving them a choice. And the greater the people's political expression, the more effective and representative parliament will become. The power of the people is the crucial element, indeed the only element, that will bring peace to the world.

Survival depends not only on military balance, but on global cooperation to ensure a world beyond capitalism and beyond socialism; a world based on balance and harmony; a world rid of weapons of mass destruction; a world that seeks non-aligned regional and international cooperation replacing "bloc" confrontation; a world where the rights of human beings are observed and respected and a world where there is a fair distribution of wealth and resources promoting social, cultural and economic liberation between the races and the sexes.

Green politics is neither left nor right, but way out in front.

We have the power within us all to see it through. Our humanity inextricably connects us all. As the Greenham Common Songbook declares:

We are the weavers, we are the web
We are the flow, we are the ebb.

4:

A GREEN PARTY: CAN THE BOYS DO WITHOUT ONE?

Ariel Salleh

ARIEL SALLEH left school in Adelaide to combine a university degree with mothering two small daughters. Not surprisingly, her first feminist campaign, Hobart 1971, was over child-care. After postgraduate studies at ANU, she worked in community health and then Aboriginal housing. She co-convened MAUM Sydney, late in 1976. Ariel is now a Senior Lecturer in Sociology at the University of Wollongong. She writes about Green politics, feminism, Marxist theory and deconstruction for both popular and academic journals and her work on eco-feminism and deep-ecology is widely known overseas. She is an editor of Thesis Eleven *and contributes to several Sydney activist groups. Apart from its rather provocative and playful title, Ariel's essay takes a rather different form from the others in the book, as it is crossed throughout by counterpoint texts. Ariel sets out to provide a "frame" inside which the voices of Movement women speak for themselves, emphasising both the decentred character of women's eco-activism and the strongly convergent political analysis developed by women—despite lived separations of space and time.*

❖

Even men who are opposed to the arms race are often fascinated by its technological and political complexities, and by the opportunities it affords for endless intellectual exercises which feed the illusion that their participants belong to the corridors of power.
Dorothy Green, *Sydney Morning Herald,* 8 October 1983

This is so true: but women, in my experience, even highly educated women, come at politics differently. I remember one night at the South Coast Conservation Society, back in 1977. A wrangle was going on between a bushwalker and a physicist, over whether the public could make informed decisions on the uranium question if they could not distinguish 238_U from 235_U. For some 40 minutes, the meeting was suspended between two powerful egos. Then, almost reluctantly, a small middle-aged woman in a grey cardigan spoke up from the back of the room: a steelworker's wife, her German accent thick and halting.

> *Well, I am only a grandmother ... but I want to be sure that my family will be born, each one ... with ten tiny fingers ... and ten tiny toes.*
> **Lucy Fisher** — housewife, Warilla, NSW.

A shamed silence fell across the room.

In the last 200 years, the major political struggles have centred on the principles of freedom and equality. Now, a far more urgent and fundamental political agenda confronts us, a Green politics, organised around the principle of survival. Scarcely a sign of progress, is it? What is more, this shift of focus produces a political dilemma for women. Not for Lucy; in her soundness and humility, she will live out her days in the conventional gender mould. But women of my generation and younger, who have tasted some emancipation, find them/ourselves in something of a bind. After a 15-year struggle, we are beginning to realise rights and freedoms which men enjoy; but now it's clear that too much emphasis on individual rights, as in liberal feminism, or on class equality, amongst socialist feminists, constrains a wider ecological consciousness.

> *We are challenging the quest for individual success and recognition which underlies Western society. We are seeking to return to community ... "Live simply, that others may simply live" is still the most succinct summary of the need for radical social change.*
> **Chris Wheeler**, social justice activist, *Getting Together* transcripts, 1986

It is often women not yet preoccupied with feminine emancipation who already organise themselves around the principle of survival. The housewives of Love Canal in New York State, battling toxic industrial waste contamination of their neighbourhood, are one example. The Chipko women of North India who hugged the trees to save them from commercial decimation, or the old Japanese granny-guerillas who daily disrupt military exercises at the Mt Fuji arsenal, are others. These women are not feminists in the usual urban-Western sense of the word, but they are radical political workers, pitted against the elaborate and irrational life-threatening activities that men persist with.

Yet it would distort reality to set up a dichotomy that too sharply polarises women's political awareness between the old and new political agendas; or as feminist versus non-feminist. Most of us juggle both traditional gender learning and feminist ideals in our daily experience; sisters in change are complex creatures and relate to their world in complex ways. But think of the beautiful diversity of age, class and colour among women who sang their common outrage in the desert heart of Australia, Pine Gap, on 11 November 1983.

❖

Women's eco-action in Australia has a substantial history which I can hardly do justice to here. A Women's Peace Army rallied against the conscription referendum in 1916; while Women's International League for Peace and Freedom (WILPF) and the Union of Australian Women (UAW) have worked consistently for peace over several decades. Further, WILPF's 1969 document on chemical and biological weapons — *New Perversions of Science* — anticipates more recent eco-feminist arguments. During the atomic tests of the fifties, women publicised the effects of strontium 90 in milk on children's bone development. Then a group called Save Our Sons emerged with the Vietnam War and did their best to sabotage the draft by registering names of family pets. At the same time, poet Kate Jennings bravely took to the soap box, urging women members of Students for a Democratic Society to confront their male comrades' bland indifference to the domestic conscription of women, sexual violence in the streets and the savaging of women's bodies in backyard abortions.

My own awareness of this politics had quickened by the mid-seventies: a conservative time, aggravated by the complacent sexism of a hippie boyfriend, of socialist colleagues in academia and of co-workers in the environment movement. So, I was reassured to learn that Friends of the Earth (FOE) women, stirred on by similar experiences, had begun to explore the overlapping ground between feminism and ecology at their 1976 Brisbane conference. Other feminists, of course, were leaving patriarchal expectations behind altogether, to set up communities of their own—Amazon Acres near Wauchope, NSW, being one of the earliest. In Adelaide, young mother and physician Helen Caldicott had started a vigorous media education campaign on the medical and genetic hazards of the uranium industry. I got involved within days of hearing her, and with Movement Against Uranium Mining (MAUM) co-convener Shirley Ryan, worked hard to extend the Sydney organisation beyond its original home in FOE and the unions to include church people, teachers, scientists, housewives and others from middle Australia. As early as 1977, we were astonished but pleased to find a piece in the Australian *Woman's Day* about women and the anti-nuclear struggle. Later, the Left fought several sectarian battles over the body of MAUM and it lost its broad community base.

Then, in 1978, FOE brought out an all-women's number of *Chain Reaction* listing addresses of feminist ecology groups in Paris, Hamburg and Copenhagen. *Chain Reaction* carried articles on recycling, animal exploitation for cosmetic manufacture, effects of radiation on Aboriginal health, and about patriarchy—progress or oppression?

> *Most of the pollution created by our society is directly attributable to the same forces that require the oppression of women. The growth ethic (supported by Labor and Liberal alike)* . . .
> **Vashti's Voice**—quoted in *Chain Reaction*, no. 13

That same year, a tribal grouping from South Dakota calling themselves WARN—Women of All Red Nations—began conscious-ness-raising on environmentally produced leukaemia and birth deformities among their people. In New York, DONT—Dykes Opposed to Nuclear Technology—called a conference on the energy crisis as a man-made pseudo-problem. Separatist collectives variously known as Feminist Anti Nuclear Group (FANG) or Women Against Nuclear Energy (WANE) were popping up in capitals around Australia. And of course, Aboriginal women from Oenpelli in the Northern Territory were coming forward to testify at the Ranger Uranium Inquiry on the devastating spiritual, social, medical and ecological impact of mining near their communities—and not only uranium, but also bauxite mining at Gove, Aurukun, Weipa; manganese at Groote.

By 1980, an Albury housewife, Margaret Morgan, was running one of the first enthusiastic rural protest groups, and the *Sun Herald* reported on ALP and Australian Democrat women's decisive intra-party stand against the lifting of our hard-won bans on uranium mining and export. Victorian Labor's Jean Meltzer—later a founding member of the Nuclear Disarmament Party (NDP) in 1984, and then, Nuclear Free Australia Party in 1986—was a significant force behind much of this. For my part, I had quit the Labor Party, totally frustrated with its male-dominated machine politics and lack of analysis. Convinced that "women are the real Left", I travelled to Europe and the States in 1981 and was affirmed by the groundswell of eco-feminist activity everywhere I went. In the USA, the first Pentagon encirclement had just occurred, using a network growing out of the Women and Life on Earth Conference which had been initiated by Ynestra King in Massachusetts earlier that year. Greenham Common in the United Kingdom followed only months later; another military installation was surrounded by women in Comiso, Sicily; and mass demonstrations of Arab women occurred at Kuneitra in Palestine. Norwegian women collected half a million signatures against NATO's cruise missile plan, then they marched from Copenhagen to Paris with their message of peace.

What do you do in case of a nuclear accident?
Kiss your children goodbye.
Australian movement poster, 1976

In the summer of 1982, the Tasmanian Hydro Electricity Commission's project to dam the beautiful Franklin River came to a head.

Men and women from all over Australia went south to block the onset of engineering work. One separatist affinity group from Canberra—the Red Emmas—quickly gained notoriety for their boldness at the blockade. Equally, the relentless energy of Wilderness Society women organisers across every State, was an impressive sustaining force in this long campaign.[1] Women's Action Against Global Violence (WAAGV) also appeared on the Australian scene around 1982. Some of its members had been part of a research and lobby organisation known as the Women's Political Coalition, but were now disillusioned with conventional political methods. Significantly, they mounted a peace cavalcade to the national War Museum in Canberra, then moved on to hold non-violence workshops and parallel parliamentary sittings, passing bills of their own.

> It is up to us to make sure the nuclear playground is the last one those boys will have.
> **Zoe Sofulis**—FANG, *Chain Reaction*, no. 13

Over in the USA, Catholic nuns were being arrested on the White House lawns, praying for peace. At home, FANG staged a rally at the Smithfield communications base, north of Adelaide. Another autonomous group, Women's Action for Nuclear Disarmament (WAND), split off from the old established International Association for Cooperation and Disarmament in order to bypass an inhibiting hierarchy. The next year saw WAND, the UAW and WILPF inject heavy emphasis on disarmament into the March 8th International Women's Day celebrations. The urgent need to transfer state expenditure from arms to welfare, housing, child-care and women's refuges is an ongoing theme of all these mobilisations.

24 May 1983 was designated International Women's Day for Disarmament and brought synchronised political responses from re/sisters around the world. European women now marched from Stockholm to Vienna via the USSR. WAAGV, also known as Women for Survival, Greenpeace women, Chrysalis and others, camped outside the Atomic Energy Commission establishment at Lucas Heights, Sydney. That year for the first time, a two-week Permaculture Design Course was offered especially for women at Tyalgum in northern

New South Wales.[2] The shift of women to rural areas was intensifying too; now along the NSW south coast. Others were taking back control of their lives through herbal medicine, meditation and therapeutic dance. Home-birthing has become a further feminist move away from the profit motive and masculine cult of expertise, towards mending the spiritual dimension of life.

We are women, we are the web,
We are the flow, and we are the ebb . . .
Protest song

1983 culminated with the first nationally coordinated on-site demonstration by women over the American "strategic presence" at Pine Gap near Alice Springs. But not without a reminder from Aboriginal women for their white sisters to remember that even radicals can have colonising attitudes. International solidarity with "Close the Gap" protesters was overwhelming; coming from as far afield as Icelandic Women for Culture and Peace and the Revolutionary Union of Congo Women. Men gave support by bike-riding to the national capital from Sydney, Melbourne and Adelaide. A further protest was held by Aboriginal women of the Arrernte people at Welatye-Therre in the Northern Territory—a sacred site threatened by planned tourist development.

About this time, the deep-ecologists, a very radical fraction of the environment movement, emerged with meetings in Canberra and in Ballina, NSW. Their philosophy, which rejects the classic Western split between Humans and Nature, is very close to the eco-feminist perception of things, yet it quite overlooked the place of women in this whole.[3]

Man's relationship with woman provides the model for his treatment of nature.
Penny Strange, *It'll Make a Man of You*, 1983

Some did not like being told this, but other deep-ecologists responded warmly to our point of view. The following year, I had an opportunity to apply this eco-feminist perspective in a course called "Women and Technology" taught for the Interdisciplinary Studies

Masters Degree program at the University of New South Wales. There we studied women as producers and re/producers in advanced industrial society; the rise of eco-feminist analyses of medicine, science, militarism and global crisis; and the ideological relation of the new movement to socialism, environmentalism and mainstream feminist politics.

Courageous ANZAC Day marches by Women Against Rape in War represent another facet of the feminine peace initiative. Likewise, elements of the UK women's peace movement such as WONT — Women Opposed to Nuclear Technology — had close ties with Reclaim the Night campaigns. The continuum between militarism, masculine identity and sexual exploitation was one concern behind the 1984 women's action during American navy visits for R & R at Cockburn Sound in Western Australia. Again that year, proposed changes in the Censorship Act led women from both Right and Left across all States, including an impressive mobilisation by Women Against Violence and Exploitation (WAVE), to step up the fight against pornography; especially snuff movies which have brought mutilation, even death to young actresses in Bangkok and Puerto Rico.

Men's fantasies are women's nightmares.
WAVE song

Germany's Green Party parliamentarian Petra Kelly toured Australia, galvanising crowds in 1984; while Sydney women architects and planners — Constructive Women — sponsored Magrit Kennedy from Berlin, an enthusiast for urban renewal using recycling, alternative technologies and permaculture principles. In inner-city Glebe, a small number of disaffected ALP people soon began to explore the idea of Green politics. But despite the efforts of a handful of us to focus on new ways of doing politics within the community, the group, calling themselves "The Greens", moved quickly into an old-style electoral campaign with organisational backing from Socialist Workers Party members. In the federal election, and after much rough and tumble in the newly formed Nuclear Disarmament Party, Quaker mother and environment activist from Perth, Jo Vallentine, was elected to the Senate on a peace platform. She is now an independent member of the House.

Around 1985, enterprising women followers of Sarkar's Progressive Utilization Theory (PROUT) started up a folk-rock band and a new magazine, *Dawn*, which looks at aspects of women's experience like workplace harassment, spirituality, physical disability, and gives special attention to the economic plight of sisters in the Third World. Women at the Public Interest Advocacy Centre (PIAC) were pursuing legal challenges over corporate malpractice in contraceptive marketing. Socialist feminists in Workers' and Migrant Health Centres continued to document occupational hazards to women in industry: abortion-inducing and teratogenic chemical emissions, and neuro-muscular stresses producing RSI. A Sydney Women and Technology (SWAT) group monitored effects of rapid technological change on women's employment conditions. The exacerbation of the dual-shift for working mothers is of particular concern, as highly skilled computer operators are encouraged into piece-work using domestic terminals. Meanwhile, investigation of what passes for development showed New Guinea men in tractors creating environmental havoc while the women continued to feed the tribe, cultivating yam crops with the digging stick.

> *Women's position in society has worsened ... linked with a male-dominated unsustainable model of development. Women's development is intimately tied up with an alternative ecological development which develops the base of sustenance ... not merely markets and cash flows.*
> **Vandana Shiva**, Science Research Foundation Director, India, *Ecoforum*, April 1985

The 1986 Marxist Summer School held at the University of Sydney gave eco-feminist politics a hearing for the first time—somewhat to the annoyance of one or two self-styled scientific socialists. Also that year, the Women in Science Enquiry Network (WISENET), already established in Canberra and Melbourne, got going in Sydney. Among other things, WISENET aims to promote communication between scientists and the community on social and environmental issues; to promote technologies appropriate to world needs, and to build a participatory science as alternative to the male-dominated tradition. Local members of the Feminist International Network on Reproductive and Genetic Engineering (FINRAGE) met with overseas visitors at the Australian National University to consider the political meaning of in-vitro technology for women. Others, including women from the political Right, were already working for a moratorium on the in-vitro fertilisation research program. Sadly, Left Labor women during the IVF parliamentary debate chose to turn a blind eye towards the horrific eugenic implications of this new commercialism, apparently in a cynical attempt to marginalise the party's Catholic Right.[4] In these same months, Malaysian women and children took to the streets — over dumping, by a largely Japanese owned multinational, of radioactive thorium near community water supplies at Bukit Merah, Perak. Farmers' wives at Coffs Harbour in New South Wales were agitating over malformities in children born near aerial crop-dusting with pesticides; and three housewives at Kurnell began to organise against a planned petro-chemical plant going ahead on the ecologically sensitive shores of Botany Bay.

Man believes he is immune from the effects of his technology, because he is above Nature . . . As long as persons with masculine values control what gets researched (and how), deadly technology will continue to be developed.
Myrna, *Man Made Madness*, 1981

Women gave a lot to both the Broad Left and Getting Together conferences which coincided over Easter 1986. Addressing the principle of equality, a Socialist Feminist Caucus from Melbourne told the Broad Left that Australian welfare recipients, mostly women, get less than 25 per cent of average male earnings to live on, while tax cuts serve to benefit the same male wage earners. They also argued a need for affirmative action in unions, to break the stranglehold of men's networks there. In the wider context of an affluent West and decimated Third World, Getting Together people agreed that the earth's finite resources could be protected and shared only by our learning to abandon an industrial-based high-consumption economics. The big question, of course, was whether a Green Party should be formed. Women favoured a looser, more organic coalition of movement organisations—wary, like sisters all over the world, of promoting any more patriarchal excursions into capital-P politics. Even as this was debated, some conference women were feeling that they were not being listened to, and had moved off into separate sessions.

One problem all wings of the [German] Party have is sexism . . . With no concrete, comprehensive plans for an alternative mode of operating, they simply slipped into the familiar, patriarchal patterns. **Charlene Spretnak**, co-author, *Green Politics*, 1984

In 1986 also, Gillian Fisher, now ex-NDP, stood for the NSW by-election in Vaucluse under the new Nuclear Free Australia Party banner. She won about 5 per cent of the vote, even while standing alongside an NDP candidate. Towards the year's close, Women for Survival renewed their campaign against the Government's lease of Pine Gap to the American defense establishment; and expiry date 19 October was marked by a women-only encampment on the lawns of Parliament House. A rhythmic spiral-dance through its precincts symbolised women's perseverance and continuity with the chain of being.[5] A team of women is now preparing to set sail across the ocean in the Pacific Peace Fleet. A late number of my *East Bay Women for Peace Newsletter* announces San Francisco WPF 25th Anniversary Dinner; War Tax Resistance; Action on War Toys; solidarity with deposed Judge Rose Bird; and Fund Raiser Concert for Nicaragua. In March 1987, women at the University of Southern California hosted a first international gathering of eco-feminists.

Yet the path is not straightforward for all women. The current Labor Minister for Education and Youth Affairs and Minister assisting the Prime Minister on the Status of Women wrote the following about our politics:

Women, as the bearers and rearers of children, have a stronger stake in the future . . . Women—being outside the power structures and the decision-making—have been the victims rather than the

perpetrators of armed warfare ... Women ... less socialised into the dominant male patterns of aggressive behaviour, are more able to see an alternative mode of human relations.
Senator Susan Ryan, Cabinet Minister, quoted in the *Sydney Morning Herald*, 8 October 1983

Why then, did not she, Ros Kelly, Jeanette McHugh and others, leave House and Party behind with the Government's 1986 Budget decision to resume uranium exports to France? How inspiring it would be, if our 16 women Senators and eight MHRs put aside their male-defined terms of reference, and dared to act in concert according to their consciences as women.

The revival of radical feminist thought with an eco-feminist diagnosis of the global crisis has helped clarify the aims of this recent international politicisation of women. The literature is a product of both despair, following the early years of feminism, and of continued hope, in the counter-cultural project of the sixties. If the penny drops for eco-feminists somewhere in the early seventies, it is already the middle of that decade before their ideas get into print. The remarkable simultaneity and similarity of these isolated analyses underline their origin as a response to quite universal circumstances encountered by this generation of women.

American theologian Rosemary Ruether's *New Woman, New Earth* and French writer Francoise D'Eaubonne's *Les femmes avant le patriarcat*, which appeared in 1975, took up archetypal feminine attitudes which had earlier been tossed aside with feminism, and argued their new relevance in the context of ecological struggle. They showed how Judaeo-Christian culture has been deforming to men — who are, in turn, appropriative and destructive of nature. The same themes were developed in "economist" Hazel Henderson's *Creating Alternative Futures* and poet Susan Griffin's *Woman and Nature: the Roaring Inside Her*, both of which were published in 1978. Griffin described the split consciousness on which the modern scientific paradigm is based: the same socially condoned mind-trick which allows prostitution or lethal pornography to coexist alongside worship of the Virgin Mary and greed to exist alongside starvation.

> *Millions starved in Africa last year where the food needs were*
> *estimated as 20 million tonnes... And yet there were 297 million*
> *tonnes of grain in storage throughout the world.*
> **Judy Henderson**, medical practitioner, *Getting Together*
> transcripts, 1986

In 1980, Carolyn Merchant's *The Death of Nature* carried the story
further with a scholarly reconstruction of the logic of domination
as it has unfolded in philosophy since the Renaissance.

Feminist magazines like *Off Our Backs, des femmes hebdo, Womenergy*
and *Heresies*, long-time advocates of a unity between personal and
political, now extended their interest to the connection between the
environmental crisis and patriarchal self-alienation. The Campaign
for Nuclear Disarmament's *Peace News* was also amenable to articles
along these lines. Following Greenham Common, the UK literature
on women, militarism and peace now exploded—with Pam
McAllister's collection *Reweaving the Web of Life* (1982), Lynne Jones's
Keeping the Peace (1983), Cynthia Enloe's *Does Khaki Become You?*
(1983) and others. A primer of eco-feminist writing came out the
same year: Leonie Caldecott and Stephanie Leland's *Reclaim the Earth*.
Its theoretical chapters are not strong, but it contains useful extracts
on issues like the dioxin disaster at Seveso, rights of animals, Mad
Women of the Plaza Mayo, carcinogenic preservatives in food and
female infanticide in India. Petra Kelly's autobiographical essays,
Fighting for Hope, an inspiring document of the Greening of one
woman's awareness, were translated from German in 1984.

Significantly, the ancient Greek word *Oikos*, which is the
etymological root of the term ecology, means the domestic environment, the sphere of basic needs inhabited by women, children and
slaves. In the classical world view, this was paired against *Polis*, the
public sphere of men and free citizens. Eco-feminism defines the contemporary global crisis as a by-product of these "abstracted" patriarchal
political institutions rather than more narrowly—say, of capitalism.
Patriarchy is understood as one possible form of social relations, which
is based on the social crippling of both men's and women's capacities

in a way that allows for the systematic domination of women by men. Capitalism is recognised as a recent historical variety of patriarchy; and economic forces are recognised as powerful determinants, having to be sustained in turn by ideological beliefs and practices.

> *Women are not inherently non-violent:*
> *they are traditionally oppressed . . .*
> *Nor are men inherently violent:*
> *they are traditionally and structurally dominant . . .*
> **Penny Strange**, *It'll Make a Man of You*, 1983

In my own research and teaching, I have been attracted by the work of neo-Marxist social thinkers known as the Frankfurt School.[6] They see the break of *Polis* from *Oikos*, the splitting of what is culturally valued from nature and life needs, as fundamental to the logic of all domination. Exploitation of nature, of one race or class by another, of woman by man . . . all these are related episodes and all equally political. The mental and ideological precondition of this "mastery" is that whatever is to be dominated and used must be seen as "other", so losing its own value and individuality. It must be turned into "an object".

Now this tendency to objectify nature and other people can also be applied to one's own self. In fact the first act of control was probably exercised over an inner "nature", as men learned to block their physical knowledge of things from feeling. The denial of sensuality is certainly identified by old Freud as the moment when patriarchal culture got underway. Then it becomes rationalised, institutionalised and reinforced as it is repeated in the biography of each successive male. Recent feminist theorists such as Dinnerstein and Chodorow assume that this splitting in men, but not women, has to do with the infant male's need to break early physical ties with a seemingly all-powerful woman/mother figure—in order to establish an identity of his own.[7] But this explanation begs the question of an already established masculine norm, and so, like most attempts to get back to the beginning of things, it is a circular argument.

Nevertheless, there is no doubt that the separation of sense from intellect is basic to the Judaeo-Christian tradition, and it leaves us with a culture that polarises everything it sees. The division between wide green unruly wilderness as against an imposed human order is a keystone of this obsessive and oppressive thought pattern. And this splitting up of reality into self/other, either/or, left/right, white/black and so on effectively keeps woman in her place too. The scientific method is similarly premised on a fractured consciousness—a so-called neutrality, an isolation of observer from field, of fact from value. Now, the industrial revolution and modern bureaucratic rationality have joined this much-prized "objectivity" to an equally mindless technological prowess.

The Frankfurt School has described these developments as the rise of "instrumental rationality". In such a culture as this, the world is viewed with abstract detachment; it is measured, analysed, taken apart and put back together again according to human design. Questions of value are reduced to cost-benefit analyses. Instrumental rational societies may be capitalist or socialist. In either system, what has evolved into a technocratic compulsion to measure and control spills over from the workplace to saturate our relationships. Unconsciously, other people become resources, commodities to be consumed, manipulated, exchanged—in a word, screwed. Some neo-Marxists like Fromm, and radical feminists such as O'Brien, suggest that the primitive origin of this disconnectedness must have come with men's recognition of their rather small role in human re/production—that strange labour of labours, which is Mother/Nature's privilege.[8] Is the alienated and destructive productivism which drives both capitalist and socialist machines nothing but one vast compensatory rage, then?

Men are fighting, not for self-determination, but for energy control.
Roslyn Livingston, *Chain Reaction*, no. 13

Carried more deeply, this writing involves a far-reaching critique of our prevailing epistemology or theory of knowledge, and also a thoroughgoing redefinition of what actually constitutes the arena of politics.[9] And while not all women eco-political workers are intellectuals who would want to formulate their conviction in terms such as these, there is pretty much tacit consensus on the guiding principles of feminist praxis. Here, two assumptions occur again and again, reappearing in multiple guises. First, there must be consistency between theory and practice. This implies no contradiction between ends and means, of course; and further, no real distinction between reform versus revolutionary activity. The second assumption—a logical corollary of the first—is that personal and political experience are not separate spheres but flow into each other. This is in contrast with the masculine way of doing things.

> *That ability to depersonalise every one and thing ... necessary for "success as a man".*
> **Jenni Dall**, *Chain Reaction*, no. 36

Thus, while feminists appreciate only too well how structural and institutional forces work—seeing themselves as one such force—they nevertheless avoid turning their politics into rigid monumental forms. Most women understand human interaction as the stuff that all political contestation is made of and are happy to work at a grass-roots level rather than create new power hierarchies.

Further, our redefinition of "the political" introduces new and unheard-of problems to be analysed and solved. In many activist contexts, women find themselves making complex decisions, with little prior experience, and in practically uncharted areas. At the same time, they struggle to maintain a democratic and nurturing group environment, in order that less articulate sisters can contribute to the process. Because of this mixture of macro and micro political awareness, women's activism is very demanding and very thorough. It is always double-edged, both inward and outer at once. Not surprisingly, many succumb to burnout and despair. There is so much to do—change at the level of self; in relationships; on child raising; within education; media; political institutions . . . To borrow another sociological term, feminist politics is reflexive. Women are particularly alert to the need to work on themselves; to cleanse and heal the scars received from childhood conditioning and from the continual abrasions of ongoing patriarchal relationships.

This means that sometimes women want to be in groups without men, so they can express ideas and feelings in non-threatening surroundings—surroundings free of the ego-games, interruptions, put-downs and non-verbal power-play which make up such a large part of masculine "communication".

Did you ever have the feeling of possessing a currency you can't use? It is just what I often felt in mixed groups.
Isabella Paoletta, *Getting Together* transcripts, 1986

Women are also encouraging men to form their own groups. In this way, men can learn how to give each other support instead of relying on an audience of women to smile and nod at what they say—as well-mannered girls always do. But separatism is an historically transitional strategy in the struggle to restore our socially crippled complementarity. Personally, I do not like it. It is at odds with consistency between means and ends and with the logic of ecology— flow, diversity, symbiosis—which could guide our action. Separatism may be appropriate for caucuses or for inward-looking exploratory or therapeutic sessions, but when the aim is to reach out and share ideas, broadening the web, it seems very hard to justify. It is also a fact that, in the present political climate, the issue can be introduced obstructively by the Left in an attempt to short-circuit meetings designed for open public discussion of the broader feminist analysis.

The reflexive nature of feminist politics also accounts for why women prefer working in collectives, with an informal rotation of roles and lateral decentralised network links. Recent history confirms that in formal organisations women generally end up taking the brunt of domestic duties like typing, research, tea-making and sex, with little opportunity to try out public spokesperson roles. There is also a certain elitism about vanguard organisations, a symptomatically "objectifying", patriarchal them/us split, quite out of touch with genuine respect and communication—that colonising tendency again. The worst excesses of this "instrumental rationality" as the neo- Marxists call it, is demonstrated by party politics, which inevitably gets down to a manipulative scramble for numbers. Yet, many radical men still have a deep need for emotional gratification in terms of the old political paradigm. Ego is still smoothed by rubbing shoulders with other men in power, it is still massaged by the general cut and thrust of capital-P politics.

So now the time has come to ask, "Should we form a Green Party?" a new question poses itself: Can the boys do without one? It is, after all, the quality of consciousness shared by men and women working together for social change, their mutual empowerment, that is the real proof of progress.

> *The number one battleground is ego, patriarchal ego, not necessarily an ego that is owned by men. Women are also capable of maintaining it.*
> **Georgina Abrahams**, peace worker, *Getting Together* transcripts, 1986

In the context of personal politics, the skills offered by women and men from Chrysalis groups all round Australia—listening, meeting facilitation, non-violent conflict resolution, have been invaluable to our movement, since affinity group training first kicked off at the Franklin blockade.[10] Nevertheless, the problem of ego is not going to be easy to solve. Some quarters of the German feminist movement argue that a separate Women's Party, entering the Bundestag on its own terms, is the only solution to this age-old problem. It would be one way of rounding out the bourgeois liberal agenda for representative democracy before moving on to the next historical phase. And no doubt, it would keep many men happy into the bargain. Eco-feminists, however, see electoral activity as essentially an educational or consciousness-raising exercise rather than a political end in itself. Process not structure; bread before stone.

> *Feminists do not want a piece of the male pie. We want a new pie ... We must withdraw physical, psychic and psychological energy from the institutions that oppress us ...*
> **Becca Miller**, *Chain Reaction*, no. 36

Instead of reinforcing abstract, depersonalising institutions, many women are already carrying out their politics directly and concretely within civil society itself. Since community empowerment is the end goal, why not go straight for it? Women are working on community access radio, organic food cooperatives, waste recycling and neighbourhood play groups. There are now self-managing tenants' unions and workplace coops in the cities, ethical investment banks and permaculture collectives further out. All replace state or private sector institutions with informal, people-negotiated economic arrangements. Power without politics . . .

Again, feminists have gone a fair way down the track with cultural criticism at the level of language and ideas—deconstructing hard and fast concepts, displacing ossified meanings, shattering stereotypes. Especially important is the dismantling of common dualisms like human/natural, masculine/feminine—both now recognised as arbitrary designations. Much of this work is done through film, through dress experimentation, in poetry and philosophy. But people with old-paradigm ideas find it difficult to recognise its results as political; of course they are equally upset by Green politics, which leaves behind old notions of Left/Right. As in other areas of feminist political practice, deconstructive work involves some subtle manoeuvering; yet it is just these existential tensions which make women's culture sensitive and astute.

To rewrite history
to reflect on the impossibility of reflection
to deconstruct reason while reasoning about difference
to read the body while speaking our minds
to denounce hierarchy but refuse equality
to make the middle ground women's space

> *without reinscribing the sexual position*
> *that leaves us*
> *always on the edge*

Joan Scott, "Occasional Verse", Feminism and the Humanities Conference, Canberra 1986

So, eco-feminist politics involves a double praxis: a move of women and "feminine values" into the *Polis* and, simultaneously, a deconstruction of irrational and excessive patriarchal institutions, by reconnecting the public sphere to its sustaining roots in *Oikos*.

❖

With its deep structural analysis of masculine identity formation and institutionalised power, with its exposure of instrumental practices in capitalism, science and family life, eco-feminism is the most un-compromisingly thorough political statement to eventuate so far. And, given the profound cultural taboo it breaches with its urge to re/member nature, it is not surprising that some people are unsettled by it, want it to go away, or pretend it says something other than what it does. But this analysis is here to stay; it is part of women's international language, and more, it has strong friends at home. It integrates concerns of radical feminists, ecologists and socialists; and while it has grown out of women's experience, it is in no way the preserve of women. Eco-feminism in Australia finds natural allies among peace workers, the deep-ecology movement, Men Opposing Patriarchy, non-violent direct action trainers, Greens, the alternative technology movement, anarchists, Permaculture, Aboriginal health and land rights workers, radical science collectives, and social justice groups.

At the same time, it is important to realise that Australian women involved in eco-politics come from several quite disparate quarters, and all do not necessarily accept the broader analysis. For example, to a large extent, concern over disarmament and uranium has grown out of socialist politics—UAW, AICD, APC, CPA and more recently SWP inspired campaigns. This kind of politics directs itself to the human costs of nuclear arms, of mining and breakdowns in the fuel processing cycle, as opposed to its technological impact on the eco-system as a whole. In as much as it remains bound by the main tenet of Marxist productivism—which is the transformation of nature according to Man's will as project of history (and I mean Man's here)—socialist feminism is compromised in relation to environ-mentalism. On the other hand, the impressive internal critique of Marxism as a gender-blind philosophy, a critique developed by socialist women during the seventies, exposes the logic of domination in a way that will serve all radical movements well.[11]

Another cluster of Australian eco-activists identify themselves as spiritual feminists. Some, including many in Women for Survival, are affiliated with established sects like Ananda Marga; others celebrate archetypal Western notions of a feminine essence. Their ideological underpinnings are in the radical feminist writing of Daly, Rich and Spretnak, so at that level, they have little in common with their materialist sisters.[12] They are mainly women in their twenties, city-based, often lesbian, unemployed and rather anti-intellectual. They also put little store by programmatic politics, preferring civil disobedience and spontaneous symbolic forms of confrontation.

A third strand of women, far less visible as movement activists, are the small cells of housewives, mothers and grandmothers— scattered as far afield as Kurnell and the Blue Mountains. They tend to be older and do not necessarily question the politics of their own womanhood. Nor do they have any particular theory behind their protest activity—it is simply based on commonsense. They are convinced that chemical plants in the neighbourhood, pornography or US bases are wrong and will do whatever they can to stop them. Some of these women ally themselves with the Australian Democrats; some are long-time WILPF members; others are active Christians. They are energetic and skilled in organising forums, delegations and submissions, appeals and petitions; they often use cake stalls and display tables in shopping centres to reach a wider public.

Still other women, quite a few tertiary trained professionals among them, put their extra-curricular time into mainstream organisations like TWS or PND. They rarely take a high profile though, and like their socialist sisters they can find themselves run off their feet with maintenance functions for the movement, scarcely finding breath to discuss possible connections between ecology, feminism and Green politics. Moreover, the formal political allegiance of many of them still lies with the ALP—despite its shaky environmental record. Some professional women carry their politics across into their work as well, influencing editorial decisions, classroom activities, or the focus of scientific research projects.

Another body of women already working for a Green future come from the Rainbow Region in northern New South Wales. Some have chosen to set up lesbian communes while others live and work with men. Some are permaculturalists and concentrate on sustainable farming techniques; others like the Nomadic Action Group (NAG) adopt a gypsy life, well suited to direct action on critical sites like the Franklin or mines at Roxby Downs. At the risk of endorsing patriarchal sentiments, these women embrace the imagery of Mother/Nature. Their response to ecology is intuitive, even mystical; and they shun the intellectual rationalism of much urban feminist politics. Conversely, many city feminists persistently censor discussion of any link—real or metaphorical—between woman and nature, identifying this as the linchpin of masculine domination.

Clearly, in face of the urgent task ahead, Australian women must put these artificial differences aside. This means learning to communicate with sisters on the Right as well. Corporate wives can be a way in to the conscience of the ruling class. They are often autonomous women, highly informed and resourceful. Many are already actively committed on public concerns. Church women too, Quakers, Catholics or fundamentalists, are already working for social justice, peace and conservation. They feel deeply; and, whatever the basis for their reasons, they hold consistently life-affirming policies on key feminist questions like in-vitro technology. Secular women need to find a way of acknowledging the human continuity with "nature" too, but one that sensitively challenges and dissolves the oppressive ideology of our Judaeo-Christian past. Whatever the patriarchy tells us, men are part of nature just as much as women are. For white people, with centuries of Enlightenment arrogance and instrumentalism to overcome, rediscovering physical ties with the earth is not easy. Jammed into our crowded, noisy and poisoned cities, we only now begin to see what Black people had got together in the first place.

> *We want to smell the clean fresh air*
> *blowing over our land, not like at*
> *Maralinga where we smelt the black*
> *dust from their bombs . . . [And] many of*
> *our people died. We want those hard*
> *thinking men of power to go away . . .*
> **Pitjantjatjara woman**, quoted in *Chain Reaction*, no. 36

In the mid-eighties, women's activism in our country and inter-
nationally is less a monolithic movement than one with many diverse
strands with apparently incompatible strategies. Feminists seem to
cluster in unsympathetic, self-righteous cliques or opt for divisive
sectarian alliances, and then become only intermittently effective in
making change. For this reason, I have argued in the past that the
movement has reached a point of crisis—a time for review and re-
orientation. On reflection, I think this pessimism comes from a failure
to think historically. The feminist movement *per se* may be fragmented
and diffuse, but women's political engagement is a strong and multi-
faceted thing. It may contain contradictory tendencies, but each of
these—liberal feminism, socialist feminism, eco-feminism—is working
away on different parts of the social fabric. With time, I think their
effects will coalesce.

Casting around New South Wales alone, the number of competent,
committed eco-political workers makes an impressive list. To name
but a few: Lyn Goldsworthy, anarcha-feminist and advocate for
Antarctica; Wendy Varney, fluoride researcher and *Tribune* columnist;
Barbara Whiteman, community worker; Nancy Shelley, non-violence
activist; Judy Lambert, at the Wilderness Society; Lilith Waud and
Kate Boyd, organisers for *Getting Together*; Lea Harrison and Robyn
Francis, Permaculture consultants; Kate Short, heart and soul of the
Total Environment Centre's toxic chemical committee; Mum Shirl,
Aboriginal health worker; Judy Messer, stalwart Plant Variety Rights
lobbyist; Jan Ardill, now on R & R from FOE; Bev Symonds, tireless
peace worker; Joan Carey, from WILPF; Ruby Emerson, Blue
Mountains Women for Peace; Val Plumwood, philosopher and forest
conservationist; Joan Staples, farmer turned ACF lobbyist, and Chris
Townend, animal liberation publicist. Some of them may not like
the label, but all would qualify as eco-feminists. All are finding a
way to reconcile the old and the new political agendas in their lives,
balancing their individual integrity as women with dedication to a
wider, ecological identity beyond themselves. [13]

And this is no mean feat. Caught between the principles of freedom
and equality on the one hand, and the global imperative on the other,
women take on two fronts at every stage of the struggle. And more,

each front in turn has to be taken on in both private and public life. Out of this complex, often painful experience so uniquely theirs, re/sisters all over the world are creating a new political sense. And their program leaves other ideologies for change looking thin, single-issue and reformist. In building a Green and sustainable future, women in the late twentieth century have a very specific energy and purpose to release.

5:
ABORIGINAL AUSTRALIA AND THE GREEN MOVEMENT

Burnam Burnam

BURNAM BURNAM was born Henry James Penrith on 10 January 1936 under the family gum tree at Mosquito Point Wallaga Lake Aboriginal Reserve in New South Wales. He was educated at Kempsey High School and at the University of Tasmania where he studied Law for three years. Subsequently he spent 13 years in the NSW Public Service and then he spent four years working for the government-owned Aboriginal Hostels Ltd as the Senior Aboriginal Executive Officer. In 1975 Burnam Burnam was a Sir Winston Churchill Fellow, travelling the world comparing the developing situation of Aboriginal Australians with other indigenous movements. Burnam Burnam has a distinguished sporting record: he played rugby for the University of Tasmania and for NSW Country; he also played cricket at intervarsity level and for the Sydney Cricket Club, and he was the first Aboriginal to gain the Bronze Medallion in surf lifesaving. Well known for his appearances in films, Burnam Burnam is a fighter for causes and has a long involvement in Aboriginal land rights struggles. He was the Parliamentary Liaison Officer to the NSW Parliamentary Select Committee on Land Rights, he stood as an independent candidate in the last Senate elections for NSW, and currently he is working as Parliamentary Liaison Officer for the NSW Minister for Aboriginal Affairs.

The emergence of the Green movement in Australia is a predictable response to the destructive pattern of an invading society which justified itself with the biblical notion that man was placed on planet Earth to tame it. The first 150 years of European occupation are a monument to the incredible energy used in denuding the landscape—from a 6 per cent tree cover back to 3 per cent.

Whereas we original Australians blessed, caressed, nurtured and worshipped the landscape in a cyclical time frame, we also became agents of destruction by our forced involvement in the tree-felling industry, once the process of dispossession of our territories was complete and once our handout dependency became secure through the system of rations and reserves. When a whole nation of native peoples is seen in inferior terms against a growing "superior" technological society supported by succeeding governments with policies of annihilation through assimilation, the inevitable happens—a very angry minority voicing appropriately angry responses follows. No amount of money can salvage the distress of dispossession for Aboriginals anywhere in the world. The appearance of non-natural boundaries like fences and the concept of land ownership, development and speculation as a commercial commodity became a passion which was to grow out of all proportion: ultimately it was to make Australia another Europe—complete with male dominance.

Few have failed to realise that Aboriginal inheritance and custodianship (the equivalent of wills and inheritance of the European system) comes down through the female line, and that in Australia today Aboriginal males identify with our mothers' country in land rights claims over traditionally occupied territory. It is the female energy which responds most readily to the threat against all things natural; and the destruction or desecration of the environment is always thwarted initially by female custodianship. So it will be the female peace-keeping energy which will save the planet from destruction by old males. Females make up three-quarters of the Green movement. More of them are active in demonstrations against any form of threat or destruction to the environment. And it is the Aboriginal woman who possesses an indisputable connection with our mother the Earth. Her spiritual strength, born out of tradition, is also acquired from male abuse, mainly sexual.

For Aboriginal women, earth connection unites—while for white people intellect dominates to the disadvantage of all. But the difference is immaterial if anyone from either group accidentally runs over a koala "bear" on the roadway: its death will never be redeemable because this beautiful, almost helpless animal has no natural enemies. The most dramatic example of female protective energy is a joy to all Aboriginals and indeed all Australians. Witness the wonderful way in which rock art, rock engravings and tree carvings have been protected by Aboriginal mothers in the educative process of their children even within the most densely populated area of Australia, the sandstone Aboriginal galleries which surround the Sydney region and which are accessible to most of us.

White Australians too have shown glimpses of custodial responsibilities—as evidenced by the cluster of *Xanthorrhoea australis* (Blackboys, Grasstree) left untouched on a cleared grazing property on the Armidale–Grafton Road in New South Wales. These magnificent specimens, so important to Aboriginals, stand 30 feet tall before the spear shaft and grass appear. The antiquity of these members of the lily family leaves one in awe: in fact they had already reached the height of 29 feet at the time of Jesus Christ, and their growth is so very, very, slow that in some species they grow only one inch every 100 years. In aboriginal mythology departed spirits repose in the trunk of the *Xanthorrhoea*. When we camp near or pass by a cluster, such as the one described, we are conscious of the countless sets of eyes watching over us in a non-judgmental, caring manner. These eyes will live long after living Aboriginals die. Unhappily, no Blackboys stand majestically in a prominent position overlooking the Sydney Opera House in the Botanical Gardens at Bennelong Point, although their protection is guaranteed forever in the green belts and National Parks around Sydney. *Xanthorrhoea* is a multi-purpose plant for traditional purposes: the soft end of the grass was chewed and eaten; the grass made good straw for mattresses in rocky areas and caves; the plant itself, which emits a gluey substance on the trunk, is the only waterproof plant in the bush—and thus it can be used as kindling for fires under rock shelter during the Wet; the fire is almost smokeless, readily combustible with a light blue flame, and conducive to meditation; the flower is hallucinogenic and headache-forming; and witchetty grubs grow big, juicy and succulent in the trunk whilst the florescence, which grows up to 10 feet tall, becomes a ready-made spear shaft that is round and straight and does not require paring; and the gluey substance, when hardened, holds the spearhead stone piece or shark tooth securely.

Aboriginal cosmology revolves around the period known as the Dreamtime, when the formations of the landscape—the trees, hills, mountains, rivers, rock, waterholes—were created by Ancestral Beings who were both men and animals at the same time, or who had the ability to transform themselves from one to another. When the creation of the physical environment was finished, the Ancestors left, leaving human children who, in turn, turned into animals, features of the environment or simply disappeared into the air, the earth or the sea. Thus the countryside is their testimonial to living humans; and it is also evidence of their existence.

Aboriginal people dislike intellectual verbalising in the Green movement. We see ourselves as descendants of the longest and most successful conservation campaign in the history of man, because we opted to become part of the environment itself. We did not mind Australia for 50,000 years to see it destroyed in 200 years of "progress". We did not expect Australia to become lighter as great shiploads of iron ore, manganese, coal and so on are being exported. The shipments have made way instead for gaping quarries which have left a scar on the landscape, deeply hurting its Aboriginal population.

Wild areas, inaccessible to the last frontier of development, last on the hit list, have fortunately had to wait. This has meant that exquisite areas like the South West Tasmanian wilderness have received a permanent stay of execution through the well-organised political activity of the Greens. But money-hungry land developers and speculators remain eager to upset the balance of nature. And at the top end of the continent, the magnificent Daintree rainforest region of North Queensland seems destined for development, with the construction of a roadway.

The area, like the Tasmanian wilderness, contains significant sites of Aboriginal value.

In Tasmania the Green movement was able to secure a land rights victory in the Franklin River area. Due acknowledgement is to be given here to each and every demonstrator and member of the Tasmanian Wilderness Society—in particular my brother, Dr Bob Brown, whom I love. It was a victory we Aboriginal people could never have won alone and we rest secure in the knowledge of its safe-keeping.

For us the victory meant the preservation of important archaeological sites of world significance, because it promises to explain why and how Aboriginal people ventured further south than any other human types during the Ice Age—20,000 years ago. The Kutikina and Deena Keena caves reveal debris of human occupation up to five metres thick, consisting of stone tools, animal bones and ancient campfires.

National Parks are an expression of land rights for the nation, and international parks and wilderness areas designated for inclusion on the World Heritage List are an expression of land rights for the world. Part of the justification for the inclusion of the Western Tasmanian Wilderness National Parks on the World Heritage List relates to Articles 1 and 2 of UNESCO's International Convention concerning the protection of the world's most important cultural and natural sites. The Convention applies to the following:

> Monuments, architectural works, works of monumental sculpture and painting, elements of structures of an archaeological nature, inscriptions, cave dwellings and combinations of features which are of outstanding value from the point of view of art, history or science.

The Kutikina and Deena Keena caves fall within this framework, and this should have been the major justification to save the area.

Both the Kakadu National Park in the Northern Territory and the Willandra Lakes region of southern New South Wales have also been nominated for inclusion on the World Heritage List. The Kakadu National Park is of outstanding universal value because the art sites there (over 1000) represent one of the major and most spectacular concentrations of Aboriginal art in Australia. The

Willandra Lakes region is important because it establishes that modern man had dispersed as far as South-eastern Australia before 30,000 years ago. Complex ritual and symbolic systems there are indicated by the 30,000-year-old ochred burial site and by the 26,000-year-old cremation site (the latter is the oldest such site in the world). Both sites clearly establish the antiquity of Australian Aboriginals.

Willandra is safe until and unless valuable minerals, oil or natural gas are discovered before it can be protected by world listing. Kakadu is far from safe because the potential for opening it up for mineral exploration and discovery is "important" for the "national interest" of Australia. A male-dominated Federal Government has created a male-oriented piece of legislation called the Northern Territory Aboriginal Land Rights Act which has seen no less than 42 amendments during its passage through Parliament. None of the amendments relate to an equal balance of females to males on the Boards of Directors of Aboriginal Land Councils created under the Act. As a direct consequence of this grave omission, the Aboriginal men have sold their Dreaming for a few shekels of silver while the women have stood by helplessly. Aboriginal women are much more formidable and honest to their Dreaming and, because of this strength and conviction, all Aboriginal Land Councils should be dominated in number by women Board members.

In Aboriginal mythology the destruction of the Green Ant Dreaming Eggs (five large boulders sitting on top of the uranium deposit) was always known to herald the destruction of humanity. Aboriginal women have silently watched their Green Ant Dreaming Eggs destroyed to enable the miners to get to their valuable uranium.

One man, a steadfast Rock of Gibraltar named Strider, did what other Greens were not able to do: he camped on the fringe of Kakadu, protesting by his very presence against the impending destruction of one of the most beautiful places on earth. Most Aboriginals have been whitewashed into thinking that gentle humans like Strider are dirty, lazy, hippy layabouts. Those responsible for such value judgments are the uptown armchair "niggers" in Canberra. In point of truth such "white hippies" are more Aboriginal than most urban Aboriginals in their treatment of, and respect for, mother earth — and in their personal relationship with her.

I sensed this breath of fresh air in white people in 1973, and so I left my Clerk Class 10 position in Canberra as a public servant to identify with these "real" people. I attended the Down to Earth Festival organised by the then Australian Treasurer and one-time Acting Prime Minister of Australia, Dr Jim Cairns, with the controversial Junie Morosi. Being dubbed "the black hippy" only made me more determined to be with these gentle folk. One Down to Earth festival followed the other—until I received a devastating shock at the Berri Festival in South Australia. An Aboriginal Arts, Craft and Musical Festival was being held simultaneously in nearby Adelaide. I journeyed from Berri and enticed a busload of traditional performers from the Oombulgarri–Kununurra area of the Kimberley region of Western Australia. By arrangement they were to perform around a campfire hosted by white "hippies". The didgeridoo players, clap stick artists, singers and dancers were performing when, to my horror, a nude male crazily picked up the end of the didgeridoo while it was being played and placed his erect penis into it.

The horror and shame of that single act made me hate whites. I was to miss the next five annual Down to Earth Festivals because of the sickness and irreverence of that one act.

My feelings of revulsion were all the more intense as I knew that the performers came from an area which had seen the destruction of their burial sites and hunting grounds by white men, following the non-consultative decision to dam the Ord River in Western Australia and create Lake Argyle which is nine times larger in volume than the mighty Sydney Harbour. I then took a job window dressing or "advising" the giant mining company CRA. The irony, however, was not lost upon me when one of CRA's subsidiaries discovered a very valuable diamond pipe which plunged deep into Lake Argyle. The company, together with the Government of Western Australia, contemplated very seriously the possibility of draining the lake to get at the treasure—thus giving the Aboriginal people a faint chance to rekindle their custodianship rites over the departed!

During the two months spent as Aboriginal Adviser to CRA I gained valuable insight into their plans to explore and exploit 49

Aboriginal reserves in the Top End for minerals. The Chairman of the Northern Land Council in Darwin, James Galarrwuy Yunupingu, used my information in his famous speech to the Press Club.

The information enabled him to be chosen as Australian of the Year, and I got sacked.

Many of my "hippy" friends banded together and bought properties in the "Rainbow Region" around Nimbin in northern New South Wales: the value of their land appreciated so much in such a small span of time that they were quickly faced with wealth. As for me, I took a position as Liaison Officer for the New South Wales Parliamentary Select Committee set up to enquire how land rights could be granted to NSW Aboriginals.

During this period, grave concern was being expressed about unwarranted logging at the Terania Creek rainforest area of northern New South Wales. When I learned of the signs of Aboriginal occupation by the Bundjalung people — in the form of stone axes and camping sites — within the logging area, I used official time and a Government vehicle to attend the concentrated Green demonstration at Terania Creek. This was at a time when the State Labor Government was very much in favour of logging at that particular rainforest. Once again I incurred the displeasure of the Government; once again I found myself without a job after I had made strong public statements against logging and Government policy. After two years of Green political agitation, and with the approach of a State election, the Labor Government did a complete reversal and stopped all logging at Terania. The Government held office — but I failed to become reinstated in my job.

Most Greens will not identify with pure Aboriginal land rights campaigns and demonstrations unless the land in question has the promise of a National (or International) Park at the end of the rainbow. But the creation of national and international parks not only robs us Aboriginals of our traditional territory; their creation is also used as a tool to deliberately prevent impending Aboriginal land claims. Thus the sudden emergence of huge chunks of land designated and gazetted by governments as "national parks" is still part of the colonial mentality, which makes governments refuse to give back to the black man what the governments know was always his.

Land rights in Australia can only refer to Government land, and in New South Wales in particular, where we have the New South Wales Aboriginal Land Rights Act 1983 in place and operating, land can only come back to inalienable Aboriginal freehold title if it is vacant Crown Land, is surplus to Government need and will not be required for future use. All Government departments have identified such land as mostly falling within one of these categories; so we find ourselves picking up the crumbs from under the bureaucratic table once again. By some strange accident the New South Wales legislation provides for ownership of all minerals — excepting the "royal" minerals, gold and silver — as well as coal, petroleum and natural gas. Should they decide to get into that particular trip, Aboriginals are free to exploit minerals on land they inherit (old existing Aboriginal reserves) and land they purchase.

The New South Wales Aboriginal Land Rights Act introduces a new concept in Australian land law. It proclaims all Aboriginal land to be "inalienable" Aboriginal title, presumably so that we Aboriginal folk can continue to have only a spiritual relationship with our land. The spirit and intent of this worthy gesture discriminates against our non-Aboriginal brothers and sisters — and I am now contemplating mounting a legal challenge in order to allow non-Aboriginals the great honour of also having a total spiritual relationship with their lands! Since inalienable title simply means that land becomes financially valueless (because it cannot be purchased or sold), all sorts of exciting ramifications follow. The so-called "hippy" properties would be first to be transferred to local Aboriginal Land Councils, and a leaseback arrangement would enable white people to camp on Aboriginal territory for 100 years or less, after which it would become re-occupied by local Aboriginal people. The Mt Oak property (3000 acres) at Bredbo near Canberra, which was the site of the 1979 Down to Earth Festival, may lead the way if I, as one of its trustees, have my way. In my opinion this type of arrangement represents the true spirit of land rights.

When I ran for a NSW Senate seat at the last two federal elections my policy on this issue was "The Land's Right For All Who Love Mother Earth".

Whilst the Greens and Aboriginals have helped each other out in times of environmental threats by linking up in demonstrations, there has not been a fusion of their commitment so that they become members of each other's various organisations. The Land Rights Support Group is very low in numbers and very few Aboriginals belong to the Tasmanian Wilderness Society, MAUM, Friends of the Earth, the National Parks Association, bushwalkers clubs and so on. Any group placed under a daily microscope over a number of generations, as Aboriginals have been, does not feel like being exposed — especially when the observing eyes behind the microscope are highly critical of any differences in lifestyle, habits and humour. The emotional security of just being together in areas like Redfern or Fitzroy is for us Aboriginals a welcome relief from a world which is hostile to our very existence and where (at best) we are seen as nuisance value and (at worst) we should be all shot at birth. How strange it is that Aboriginals are made to feel more alienated than a brand new Australian just arrived from overseas for the first time! Are we not entitled to feel historically bewildered? Naturally, there is a strong element of mistrust . . . and naturally urban Aboriginals will not be seen on Australian beaches in the summer, or walking down bush tracks frequented by other people.

While we cannot expect a subterranean relationship between introduced European trees and eucalypts to develop overnight, we should observe the compatible habits of companion plants in Australia. It is reassuring to find, when passing through such suburban areas as Toorak, Mt Eliza, St Ives, Wahroonga and Indooroopilly, that their original tree cover and vegetation is still intact. There, property value is enhanced *because* the original white settlers refused to clear their blocks of land. And, conversely, it is sad to note the mentality which has allowed western suburban Sydney and Melbourne blocks to be valued on their total clearance of all trees and vegetation. And in this context, it is important to take note of the development of our capital city, Canberra, which carried a free gift of 15 trees for every house built till the point has now been reached where the houses are sinking below the treeline.

The physical environment in Australia is more powerful than the total sum of all the human beings who have lived on this continent in the long distant past and who will live on it in the future. Aboriginals have always operated by the cyclical time-frame of nature; and our gentle nature, silent strengths, and undeniable link with the land testify to the special energy that can be gained from our environment. We all automatically acquire a soft, laid-back Australian way of living the longer we remain here.

There are certain dire consequences for those who refuse to listen to nature. An example of this was Mr Malcolm Fraser's sudden call for an early federal election in 1983. Although a farmer, "big Mal" disregarded natural elements like the effects of a long drought, and he campaigned when Australia was a tinder box. In the middle of that political campaign, bushfire descended upon Melbourne and Adelaide on Ash Wednesday, leaving a trail of devastation and death behind. Malcolm hovered around the devastation while Bob Hawke, far removed from the area, was campaigning in places like Townsville and Cairns in North Queensland. The moment Bob Hawke was elected the drought broke. It rained non-stop in Sydney for almost his first six weeks in office. The day he left Australia to make his first visit to President Reagan it stopped raining, and the sun shone brightly for the next three weeks. The day Bob arrived back in Sydney it poured with rain. Political advisers should observe the politics of nature and advise governments to call elections during the first full-moon Saturday of either Spring or Autumn; preferably it should be Spring, with its fine array of bottlebrush, banksia and so on. The Prime Minister should plan his television advertisements during the full moon before the elections. He should be televised silhouetting himself against the full moon as it pops over the sea horizon at dusk while he makes his policy speech. By playing on the goodwill of moonstruck Australians he could find that nature might help where economic policies fail.

The 1988 Australian Bicentennial celebrations serve to highlight the illegal dispossession of Australia from the Aboriginal nations. I do not deny my neighbour his right to celebrate in party form for whatever reason, so long as he observes normal courtesies and behavioural standards. My sincere hope is that sometime between 1990 and 2000 the Australian people will also share the celebrations of our first 250 Bicentenaries, which will mark the continuous and unbroken occupation of this continent by the first *Australians*, who probably arrived on the *first fleet* 50,000 years ago.

In an appropriate gift back to the Aboriginal community, any and all governments should celebrate the various Aboriginal Bicentenaries by handing back to Aboriginals their inalienable freehold title to all State forests and all national parks within Australia. This would be a book transfer only: the parks and forests would not change their current management styles too greatly. The Fraser Liberal Government has already given back the Kakadu National Park to the Aboriginal communities of Arnhem Land; and in 1984 the Hawke Labor Government did likewise with the Uluru National Park. Both parties have leaseback arrangements whereby white management is maintained with good Aboriginal representation at Board level. These arrangements have hastened the process of appointment of Aboriginal rangers, initially in training roles and ultimately in management control positions. State governments have recognised the training needs and appointments of Aboriginal rangers in National Parks and Wildlife Departments, but they have failed to follow the important precedent created by the successive Liberal and Labor federal governments.

New South Wales is the leading State for Aboriginal preparation of Aboriginal ranger training: during 1982 22 Aboriginal trainees enrolled in the ranger course at the Aboriginal Training College at Tranby, in the Sydney suburb of Glebe.

While I worked with the Keane Parliamentary Committee on Land Rights in 1981, I came up with the notion of the need for State and federal governments to create Aboriginal Heritage Commissions so that the Aboriginals of New South Wales, for instance, could ultimately take over from the NSW National Parks and Wildlife Department those matters relating to Aboriginal Heritage. Aboriginal people would take camping, hunting and rehabilitation rights. As owners of State forests we would give ourselves flora and fauna rights over such areas. In fauna rights, the creation of native animal hospitals for treatment and for resting purposes before their release back to the bush would provide significant transitional employment opportunities for reserve Aboriginals.

The NSW National Parks and Wildlife Service has already successfully identified 10,000 Aboriginal sites, and indications are that there are still 20,000 sites to be identified. The most vexing problem here is obviously the reluctance of white property owners to reveal obvious Aboriginal sites for fear of Aboriginal acquisition under the National Parks and Wildlife Service Act. All people are required, by law in New South Wales, to report any finding of ancient Aboriginal artefacts, stone tools and other implements. But in this area silence reigns supreme.

Still, to have exclusive Australia-wide franchise over native flora (birds' nests, staghorns, ferns, lilies, orchids) in State forests would be a major boost to the horrific unemployment statistics of Aboriginal people on reserves (98 per cent for males). All Aboriginal reserves would then contain a four-hectare native plant nursery where rescued plants from the logged sections of state forests would be potted and cared for by local Aboriginal people. An Aboriginal trucking company would take the plants from their original home to the reserve, and then from the reserve to the wholesale Aboriginal nursery in each of the major cities—Brisbane, Sydney, Melbourne, Adelaide and Perth. The trucking company would subsequently disperse the plants to Aboriginal retail outlets, which would use the plants to landscape all new government housing estates as well as to Green all Aboriginal reserves—and even the Aboriginal urban areas of Redfern, Fitzroy, inner Brisbane, Adelaide and Perth.

Governments are notoriously non-entrepreneurial by nature and their slowness of pace stifles exciting development. People like me are seen as eccentrics and, unfortunately, governments do not offer financial rewards for new ideas. It seems a great pity that our own round-leafed alpine gum (*Eucalyptus pulveralenta*), used so successfully in the florist industry and imported into Australia from the United States at $1.50 a stem, should not be available in Australia from Aboriginal sources. High-altitude state forests could be used as farms for Aboriginals to cultivate *Eucalyptus pulveralenta* from seed. At a later phase, the glycerined, coloured product would be manufactured.

It also seems incongruous that 80 per cent of eucalyptus oil is imported into Australia from China and unfair that a country like Japan with a 25 per cent tree cover should denude our trees for its wood-chipping industry. The Greening of Australia and the use of 1988 as the International Earth Repair Year should attract great interest and contributions from our State and federal governments.

Let us all renew our Dreaming on this our Sacred Island Gondwanaland.

6:
FROM RED TO GREEN: CITIZEN-WORKER ALLIANCE

Jack Mundey

JACK MUNDEY *was born on the Atherton Tablelands in 1932. He came to Sydney in the early fifties to play Rugby League for Parramatta. In 1962 Jack was elected Organiser of the NSW Builders Labourers Federation. Subsequently in 1968, he became Secretary of the NSW Builders Labourers Federation—a position which he voluntarily relinquished in 1974, after leading many of the now world-famous Green Bans. Jack has been a NSW delegate to the Australian Conservation Foundation National Council since 1973, and he has also lectured worldwide on Green issues, notably in the United Kingdom in 1975, at the United Nations Habitat Conference in Vancouver in 1976, at the World Wildlife Foundation in San Francisco in 1977. In 1984 he was elected Alderman of the Sydney City Council, where he was appointed Chairman of the Planning Committee in 1984 as well as 1985. Jack's well-known activities within the radical movement have taken a momentum of their own since the NSW Labor Government's summary and anti-democratic sacking of the Sydney City Council in April 1987.*

The Green Ban movement in New South Wales in the early seventies was unique and attracted the attention of environmentalists the world over. The main reason for this interest was the unlikely alliance of generally middle-class environmentalists with a militant trade union, the NSW Builders Labourers. It is an unfortunate fact that the trade union movement in Australia, as in other industrialised countries, has a poor record of environmental consciousness. Likewise the environment and conservation movement has an equally poor record of concern for trade union struggles over wages, conditions and the standard of living of workers.

Environmentalists are generally the more enlightened of the middle-upper classes. They give a much higher priority to nature conservation than they give to urban environmental issues. Yet we live in the most urbanised country on earth, with 90 per cent of our people living in six cities: if you take Melbourne–Geelong and Sydney–Newcastle–Wollongong (which are almost connected) we have nearly half of Australia's population in two huge metropolitan areas, and all these urban areas have many and varied environmental problems. Trade unions, on the other hand, all too often confine themselves to mere economism (ie wages and conditions only). The Green Ban experience was therefore tremendously important from a historical point of view because one particular union articulated why it fought to save workers' housing, historical buildings and open spaces. That particular union also expressed a definite viewpoint on the quality of life of urban workers and other citizens.

The corporate sector and bureaucratic institutions have often succeeded in driving a wedge between environmentalists and trade unionists. They have falsely portrayed environmentalists as selfish "greenies", who are not really worried about workers. So instead of unionists and environmentalists being allies in the common fight for a decent quality of living in noisy, polluted cities dominated by private motor vehicles, we often find that environmentalists and trade unionists are cynically exploited by both private corporations and public sector bureaucrats for their own vested interests. In the Green Ban movement, however, residents, environmentalists and trade unions with a social conscience all worked in common cause. They argued that the two ingredients—work and a clean environment—were not necessarily in conflict. Indeed, citizens in huge modern cities demand *both* employment and a decent urban environment.

This remarkable movement had its birth when a group of women from the select suburb of Hunters Hill banded together to fight to save the last remaining bushland on the Parramatta River, called Kellys Bush. This was June, 1971. The biggest building boom in Sydney's history was in full flight. The conservative, and now universally condemned, corrupt NSW State Government of Sir Robert Askin was in power. The big developers were having a field day. It was open slather, as there wasn't any provision for public participation, and the National Trust was powerless to prevent the demolition of historically or architecturally significant buildings.

After exhausting all known channels of protest this group of women, called the "Battlers For Kellys Bush", came to the NSW Builders Labourers Federation because of a newspaper report in which I was quoted as saying, "In a modern society, trade unions must broaden their vision and horizons and become involved in wide-range social, political and environmental activities. The struggle for improvement in wages and conditions must continue, but the broader issues should be addressed. Not only has the trade union movement the right to intervene, it has the responsibility to do so."

When the "Battlers For Kellys Bush" came to address the NSW Builders Labourers Federation's State Executive requesting our support, some of the less environmentalist thinking Executive members asked: "Why should we the working class be fighting to save open space for these well-heeled upper-class people from the fashionable suburb of Hunters Hill? There is nothing in it for our members." On the other hand I, and some of my colleagues, argued that it was not simply an old fashioned "class" question. To fight for the retention of precious open space went beyond narrow class considerations. It was a social, political and environmental issue. In fact these environmentally aware middle-class women had much in common with an environmentally aware and concerned trade union, which was expressing a social conscience. At the time I described it as "an alliance between the enlightened middle class from Hunters

Hill and the enlightened working class from the NSW Builders Labourers Federation enjoined in common environmental struggle".

The Builders Labourers Federation or BLF produced a sound policy for implementing our work-bans for environmental considerations. We said to the women from Kellys Bush that we would accede to their request to impose a ban provided they called a public meeting of Hunters Hill residents so as to demonstrate that there was strong public support for the retention of open space. A meeting of over 600 residents took place. There was a unanimous resolution requesting the ban and so the first of the famous Green Bans was imposed. This democratic method of imposition of Green Bans stood the union in good stead. It clearly demonstrated that it wasn't Mundey or some other union leader arbitrarily deciding to act on the basis of his own particular judgmental values. Every ban was only imposed *after* a full and open public meeting had been held.

Historically trade unions have generally imposed "black bans" on certain work so as to improve their wages and conditions. Originally our bans for environmental reasons were also called black bans, but I considered our new bans to be more far-reaching, more moral — and thus the more apt and descriptive term "Green Ban" came into the language. With the Kellys Bush Green Ban came uproar from Sir Robert Askin and his developer friends. Sir Robert in his best sarcastic mood said, "Who do the NSW BLF think they are? Mere labourers setting themselves up as Urban Town Planners!" He went on to say that the new bans would not be tolerated. The property developer concerned — A. V. Jennings — said they would ignore the ban and use non-union labour. However they hastily withdrew that threat after building workers on an A. V. Jennings project being constructed in North Sydney declared: "If one tree or shrub is destroyed in Kellys Bush, this half completed office block will remain uncompleted, as a monument to Kellys Bush." This action really set the cat amongst the pigeons. Despite all Askin's blustering and threats, people began to realise that the Green Ban on Kellys Bush had the support of very diverse strata of Sydney's population — including many conservative citizens, who would normally be voters for Sir Robert Askin's Liberal Party.

The Green Ban movement struck a chord. For the first half of the sixties, the unelected, remote and elitist State Planning Authority (SPA) had decided what was best for Sydney and New South Wales. There was no avenue for public participation in the planning process. There was an air of hopelessness as residents, environmentalists and other citizen organisations fought to have some say in the political and planning decisions. For instance, Resident Action Groups had sprung up all over New South Wales in the late sixties and an umbrella organisation, the "Coalition of Residents Action Groups" or CRAG, had begun to coordinate citizen protest against the NSW Government.

Now the Green Ban success in Kellys Bush gave great heart to CRAG, and the BLF was inundated with requests for similar Green Bans. In the subsequent actions the same formula adopted for Kellys Bush was followed: there would have to be a public expression by the people or organisations requesting the ban before the BLF would accede to each request. In this way allegations that the union leaders were making personal value judgments and flexing their industrial and political muscles in an arrogant manner were prevented.

A UNION WITH A DIFFERENCE

The NSW Builders Labourers Federation in the forties and fifties had been a corrupt union, with its right-wing and reactionary leadership working in open collusion with the employers in the Master Builders Association (MBA). Left-wing militant workers fighting to civilise the very harsh and dangerous building industry were victimised. A "blacklist" existed and the union leaders and the employers cooperated to drive militant activists off building sites and out of the industry. In one year in the fifties I had 17 jobs because of this treachery. The employer would discover that I was a union activist, and one of the leaders of the Rank and File Committee — whose aim was to cleanse the union, and to democratise and civilise the industry. I would then be promptly sacked. The same thing happened to Michael McNamara, Bob Pringle, Joe Owens, Bud Cook, Harry Connell, Tom Hogan, Eddie Gordon, Darcy Duggan and literally hundreds of other militant BLF members in the fifties. However, with the high-rise building boom of the late fifties and early sixties the concentration of labourers on big projects became greater, and so it became more difficult to victimise the militants (who at that stage were merely fighting for decent wages and conditions and for a certain degree of human dignity). Finally the rank and file broke through. Michael McNamara, only 22 years of age, became the secretary of the BLF. Wages, conditions of work, safety, hygiene began to improve. The ordinary BLF member was for the first time proud of the union.

Michael McNamara resigned of his own volition in 1968, and I then became the secretary. As the rank and file extended their control of the BLF, some of their policies and decisions clearly showed the new nature of the BLF's philosophy—a philosophy which really allowed the union to take that vital environmental action a little later on. From the early sixties we were very involved against the war in Vietnam. Many of our members were arrested in the huge moratorium marches and other actions against that war. The union was to be in the forefront in the fight in support of Aboriginal Land Rights and against racism wherever it manifested itself. Ninety per cent of our members were migrants, and we elected Greek, Italian, Portuguese, Spanish, Yugoslav and other migrant organisers. We were the first building union in Australia to compel the employers to employ women. In what up to then had been an all-male enclave, women were also elected to the State Executive as Organisers. To combat entrenched trade union bureaucracy, we introduced a very controversial union rule—limited tenure to office. All full-time officials, after being elected each three years, must relinquish their position after six years (two terms) and return to the job for at least three years before being eligible for reelection. Besides, all full-time union officials received exactly the same wages as the worker on the job. Naturally the limited tenure policy was not popular with many trade union bureaucrats who really believed in life tenure or better if it could be organised!

Two other political and industrial actions undertaken by the BLF in the early seventies showed its better mettle and its increasing social and political sensitivity. Jeremy Fisher was kicked out of the Robert Menzies College at Macquarie University solely because he was a homosexual. Builders Labourers working on the campus stopped work on urgently required buildings and forced the authorities to reinstate Fisher. The following year at Sydney University, Elizabeth Jacka and Jean Curthoys were prevented from running a Women Social Liberation Course, and both staff and students of the Philosophy Department went on strike. Again, Sydney University was engaged in extensive building developments which were urgently required for the next university year. The BLF members went out on strike in support, and Jacka and Curthoys won the day. I cite these wider political and social actions to demonstrate the heightened awareness of the union. When, therefore, the Green Ban requests began to arrive, the union became actively *responsive*. It did not merely arrange to send a telegram or letter off to the Government as most unions would have done, claiming they had done all they could.

GREEN BANS MUSHROOM

The mushrooming of the bans continued apace. From June 1971 with Kellys Bush through to the end of the Green Ban period in March 1975, 42 Green Bans were imposed. They held up an estimated $5000 million of so-called development (1970 valuation). The Bans were diverse and affected every socio-economic group in Australian society.

The Rocks, the oldest settlement of European Australia, had been under threat since 1970 when the Askin Government had set up the Sydney Cove Redevelopment Authority (SCRA). The intention was to carry out widespread demolition of this historic area and then massive construction of high-rise commercial development worth more than $700 million. The Rocks residents were different from the Hunters Hill middle-upper classes. They were working-class, and many of their ancestors could be traced to the early settlement. The workers from the Rocks worked in jobs servicing the city, on the waterfront, in the offices and factories and on the ferries. Now the dwindling number of Rocks residents were to be shifted to suburbia, thereby losing all their links with their eighteenth- and nineteenth-century heritage. Led by a former barmaid, Nita McRae, a fiery and capable spokesperson, the Rocks Resident Action Group was formed. It heard about Kellys Bush and wrote to every trade union affiliated with the Labour Council. Nita related in *Rocking the Foundations* — an award-winning documentary by Pat Fiske — how only one union replied to her request for assistance.

That union was the BLF.

Over 1000 people attended the public meeting at the Rocks in late 1971. The breadth of the mounting opposition to the re-development became clear. Tom Uren, later to become Gough Whitlam's Minister of Urban and Regional Development; Milo Dunphy, conservationist; both the Catholic and Anglican Churches; Neville Gruzman, architect; John Morris of the National Trust — all opposed the massive destruction of this enormously important part of our history. The meeting unanimously requested that the Green Ban be imposed so as to allow the Resident Action Group to draw up a genuine "Peoples Plan" for the area. This "Peoples Plan" clearly showed that the BLF was not against *all* development *per se* — as Askin had been claiming; but the union *was* against insensitive, gross development — particularly when ordinary citizens hadn't been notified, consulted or allowed to advance their views on redevelopment proposals. During the following three years, before the historic area was saved, there were many bitter physical clashes as Askin used police and scab labour in attempts to smash the Rocks Green Ban. But the Green Ban held, and it saved the Rocks.

Neville Wran, who was to become NSW ALP Opposition Leader, declared that a Labor Government would abolish the SCRA. This promise wasn't honoured when Labor came to power in 1976. However SCRA's bureaucracy did change — Askin's Colonel McGee was replaced by Wran's Janet Thompson, who is more aware of urban environmentalism. How ironic it is that now SCRA boasts that over two million people annually visit the birthplace of European settlement in this country! How many people would bother to visit there if those concrete and glass canyons around Circular Quay had gone right down to the water's edge adjacent to the Harbour Bridge?

Woolloomooloo, one of Sydney's oldest suburbs, was also to be transformed from a working-class port area to a $600 million commercial development. Again, the hapless citizens who lived in the 'Loo were to be uprooted and distributed around the far-flung western and south western outer suburbs. Victoria Street is a famous landmark between Kings Cross and the 'Loo; in fact it is on a cliff which overlooks the 'Loo. Frank Theeman, director of the developing company Victoria Point Pty Ltd, began to forcibly evict squatters who were fighting to retain medium density and low-cost housing. The street had traditionally been inhabited by a pot pourri — bohemians, seamen, actors, labourers, writers and artists. Victoria Street, Theeman had hoped, would be turned into two giant 45-storey tower blocks, something which would have completely changed the street's character. The Green Ban cost Theeman millions of dollars in interest payments, and finally blocks of fewer storeys (14) were constructed and most of the streetscape and better buildings were retained. Juanita Neilsen, who ran a Kings Cross newspaper, *Now*, and who had campaigned against the high-rise development, vanished and was never found. It is believed she was murdered, but an inquest returned an open finding.

Sidney Londish (who has many friends in high places, one of whom is Paul Keating) was the main developer in the proposed 'Loo scheme. He was a close personal friend of Sir Robert Askin, who together with John Charody, an Hungarian-born developer, raised finance for Londish's ambitious Woolloomooloo development from the USSR's Narodny Bank in Singapore. More irony: here was our anti-communist premier of NSW raising money for his developer friend from a Russian bank. It was all in vain, because the communist secretary of the NSW BLF, Jack Mundey, imposed a Green Ban at the request of the residents. (When later told of the odd twist of a communist union official holding up the Londish–Narodny development, the manager of the Narodny Bank said, "This union man must be a strange sort of person if he is opposed to progress!")

One of the driving forces against the Woolloomooloo high-rise was the local progressive priest Father Ed Campion, author of *The Rockchoppers* and *The Irish In Australia*. It was Father Campion who urged the local Action Group led by Mrs Wilkinson and Nell and

Jerry Leonard to contact the BLF. The Woolloomooloo ban held firm despite legal, political and personal threats. Both the reactionary Askin government and a conservative Sydney City Council were applying pressure, but by this time the first federal Labor Government in nearly a quarter of a century had been elected, and Whitlam promised to improve the quality of life in our cities. The Department of Urban and Regional Development under Tom Uren with a very innovative Town Planner (Pat Troy) at its helm started to make an impact. On Troy's initiative a splendid plan for medium density Housing Commission flat development was advanced. This was an acceptable alternative and the residents gave it their endorsement. Finally the State Government and the City Council came to their senses and a joint venture saw the sensitive construction of a Housing Commission development which is now looked upon as a prototype of desirable medium density housing in an inner-city area.

It was also very significant that, with the successes of the Green Bans, the frustrated developers changed their tactics. In the beginning they and Askin tried to bludgeon the union, but when this failed they resorted to trying to bribe the union leaders to break the bans. If I had accepted only some of the bribes offered to me during the four years of the Green Bans (1971–75) I would be a multi-millionaire today. It shot home to me the corrupt nature of late industrial capitalism in general, and the widespread nature of corruption in NSW in particular.

In 1972 a group of people, led by the then Lord Mayor and former Rugby great, Nick Shehadie, and by developer Dick Baker of the Mainline Group, hit upon a bright idea. To celebrate 200 years of White Australian rule, Sydney could host the Olympic Games in 1988! And where better to have the games than in the 400-acre Centennial Park in the Eastern Suburbs of Sydney—a site which Lord Carrington had decreed open space for posterity at the celebrations of the first centenary? What myopic thinking to destroy it! A diverse group of citizens rose up in anger against the proposed desecration of Centennial Park—against turning it into concrete sport stadiums, gymnasiums, swimming pools and the like, with of course high areas for parking facilities for God-car. Novelist Patrick White rubbed

shoulders with unlikely allies: Cardinal Gilroy; entrepreneur Harry
M. Miller; Neville Wran (at the time still a remote MLC); Pat Hills,
the then leader of the NSW Opposition; novelist Kylie Tennant;
actor Noel Ferrier; economist Professor Neil Runcie and many other
notables. Three thousand people attended a rally in the Park, then
marched to Sydney Town Hall, where once again the NSW BLF
acceded to the unanimous call, from an overflow audience, to impose
a Green Ban. The speakers argued that any sporting stadiums of such
a magnitude, if built, should be in the western suburbs of Sydney
where the great majority of Sydney's four million people live. So
once again the protest was not against sport stadiums as such, but
against the incredible proposition of destroying lovely Centennial
Park. Fifteen years on, who, except possibly the most avaricious
developers, would now suggest that Centennial Park be destroyed?

Changing community values have been such that thankfully
Centennial Park is now safe. Again this is an example of the value
of the Green Bans and how they raised the consciousness of people
in relation to the urban environment. Fifteen years ago we were
vilified for our Centennial Park Green Ban. Today we have been
well and truly vindicated.

Moreover, after discussions with representatives of the National
Trust, and because so many historical buildings were being demolished
during the building boom, it was also decided that a demolition ban
should be imposed on any building classified by the National Trust
to be worthy of preservation for historical or architectural reasons.
During those years of the Green Bans there were virtually no impedi-
ments to prevent any owner of an historical building from demolishing
it. Thus over 100 historical buildings owe their existence to our bans,
and our action encouraged the Wran Labor Government when it
came to power in 1976 to introduce stronger demolition laws on
classified buildings.

One building, the historic 155-year-old Pitt Street Uniting Church,
caused much controversy when the minister, Reverend Bryant, much
to the dismay of his congregation, declared he was going to demolish
the fine two-storey building and build a 30-storey commercial office
block on the site. The parishioners came to us to oppose the minister's

plans. The church was saved—and on the occasion of the Church's 150th anniversary, the first Uniting Church's woman minister, Reverend Dorothy McMahon, and the NSW Governor unveiled a plaque honouring the NSW BLF for saving the building. In the same year, 1972, the Askin Government announced plans to cut down three lovely Moreton Bay fig trees, over 160 years old, which stood in the Outer Domain adjacent to the Botanical Gardens. The plan was to build a carpark for the Opera House. The Opera House was nearing completion when it was suddenly realised a parking place for God-car had been forgotten! The idea was to cut down the trees, cut into the cliff face in lower Macquarie Street and build the carpark partially underground. The damage to the Botanical Gardens and the old Government House nearby would have been extensive. The BLF Green Ban was welcomed by the NSW Governor, Sir Roden Cutler, who was reported as saying, "Thank God for Jack Mundey and the Builders Labourers."

A teary final night crowd at the old Theatre Royal was bewailing the fact that the theatre—the last live theatre in the commercial heart of Sydney, on the corner of Castlereagh and King Streets—was soon to be demolished. John Tasker, a prominent producer, organised a "Save the Theatre Royal" campaign, and the first port-of-call was the BLF office and another Green Ban request. At a large public meeting in the Town Hall, attended by 2500 people, the ban was imposed. Then Dick Dusseldorp, head of the Lend Lease company, called to see me. He proposed that in the giant complex which was to be built on the site of the old theatre his company would build a new Theatre Royal, incorporating all the features demanded by the "Save the Theatre Royal" Committee. A further public meeting was held and the compromise was accepted. I might add that in all my dealings with developers, Dick Dusseldorp was one of the few who were trustworthy.

The Green Bans were now very controversial and Australian society was becoming polarised in quite strange ways. Naturally the Askin Government and their developer friends opposed them—as did right-wing trade union leaders such as John Ducker and Barrie Unsworth. But they were joined by some conservative and orthodox left-wing union leaders, such as Soviet-oriented Pat Clancy. Clancy felt we were "going too far" and "going beyond the bounds of unionism". On the other hand, many people who were normally against trade unions found themselves on-side the BLF and the Green Bans. Many people who had voted conservative all their lives uncomfortably found themselves supporting a trade union led by Marxists.

Green Bans fell into many different categories. Some, such as Centennial Park, were non-negotiable—the Park simply had to be kept as an open space. Others, such as the Theatre Royal, were negotiable; and compromise solutions could be worked out. The union was answering those critics who were saying "Mundey and the BLF will bring Sydney's development to a halt". We were constantly demonstrating that we were not against *all* development, though we argued that there should be genuine public participation, and that the twin issues of a building's usefulness and of social considerations must always be addressed.

In fact this hit the raw nerve of conservative governments and developers alike. We were arguing strongly for a degree of worker control. Why should corporations and bureaucrats alone determine what should be built? How should a country be developed? When one considers that we supposedly live in an enlightened and civilised society, really important decisions are made by a very tiny minority, albeit a very powerful one. Really vital decisions affecting the public at large are often made in secret, sometimes in trans-national board rooms in countries thousands of miles away.

We were saying that all development is not necessarily "good". Both of the longest serving regimes in NSW, those of Askin and of Wran, adopted the same "development ethos": *all* development was good; the number of job opportunities was always exaggerated; and if development such as the Darling Harbour Scheme or the Monorail attracted hostile public opposition, or if the Sydney City Council questioned certain aspects, the Government would ignore environment impact statements and introduce special legislation, thus overriding any existing environmental laws.

The Green Ban movement covered both the natural and man-built environments, though because of the building boom in Sydney in the seventies, the built environment was under the greatest pressure. On my lecture tours in the United States, Canada and Europe, conservationists were always amazed that the movement in Sydney could bring together conservationists and trade unionists in a common struggle and achieve so much. To give an example of the yawning chasm that exists in the United States, when I organised a meeting between a group of trade unionists and environmentalists at the Sierra Club (the oldest conservation organisation in the world) in San Francisco in 1977, it was the first-ever such meeting this century!

Trade unionists and environmentalists can be natural allies if both consider and have real respect for each other's standpoint.

WORK IN A SUSTAINABLE SOCIETY

It has never ceased to amaze me that the Protestant work ethic is never seriously questioned, particularly when there has been so much ecological destruction. All of the main philosophical strands of both capitalism and socialism have remained locked into the economic-growth-at-any-cost straitjacket. There is precious little debate on making ecological thinking an integral part of all economic and political decisions, yet surely this must happen if the planet is to be saved.

On the one hand the ever-present reality is that humankind is now capable of unleashing such nuclear weapons as to annihilate itself, and much of nature as well. On the other hand if sanity prevails and the forces for peace succeed against the forces that would bring nuclear destruction upon us, we could still destroy the globe through human greed and ecological ignorance. Paul and Ann Ehrlich, Barry Commoner, Murray Bookchin, Richard Grossman and other such thinkers have done much to make people in "advanced"[?] industrial societies begin to think about ecology. Yet a number of well-educated people remain who, when confronted with the enormity of the ecological problems, shrug their shoulders and mutter, "Yes, but something will turn up." An even more selfish approach can be found among many middle-aged people who say, "Yes it is serious, but I only have another 20 or 30 years on earth, so why should I worry too much about such things?"

Environmentalists must forge closer links with the labour movement. Furthermore environmentalists have an educating role to play because of their greater understanding of ecology. The central theme must be an insistence that all work performed should be of a socially useful and ecologically benign nature. A tall order indeed, but there isn't any alternative. Once judgmental values relating to ecology are introduced then people will realise the primary importance of things ecological. Glimmers of hope can be seen with the advent of the West German Greens and their ecological influence on the labour movement and specifically the West German social-democrats.

In the early seventies, at about the same time that the Green Bans in Australia were making an impact, in the United Kingdom the Lucas Aerospace Workers' Corporate Plan for making products of a "socially useful nature" was attracting considerable attention in both the environmental and labour movements. The Lucas management was restructuring its operations following the loss of a number of military contracts, and was threatening redundancies amongst the workforce. Led by Tom Scarborough and Mike Cooley, the Combined Trade Union Shop Committee embraced a wide range of worker skills—from scientific and technical know-how right across to labouring work. Fighting back against the sack, the workers drew up a Corporate Plan of "socially useful" products instead of manufacturing military hardware. The actual products varied from kidney machines right through to specially manufactured vehicles suitable for Third World countries. These vehicles would be so sound they would last for 30 years or more. The Corporate Plan was widely discussed in Europe and North America, and there was a feeling in environmental circles that a breakthrough was imminent. Labour was in power in Britain; and some Left-Labour MPs such as Tony Benn were very supportive. However, Harold Wilson, the Prime Minister, was less enthusiastic—and the Lucas management itself would have no truck with the Corporate Plan. Their stand was the old fashioned one that management decisions should rest solely with them. So a great idea was stillborn. While in England in 1975 and 1976, I suggested to the Lucas union leaders that the workers should actually occupy the factory and manufacture some of the products in their Corporate Plan. In this way they would dramatically prove that these "socially useful" products could be made.

The Lucas Aerospace Workers' Corporate Plan and the Australian Green Bans were the most imaginative Labour–environmental coalitions of the seventies. The Lucas Plan was more advanced in theory, but the Green Ban movement actually achieved much more, and had a lasting effect. It clearly demonstrated that it was possible, given the political will, to unite environmentalists and trade unionists in community action and achieve significant victories which enhanced the reputations of both the environment movements and the trade unions involved. The impact of the Green Ban movement led to greatly improved environmental legislation being introduced into the NSW Parliament in the late seventies; particularly provisions were made to allow greater opportunities for public participation.

It is disturbing to note, however, that the Wran government in the early eighties often ignored its own environmental legislation and introduced special legislation such as the Darling Harbour Act and the Monorail Act to deliberately bypass its own environmental laws! When it comes to environmental issues, eternal vigilance is necessary — otherwise developers will use their political influence to win every time.

In recent times it is obvious that some nature conservationists have been conned by the NSW Labor Government, which has a reasonably good record of extending National Parks. However Labor's urban environment record is very poor. Developers have had many victories, and it is in the *urban* area that billions of dollars are involved on various development projects. Labor's approach has been succinctly described as "pristine wilderness for nature conservationists and their National Parks, but urban blight for urban environmentalists fighting for a liveable urban environment". So it's a question of environmentalists considering *both* nature conservation *and* improvement of our urban environment.

The Green Ban story is certainly an exciting one, and those of us who were fortunate enough to have been involved in it can see the necessity for similar alliances to be forged in the interests of our environment. It is interesting to remember that when the developers and the corrupt Askin Government couldn't bribe, coerce or bludgeon the NSW BLF and break the union, the developers got the Federal BLF under Norm Gallagher to smash the NSW union, and to illegally expel its democratically elected leadership. Later on it was revealed that Gallagher had received secret commissions from two of the biggest developers—George Herscu of the Hooker Corporation and Bruno Grollo of Grollo Brothers. Gallagher was gaoled.

Pat Fiske's story of the NSW BLF, *Rocking The Foundations*, was a very successful documentary which was applauded wherever it was shown, and received rave notices from the critics both here and overseas. It showed that enlightened public opinion not only agreed that trade unions have a role to play in environment issues, but indeed that trade unions, just like other public bodies, have a responsibility on matters affecting the environment. There will be many ebbs and flows when facing environmental issues, but ecological pressures are such that Green political issues will increasingly impinge on the organised labour movement. The labour movement must respond to its responsibilities, or else its influence will wane. However it is the role of the organised environment movement to ensure that doesn't happen.

Despite some apparent contradictions, trade unionists and conservationists *should* be allies.

The Green Ban movement proved it could really happen.

It can happen again. In fact it should happen, must happen.

7:
BUILDING A SUSTAINABLE GREEN ECONOMY: ETHICAL INVESTMENT, ETHICAL WORK

Merv Partridge

MERV PARTRIDGE now lives in Sydney where he works as a training manager in the cooperative sector. A refugee from Queensland, he began his political involvement in Sydney with the Queensland Democracy Support Group and the Getting Together Conference, where he organised joint sessions with the Broad Left Movement. He is now involved with a working party, planning a formal linkage of progressive social movements into a national alliance. While in Queensland Merv lectured in Social Sciences for four years at Brisbane CAE. As an activist, he participated in the formation of the Australian Association of Sustainable Communities and the Queensland Green Party. He was Secretary of the Queensland Coalition for Democratic Rights during the 1985 Queensland political crisis that developed from the electricity strike, and did the Solidarity Radio Program on 4ZZZ. Merv was led into social activism by the increasingly oppressive political atmosphere and the decay of democratic institutions in his home State of Queensland. While Merv's concern with the appropriateness of technologies extends to the transformation of consciousness, his aim in this chapter is to concentrate on the problems generated by the Technological Revolution when transforming nature—in order to facilitate change within the economic realm.

Thus Athens went from strength to strength, and proved, if proof were needed, how noble a thing freedom is, not in one respect only, but in all; for while they were oppressed under a despotic government, they had no better success in war than any of their neighbours, yet, once the yoke was flung off, they proved the finest fighters in the world. This clearly shows that, so long as they were held down by authority, they deliberately shirked their duty in the field, as slaves shirk working for their masters; but when freedom was won, then every man amongst them was interested in his own cause.[1]

So wrote Herodotus almost 2500 years ago. Yet his description of the rise of Athens, the first city-scale experiment in participatory democracy, still shines like a steadying beacon today. Ours is a time when the tenuous hold that modern societies have on democracy seems to be breaking apart, caught between the crushing weight of a growing militarisation and the hurricane-force wind of industrial automation. At the end of 1984 13,000 industrial robots had been installed in the United States, 20,500 in Europe and 64,000 in Japan.[2] The Japanese, well ahead in the race, predict that they will have one million industrial robots in operation by the year 2000.[3] That is 13 years from now. Already in automated factories robots are making more robots with negligible human involvement while schools churn out carefully tailored machine minders.

We are being swept across a threshold into a new world with new rules. A techno-totalitarian world. Prophecy of this "brave new world" was offered just 30 years ago by Norbert Weiner, pioneer in the science of cybernetics, or human-machine systems. Weiner warned of the danger, now being realised, that automatic machines would see the reinstitution of slave labour, or worse.

Let us remember that the automatic machine ... is the precise economic equivalent of slave labour. Any labour which competes with slave labour must accept the conditions of slave labour. It is perfectly clear that this will produce an unemployment situation, in comparison with which the present recession and even the depression of the thirties will seem like a pleasant joke.[4]

The power of people over their lives, over incomes, over jobs, over the products and conditions of their work and even over their own minds is being sucked at an ever increasing rate into automatic machines controlled by an oligarchy who, while extravagantly pretending to be the determined defenders of democracy and freedom, are by their acts its mortal enemies. And yet, in stark contrast to their long-term interests, masses of people are flocking, like lemmings to the precipice, after the false "promise of technology": the journey to the stars.

We have only about two decades in which to democratise industry; otherwise we shall become slaves again to technocratic despotism. Already a small number of people control the rapid process of robotising the world's manufacturing industry. Shortly the rulers and the ruled will again be separated by a great wall of self-perpetuating automatic machines tended by a small herd of highly paid, subservient machine watchers. And nothing short of world-wide catastrophe is likely to stop this inexorable advent of automation.

So if we care for human freedom then we are faced with fundamental questions that most people have preferred to toss into the "too hard" basket and leave for another generation. There is no more time for the luxury of hesitation. If we are to meet the complex problems posed by the technological revolution then we must go to their source without distraction. E. F. Schumacher came close to the heart when, in *Good Work*, he wrote,

> *The question of* what the work does to the worker *is hardly ever asked, not to mention the question of whether the real task might not be to adapt the work to the needs of the worker rather than to demand that the worker adapt himself to the needs of the work— which means, of course, primarily to the needs of the machine.* [5]

If we undertake to adapt machines to the needs of the people who use them then the practical question arises: what methods of organising can we use to break up the dominant centralising trend in the control of technology? How can we bring the robots, and any decisions to be made about their uses, under the democratic control of the wider community? Australia's trade-based unions have concentrated all their efforts on wage rates and workplace conditions. They have not, so far, succeeded in any way in lifting the yoke of authority from the workplace; at best they have merely slowed the rate of displacement of jobs as this is brought about by the introduction of new technology. Moreover, as many people are now arguing, the power of union officials as *representatives* of workers' interests will quite possibly become diminished. If so, then clearly that power must be transferred to workers themselves in a more directly democratic and rational organising of workplaces and between workplaces. To simply allow unions to be disempowered and to leave individual workers in an unequal bargaining position in undemocratic workplaces would be to make the power flow back, by default, to the oligarchy who own the machines.

We can expect people to assume responsibility for their work and for its effects on their environment only if they are themselves able to determine through a democratic process how their work is managed, only if they can participate in decisions about investment, about the sorts of technologies they use and about the sorts of products they produce.

Athens was able to withstand and prevail over the military might of the immense Persian empire precisely because of the total commitment engendered in its citizens by institutions of direct democracy. And the Athenians ultimately failed precisely because they then selfishly limited their concept of who could be a free citizen, and because they selfishly then oppressed those excluded from the "free state". Women were locked in their houses, enemies were made slaves and allies were ruthlessly exploited for the wealth that they could bring to aggrandise the city–state. Such militarism and despotism is again characteristic of our modern world. For the West too has failed to extend democracy into its industry or to the poor countries that it economically dominates.

Modern democracy is in crisis. People do not feel they have control over their own destinies. They no longer even believe that self-determination is possible. So many Australians now seem prepared to turn to despots like Joh Bjelke-Petersen simply because he shows uncompromising will and confidence: the very qualities which are draining out of their own experience. Petersen is a figure from a dream, a wish-fulfilment. He is a simplistic symbol of force that compensates for powerlessness. In the face of the hollow promise of authoritarian power offered by the New Right and its Petersens it is futile to fight to preserve our current unsatisfying pseudo-democratic institutions. Rather we have to begin the building of totally new, immediately responsive democratic structures that extend down into the deeper roots of society.

Where to begin? There are many layers of economic decision-making where participation must be strengthened if we are to build a democratic economy that will be enduring. As has been shown by Nader and by the consumer cooperative movement, consumer control over product quality and price can be strengthened through organisation. The process of production needs to be democratised. People who produce should have a high degree of control over their conditions of work, the machines they use and the product they make. Further, investment in enterprises and in research and the development of new technologies ought to be brought under more direct democratic control. Where there is planning and coordination of investment, this process should also be by open and democratic negotiation. The design and application of new technologies, like nuclear reactors and robots, which have a significant social impact, should involve public education and decision. Finally, the values by which people live should be chosen by them through conscious deliberation. In our society at present, advertising and mass media are extremely sophisticated value-shaping technologies which a small number of powerful people are able to use subtly to manipulate others without being accountable for their effects. These institutions should be democratised and made answerable to the people they influence. Community radio, public access television and cooperative newspapers are emerging models.

In the following pages I want to discuss practical methods of building direct democratic control over *investment, work* and *production*. To begin let me pose a question.

What do the following three people have in common? A Queensland policeman physically drags an unresisting Santa Claus to a paddy wagon after the latter has made a political speech in the Queen Street Mall, protesting against the presence of nuclear-armed warships in Brisbane.[6] A logger rips his chainsaw through the last thousand-year-old tree in a rainforest. An adman works his skilled imagination to package the idea of a sweet, black, carbonated liquid as the "real thing", even "life" itself, and next he may package the "freshness" of burning tobacco, then of toothpastes.

The answer, of course, is that the policeman, the logger and the adman were all *just* doing their job. They were taking orders. They did not define the task to which they applied their skills, and they all claim that they are not responsible. If they don't follow orders they are afraid they will lose their jobs and sully their reputations for unquestioning obedience.

In this way a socially accepted and routine pattern is created for passing the buck of responsibility along a "chain of command". This is one social structure. Another sort of buck is passed back down the chain in return. This buck can be used to buy another person's unquestioning labour or its products. Thus we work at tasks set by others who are not accountable to us, out of the fear that we will lose our jobs and hence the power to, in turn, buy other people's labour or its products.[7] The buck then stops at the top of the chain of command, with the owners, the board of directors or the senior bureaucrats, the generals and the politicians. At the top it is converted into yet another sort of transferable responsibility. Expediency and efficiency. Profit. Control. Accumulation. Because of faithful service to these false gods the danger of war and the means of waging it are blossoming. Torture becomes an art taught by international schools. Poverty flourishes. Destruction of the environment that sustains us grows, with GNP, at an ever increasing pace.

How do we restore individual responsibility to skilled work? How do we make responsibility for our work and its effects into a *normal* behaviour, into a social structure . . . in an age when one half of the world's scientists and engineers are building weapons of mass destruction, just for a buck, while a thousand times their number are undernourished through lack of skilled assistance and withdrawal of resources? I hold that people will take responsibility for their work and its consequences only when they are given the power to define it by the ways in which their workplaces are structured. Only when there is democratic control of work and its products will relationships of trust and cooperation develop in our industries. Only when people are given their fair share in the fruits of their labour will they develop the sense of commitment and responsibility for the common good that is so desperately needed in Australia today.

There is nothing terribly controversial in the argument. Workplace democracy and cooperation is recognised as a legitimate goal by all sides of politics. Since the last century, liberals as well as socialists have both put workplace democracy forward as a model of participation in a more evolved economy. The father of liberalism, John Stuart Mill, wrote:

> *The form of association . . . which, if mankind continue to improve, must be expected to predominate, is not that which can exist between a capitalist as chief, and workpeople without a voice in the management, but the association of the labourers themselves on terms of equality, collectively owning the capital with which they carry on their operations, and working under managers elected and removable by themselves.* [8]

What *is* controversial, however, is to actually *work* towards workplace democracy—to organise the political will to make it happen. For this means challenging the privilege of the most powerful among us, and making them institutionally share prerogatives that they now retain as *exclusive* rights. Choices of investment, of technology, and of product.

The Fraser Liberal–National coalition government was the first to introduce policies of industrial democracy and employee participation. These were so timid that in effect they said to employers, "Please, sir, think about sharing some information, and some profits with your employees. Take all the time you like. If you choose to share a little you will find your employees are more committed, more motivated. They will work harder at doing what you tell them to do." Then, in December 1986 the Hawke Labor Government distributed a "green" pre-policy discussion paper on *Industrial*

Democracy and Employee Participation which suggests they too may consider following Fraser's "Please sir" with taxation carrots and gentle legal sticks to encourage a very, very gradual democratisation of the workplace. Cooperatives rate only passing mentions.

This seems absurd when tried and tested cooperative structures offer some of the most advanced and uncompromising structures for democratic control and industrial harmony. They also offer a greatly enhanced sensitivity to human and environmental well-being, through their integration with the local communities in which their members live and work. If the correct structures are used, integrated systems of cooperatives also offer greatly *increased* economic efficiency, no strikes, and the generation of new, secure, and well-paid employment in capital-intensive industries which are undergoing automation.

The evidence for these claims is solid (I will refer to some of it later) but the *communication* of this evidence is restrained: our main channels of information, and of opinion formation, are government and privately owned media; and both government and big business have as their structural dynamics the accumulation and centralisation of power and control. Neither therefore has a clear interest in promoting cooperative development whose dynamic is towards the decentralisation of power and control. Still, as they currently face seemingly insoluble problems of unemployment, economic stagnation and industrial conflict, governments of all shades, from Victoria and New South Wales to Queensland, are at last turning some attention and resources towards the cooperative sector. This is not because they suddenly wish to redistribute power, but simply because they are desperate. In other words they are beginning to address long-term structural problems in order to conserve what power they can.

But while governments can facilitate or obstruct cooperative development, it is the organised self-activity of ordinary people that really makes it happen. Thus the capital needed to finance the development of democratic ways of producing environmentally and socially benign products will have to be provided by all of us, even if our contribution only amounts to a few dollars. This involves the mobilisation of many thousands of people, to consciously demand and practise the ethical and democratic investment of their own wealth as well as of public wealth. Organised ethical investment will be most effective if it is coordinated in accordance with planning processes which are democratic and open for negotiation and which offer guidance rather than coercion.

The process has begun. Enough of the necessary, people-controlled institutions are already in place. Whether the seeds that are offered grow depends on the attention that people will give them.

MAKING TECHNOLOGY WORK FOR PEOPLE

Australia was initially colonised under military rule as a consequence of the industrial revolution, a revolution which represented a momentous escalation of the age-old bid made by the generations of men ruling Western civilisation to control a nature which they have experienced not as a home to be cared for but as an alien and at times threatening realm to be appropriated and dominated. The futility of the bid lies, of course, in the simple fact that people are inherently beings *of* and *in* nature. There can be no more extravagant human ambition than this project of achieving complete domination over nature, for it places human rulers in the role reserved for the ultimate state of being that Western religions call God.

Today the men who struggle for absolute power over non-human and human nature are more than ever reaching out. But just as their grasp seems to be closing on their goal, so does the fundamentally paradoxical nature of their project come into sharper and sharper focus. The contradiction inherent in their quest has been neatly portrayed by the conservative British historian Arnold Toynbee:

> The Industrial Revolution exposed the biosphere to the risk of being extinguished by Man [sic]. Since Man is rooted in the biosphere and could not survive apart from it, Man's acquisition of the power to make the biosphere uninhabitable is a threat by Man to Man's own survival. [9]

Indeed, Toynbee recognised far more clearly than most the peril into which the earth and its people have been swept as a result of the convergence of the military quest (for domination of human nature) and the industrial quest (for domination of non-human nature):

> *In the eventful century 1763–1871, by far the most important event was a sudden vast increase in human power both over human beings themselves and over non-human Nature. This increase in human power was achieved by the combination of a social innovation with a technological one. The efficiency of soldiers and of industrial workers was increased by subjecting them to a strict discipline, by setting them to work with machinery and weapons of an unprecedented potency, and by organising their work intensively. Disciplined professional armies began to be created in the West towards the close of the seventeenth century. In the later decades of the eighteenth century the regimentation already imposed in military parade grounds was applied in civilian factories, and a technique that had been invented for boring cannon-barrels was applied to the fitting of pistons for steam-engines.* [10]

Such a fusion of the military and industrial projects is an integral characteristic of the present technological revolution. Today more than half of the world's scientists and engineers, our most skilled minds, are engaged in work where they produce the means of mass destruction in exchange for money. Given the structural manner in which their work is organised, they do not have the right to question the very nature of their work and its products. Nor, in general, do they even struggle for this right or do they accept responsibility for what is done. This general irresponsibility is highlighted by the exceptions — the dedicated activities of groups such as The Society for Social Responsibility in Science.

While disciplining the order of "outer" nature, industry is also, and simultaneously, disciplining human natures. It is in the regulated space called work that the vast majority of highly disciplined human skills are developed and exercised. Work is where and when people are most prepared to deny and repress their natural dispositions for sustained periods. And since the development of the wage labour relationship, where each participant is formally "free" to leave employment, each worker is set up so as to personally choose complicity in the project — or else to suffer marginality. Therefore our generation has to complete the democratic revolution by thoroughly democratising our institutions and workplaces or it will deliver a world to the next generation that is dead in spirit under totalitarian rule, or dead indeed if the products of our most skilled labour are put to the use for which they are intended.

Our entire education today is shaped around the "needs" of industry; today the human is fitted to the machine. And already today in Japanese factories robots are building new robots. What we are faced with, therefore, is a substantial obsolescence of both unskilled and skilled human labour within a couple of decades. For instance any political efforts to make Australia's manufacturing industry competitive are absurd—unless the strategy involved aims precisely at a rapid and thoroughgoing automation of Australian industry, a necessary consequence of which is to render unnecessary most of the hours now worked by our industrial and white collar workforce: in other words, the aim of this *planned obsolescence of people* is to greatly reduce the total number of 40-hour workers, thereby reducing the overall wage bill and allowing the extra productivity built into the machines to benefit the minority who own the machines. Thus a consequence of this strategy is massive unemployment, underemployment and poverty. It also means a massive welfare bill, unless the welfare state is dismantled, which means firstly dismantling the power of trade unions and the organised ability of workers to resist. This is the openly proclaimed strategy of the New Right and of the Queensland Government. But an alternative to this strategy is to reduce working hours to a standard of about 20 per week by the turn of the century. In this situation, incomes could only be maintained by sharing the benefits of the increased productivity of the machines with the workers whose skills are being absorbed by the computers and robots. Such a counter-strategy depends upon people being organised strongly enough to assert a claim for a fair share in the increased production per hour of labour. Such organised claims may be asserted indirectly, through trade unions or political parties, or directly by democratising control of the machines and what they produce through cooperativisation or through universal stock ownership.[11] The counter-strategy would also be heavily dependent on developing an indigenous national capacity to produce automatic machines: people in Australia would have to be in a position to exercise local democratic control over decisions about appropriate designs for the technologies they use.

Development strategies which do not pursue rapid automation will, if we remain engaged in the competitive international economy, lead to an ever-increasing reduction in national income—especially relative to those trading partners from whom we continue to purchase the products of the robot factories. To choose neither to automate nor to consume the products of automated factories therefore means a significant disengagement from the international economy. This national choice may emerge from one of the range of scenarios of global crisis which now confront us as real possibilities.

However, if achievable change is the aim, the likelihood of the Australian population choosing autarky and not the machine is too remote to dwell upon. Automation of everything is happening whether we like it or not. It will not be wished away nor resisted to a standstill. The alienating horrors of automation, already manifest in the advent of Star Wars and of a marginalised human majority who are technocratically mind-managed, will only be cured by going clear to the heart of the process. We must do this in an organised manner, aiming to transform the *fundamental* structures of technological decision-making and control. If we simply try to repress or abandon the machine we are doomed to failure. The military–industrial project will then maintain its momentum on the face of the planet; and we or our descendants will inexorably be brought back into its framework. Accordingly we must transmute the paranoid project *where it is most fervent*: that is in the workplaces, where the project of domination is being most dramatically chosen and re-chosen in the here and now; and in the investment centres, from which the crucial choices are made about how to convert promises of allegiance (money) into human and mechanical action.

Nevertheless, while it is vitally important to establish new more humane models of work, an exclusive focus on alternative ways which fails also to contend with the vast momentum of the old and alienated ways must inevitably concede the world to robots and weapons factories. Even an elaborated alternative economy and culture cannot provide the basis for a confident, healthy and sustainable partnership with nature while leaving the now immensely powerful modern industrial–technological project loose on the planet in its present form. We cannot be merely content to romantically repress or to expel the industrial project and its growth points from our consciousness, to separate it out from an abstract, purified "nature". This is a deadly trap triggered by fear. And it is precisely fear of the alien which is the *source* of the military–industrial project.

Rather, to make our world a home for all again we need to tease the fear of the alien out of the collective projecting of our culture — so that its dynamic towards domination can then be relaxed into a wonder-filled project of active appreciation, and so that work can then become fulfilling creation. We will always need to understand and attend to the sources of the will to domination and its technological progeny, just as the German Greens actively keep alive the memories and lessons of Nazism. To forget is to become unconscious and vulnerable to an *ever-present* danger. We only cosmetically tinker with a culture, we do not change it, *until we successfully transform the relations of human to human, human to machine, and human to nature at the sites of production.*

In modern industrial societies, the predominant relations at sites of production are relations of domination and subordination. Furthermore, the *decisions* about what to produce, as well as the *products* of people's labour, are at most workplaces controlled and disposed of by remote super-ordinates. They are not controlled by the people who actually do the producing, the people who consume the products, or the community in which the industry is located and whose lifestyles are affected by its operations. So weapon-making, warrior-making, poverty-making and environmental-unmaking will only effectively cease once we have succeeded in resolving the relations of domination that people habitually repeat at the majority of workplaces.

If we can alleviate the alienation of the modern workplace, we may then be able to restore a creative relationship to nature, and we can place that relationship at the centre of human activity and skill development. Our task is to reduce the coercive compulsion and the fear of loss of livelihood which induce people to squeeze their bodies and minds and imaginations and feelings into an ordered and ever-contracting mechanical time and motion. Our generation must begin the long and arduous task of replacing fear at work with the positive incentives which derive from workers having a high degree of responsibility and control in the work process. This means the simultaneous pursuit of industrial and economic democracy, together with the general cultivation of skills and attitudes of self-reliance and personal, social and environmental responsibility. If we can succeed in that on any scale, we may shape a world in which all people can feel relatively at home with each other, and with the technologies we choose to apply, and with the products of our activities. We may then quite naturally come to cease wrecking, dominating or appropriating everything we can lay hand, tool or mind upon.

While it is crucial to make sure that *new* workplaces are healthier and more democratic, if we are seriously pursuing a sustainable culture then we must transform the existing alienated workplaces so as to make the work processes humane, the products useful, enduring and benign, and the technologies appropriate. More democratic and community-oriented unions could, theoretically, play a significant role in this effort. In my view, however, a decisive new influence will be the *strategically organised control of investment*, together with a set of *supporting institutions* which can at the same time deliver both superb *management and planning skills* and a *rigorous commitment to the widest possible sharing of those skills*. With good institutions and the pooled capital of millions of ordinary people, companies can be *legally* taken over and democratised. And their resources can be turned, if necessary, to more appropriate production.

This approach to democratic industry-planning is achievable within existing legal frameworks. It does not depend upon being established as policy at the level of central government, though of course the attitude of central government is extremely important, as it can move to inhibit or facilitate the evolution of ethical financial institutions. The means are already available; many of the building blocks are already in place for establishing a decentralised system of democratic and ethical financial decision-making. The resources that can be mobilised as these institutions gain in credibility extends to a rapidly organising international pool of "ethical capital".

In order to thoroughly decentralise and extend democratic control into *all levels* of power in the society it is necessary to cultivate, both through education and through institutions, the highest degree of individual self-reliance, responsibility and local self-management which is possible in the society. Individual self-reliance would need to be accompanied by a strong *general* commitment to the development of skills, knowledge and confidence in even the weakest members of the community. And the combination of emphasis on self-reliance and mutual responsibility is already a deep common thread in all of the traditions which make up the cooperative movement. The co-operative movement thus provides the best developed point of departure that I can see for a general transition to a sustainable economy which may avoid the spilling of large amounts of blood. I will come back to a discussion of industrial democracy and to the cooperative approach to democratising workplaces and consumption. First, though, I want to examine some strategies for pursuing economic democracy, the direct democratisation of the control of investment decisions. This means democratisation of control of decisions about what sorts of research and development should be financially supported; about what sorts of technologies should be developed as appropriate for a decent society; and about what levels of concentration or dispersal of control over machines and their products, as well as over the media, should shape our behaviour.

INSTITUTING SUSTAINABLE INVESTMENT

When choosing what to purchase (and from whom), people express their values. At the same time they contribute to demand for that product or service, and they assist the growth of the producer whose goods they have selected. As consumers, people are quite discriminating about what they vote for with their dollars. Yet things have been different when people *invest* their money. They usually seek only to maximise the return and the security of their investment. They give their money to financial managers, who then *decide for them* what sorts of activities to support through their investment.

This state of affairs is now changing rapidly. The movement towards "ethical investment" is a move by ordinary people to assume responsibility for decisions about where their money is invested and hence about what sorts of production they want to support. The central concern that the movement is responding to is summed up in the now-popular slogan "It's an hour before midnight. Do you know what your money is doing tonight?" The degree of responsibility assumed varies: some ethical investors still try to maximise returns and so restrict their investment choices only a little. Others are prepared to be more rigorous in their choices: so they accept lower returns as the price for more fundamental change. In the United States, where it is often called "social investment", ethical investment began in the early seventies with a few thousand dollars but by 1986 a multitude of ethical funds had attracted $55 billion.

The North American experience has shown that well managed ethical funds can match and often outperform conventional profit-maximising funds in levels of return. As an example, in 1984 the Calvert Social Investment Fund increased its assets by 83 per cent. In 1985 its rate of return was 26 per cent which was 4 per cent above the Mutual Funds Industry Average.[11] Explanations offered for this rather surprising phenomenon are as follows: firms with good work-place relations that produce ethically tend to be more productive and stable and do not have to bear such disaster and loss-of-confidence costs as occurred within the nuclear industry after Chernobyl, or with Union Carbide after the Bhopal chemical factory explosion.

Ethical dis-investment: the grass-roots capital strike:
In addition to positively directed investment, the social investment movement also encompasses organised *dis*-investment. You could call this the investor's equivalent of a consumer boycott. History offers abundant examples of capital strikes by international financiers being used to discipline or destabilise wayward governments. Social divest-ment is the progressive use of the capital strike by multitudes of ordinary mortals who have come to realise that the gods *are* crazy. For instance, since 1977 pressure has been mounted on American

educational institutions to divest themselves of securities in companies that do business in or with South Africa. By the end of 1985, of 28 major New England colleges and universities seven had adopted policies of total divestment, 14 were in the process of partial divestment and three were reviewing divestment options. Only four had taken no action.[12]

It is now becoming common for people to "give the stick" to their money manager. They confront their bank or credit union manager with a request to give account of the bank's investment policies. If the answer shows investment in unethical areas, or even *ignorance* about where the bank is putting their money, then the conscious investor cries foul, instantly closes his or her account and runs with the money to an institution that shows a more mature approach. Needless to say, even the gods can take only so much stick before putting a review of investment policies onto the agenda of the bank's board. Try it. Find five or ten friends with accounts in a particular financial institution and have each one call the manager to account within about a week. Give the stick in person and maybe follow up in writing. You may need to repeat this in several branches — but American experience does show that this method can have a disciplining effect on bank investment policies once enough people become involved.

Ethical investment in Australia:
Ethical investment came to life in Australia out of the Alternative Economic Summit held in the living room of Bill Mollison, the Tasmanian father of the permaculture movement, just after Bob Hawke's Super Economic Summit in 1983. Jill Jordan went back to Queensland to organise a working party from the ranks of an existing food coop, and with $200 the Maleny and District Community Credit Union was born in a little room attached to the Maple Street Food Coop. Then Geoff Young started the Earthbank Society. He ran it as a very active Secretary and his work culminated in the organisation of the Earthbank Conference in Sydney in May 1986.[13] The Earthbank Society is an Australia-wide organisation that encourages and provides information about ethical investment.

It offers support and advice in the establishment of ethical investment facilities.

Sydney is the home of a private ethical investment company called August Investments; this company is just completing the establishment of a Trust Fund which invests according to ethical criteria but still aims to maximise returns. Another option for ethical investment is the Southern Cross Capital Exchange in the Blue Mountains which is inspired by the philosophy of Rudolf Steiner. The Southern Cross Capital Exchange allows members to invest for a minimum of three months at variable interest rates depending on the type of project in which they elect to have their money invested. These range from schools to environmental projects and community businesses.

The Earthbank Conference held in May 1986 stimulated a wave of media attention which greatly boosted community awareness of ethical investment. Interest was also stirred in some large existing financial institutions. Two representatives of the NSW Cooperative Federation (now the Australian Association of Cooperatives) addressed the conference, describing their Centralised Banking Scheme as an ethical investment institution which lends only to cooperatives. They also offered to assist interested groups with the incorporation of ethical investment societies and to consider the establishment of special funds given sufficient member demand. A plan is now afoot in Sydney to convert the old pioneer Mutual Fund Cooperative into a strategic ethical investment cooperative. The term *social audit* is now in their vocabulary (but not yet in their policies I think).

Within two months of the Conference the Friends' Provident Life Office was offering a new Ethical Managed Fund, which "as far as is practicable" does not invest in companies involved with armaments, alcohol, tobacco, gambling, uranium or trade with South Africa. This national fund attracted $800,000 in its first month of operation. In addition to the Maleny Credit Union, which I shall come back to, there are now several financial institutions operating in local areas and under community control which invest according to ethical criteria consistent with a sustainable way of living. Two are Trusts incorporated as companies limited by guarantee, which means they are non-profit. At the time of writing, the Bellingen Community Loan Fund had just started operation in northern New South Wales. The Channon Trust near Lismore, formed earlier in 1986 as a vehicle to finance the establishment of a local craft market and restaurant, aims to develop a pool of community-controlled assets and money. There are two classes of shares: profit-seeking and non-profit seeking. Voting is on number of shares held rather than on the "one member one vote" cooperative structure. The Channon Trust is experimenting with the concept of using "Green Dollars" in combination with conventional dollars as a local currency backed by local assets. Discussion of this experiment will be taken up later.

Security of investments is vital if ethical investment is to become popular on the broad scale necessary to really change our society. To date, the security record of the existing ethical investment institutions is impeccable. The strong trend towards bio-regional community bases for ethical investment institutions should further strengthen this security. This is because local communities can usually judge well the level of loan repayments a person can sustain or their capacity to succeed in a proposed venture: the community becomes quickly aware if any problems arise and can quickly offer support, and there is always strong pressure to be responsible about money borrowed—since it has come from people you know! Thus, according to figures quoted by Robert Rosen, the current Earthbank Secretary, the loan loss rate for 20 North American community funds represented at the 1985 National Conference of Community Loan Funds was below 0.7 per cent.[14]

Democratically controlled investment:
It is possible to have institutions which invest ethically but in which choices of policy and staffing are not made democratically. If the policies and investment choices are good, then surely this is acceptable in the short term. Indeed, in some cases more progressive investment policies may be proclaimed by a powerful but enlightened individual than by democratic negotiation.

However, if in the long term we are aiming to reform our investment institutions into forms that are sustainable because they are guaranteed (by their structures) to be responsive to community and environmental needs, then it is crucial that the institutional structure of economic decision-making become as directly democratic as is feasible. This is an area in which the new information technologies *could* be put to constructive use in decentralising power. Any unusually enlightened individuals should be elected onto boards or employed as managers or advisers, not allowed dictatorial powers.

A democratic financial institution is legally incorporated when a cooperative or a company is formed, with a "one member one vote" democratic structure unequivocally entrenched in its articles of association. A cooperative may be either a credit union, whose purpose is to lend money back to members, or an investment society, whose purpose is to collectively invest members' funds in agreed ways. Both are required by law to have a range of powers and responsibilities vested in a board, which is elected by the members on the cooperative basis of one vote per member. Certain of these powers are reserved to the board and cannot be returned to the membership by changing the rules. As far as I know a truly *collective* structure, in which *all* powers can be exercised directly *by the membership*, is not possible for a financial institution under Australian laws. This is not an acute problem at present since a collective structure can only operate effectively with an extremely mature and responsible membership. It will, in fact, take us more than a generation of grass-roots skill development before this direct democratic structure can become widely practicable for investment planning.

The elected board of a cooperative appoints staff and advisers and decides on an investment policy and possibly a strategy. The membership should have full access to information about how these decisions are made and the means, via meetings and preferably other avenues as well, of debating these decisions amongst themselves. If decisions are found unacceptable, the board can be voted out. Recommendations can be put to the board by a meeting and, stronger than this, the board can also be constrained by members voting to include specific principles into the rules and objects of the organisation. The appointed staff are accountable to the board, and the board is accountable to the membership.

Until the cooperative movement can get the cooperative laws changed to make them less patronising, new financial institutions will continue to be set up more often under the *Companies Code*. The *Code* is more flexible and less regulated than the cooperative laws, though penalties for misconduct are sometimes higher. Unlike cooperative laws the *Companies Code* does not require or even encourage a democratic structure. What is usual with companies is to allow some individuals to have more voting power, because they can afford to own more shares, but if there is the will it is *possible*, and not uncommon, for companies to be set up so that each member has just one vote. It is up to individual ethical investors to decide if they wish to support the democratisation of the structures as an added dimension of ethical investment.

By virtue of the laws they operate under, all credit unions are, potentially, democratically controlled ethical investment institutions. The practical reality, however, is that most have passive memberships. Few of the members ever play any role in decision-making. Credit unions are usually controlled by professional corporate management, whose touchstones for successful performance are strictly the profit maximising and technological "imperatives" of the unrestrained market.

Community Credit Cooperatives:
The only credit union that I know of which operates according to an ethical charter is the community-based credit union set up in the small country town of Maleny in Queensland in September 1984. After two and a half years of operation the *Maleny and District Community Credit Union* has over 560 members and over $900,000 in deposits. Money is still flowing in from all over the country.

The Maleny Credit Union may also have the highest degree of member participation of any in the country. Board meetings and minutes are open to *all* members (except for credit committee reports on loan applications). Members are also encouraged to participate in the cooperative study group which has been set up in the region. Ordinary people are running this institution and their collective capital is serving local needs. These needs are met in an ethical order of priority set down in an investment policy which is negotiated democratically by the membership and has been written into their objects. The four principal goals of the Maleny Credit Union are as follows:

- *To promote regional financial autonomy*
- *To promote socially responsible use of money*
- *To promote social change*
- *To promote individual financial empowerment*

The Maleny Credit Union has also established two special funds into which members may choose to deposit donations or have a percentage of their interest on deposits paid. Members decide at a general meeting which community project will receive the annual grant from the Community Development Fund. The board has discretion in allocation of the Community Assistance Fund to victims of hardship in the region.

For several years now a group has been working on establishing a similar ethical credit union in Brisbane. It seems to be impossible to set up new credit unions in New South Wales, where ordinary people apparently can't be trusted to manage their own money.

At the moment there are two ways in which a credit union can be used as an institution for ethical investment. One is by simply fulfilling its basic function of lending money to members. By this route, if the majority of the membership of a credit union have a commitment to setting a scale of ethical preferences for lending to members, as has occurred in Maleny, this can become credit union policy. Preference in loans and possibly lower interest rates may be offered to members depending on the social and environmental soundness of the project to which they plan to devote their loan. The other path is for credit unions to lodge "deposits with any prescribed body corporate or with any body corporate of a prescribed class of bodies corporate".

By law NSW credit unions can invest in common ownership companies or cooperatives (or other corporate bodies) if they have been *prescribed* by the State. That seems promising, except that at present *not one* corporate body or class of corporate bodies has yet been prescribed. At least, though, it is already possible by law. Concerted lobbying may be able to come up with the prescription of cooperatives, or of environmentally and socially ethical companies, as "prescribed" classes of bodies corporate. Procedures are now being drawn up for lending to coops and small businesses within a credit union bond area. But in Queensland credit unions have just been refused the right to lend to cooperatives in spite of lobbying from the movement.

Standard practice at present seems to be for members to use their credit union as a source of credit for consumption rather than for investment in new production capacities. Again, this is well and good—but ordinary consumption isn't the fastest way to transform an economy, in spite of the claims made about consumer sovereignty!

There is thus a lot of potential for community credit unions. I think existing deficiencies can be overcome with an increase in experience and awareness; some effective political lobbying to loosen aspects of the laws and the regulation of credit unions may also be necessary, most particularly in order to facilitate the setting up of new community credit unions.

The established larger credit unions, with their financial expertise and national electronic fund transfer networks, provide both security and easy accessibility to a very large number of people. If their members can become more aware of their collective democratic power, and more willing to actively exercise it to institute ethical investment practices in their cooperatives, they could prove to be one of Australia's greatest assets for social change.

Livening up mainstream credit unions:
So far policies of socially and environmentally appropriate investment have occurred only in new and small credit unions. The possibility is certainly open for ethical investment policies in some of the large existing credit unions. One way to encourage this process is to run campaigns for board representation on ethical investment "tickets". I tried this in a very amateur way with the Queensland Teachers Credit Union in 1984. My application was refused on a technicality. I was more relieved than disappointed. The remotest possibility of

being elected horrified me at that time. My aim was to put ethical investment up for debate amongst the membership so as to lay the ground for a serious campaign in a later year. I have since come to realise what an unnecessary barrier that fear of taking responsibility for public decisions about money presents for most people. This is another area in which the Maleny Credit Union presents a model for other credit unions that wish to empower their membership: consistent with their fourth goal, the Maleny board ensures that the membership is educated in ways that demystify financial management and reduce their fears.

When people think of conducting election campaigns they almost invariably think of high-flying levels of representative government. If our aim is to decentralise control, why should such a movement for change as ours focus most of its resources and attention on gaining representation in political forums? The prospect of gaining sufficient parliamentary representation to institute significant legislative changes, even within a decade, is in any case fairly remote. In my view, it is much more meaningful to devote a greater part of organisation and resources to developing stronger grass-roots control of new or existing organisations, especially with respect to their investment and technological decisions and to their workplace relationships.

If, from the multitude of discussions during 1986–87, a new progressive political party or electoral alliance finally emerges, I hope it can maintain sufficient awareness of past lessons to release people's energies from parliamentary-focused politics. I hope this political movement can turn the spotlight downwards towards grass-roots productive activity, for success in direct empowerment of people in their everyday lives will echo far more loudly through the corridors of parliament than the most articulate of alternative politicians. No doubt the latter are still needed to project the voice of a grass-roots mobilisation and to lend it confidence, but they must not be a substitute for direct democracy; and the movement must not repeat the mistake of the other parties in focusing all resources on building a hungry party machine aimed merely at conquering power. The Greens' ambition is to lower the summit of political power, not to conquer it.

Credit unions are financial institutions with a formal democratic structure, and they are based on the premise that the power of the people can be woken from its slumber. In practice, as credit unions grow and command more funds they tend to become more like banks. They develop traditional management structures: boards, controlled by financial "experts", who set policies aimed at maximising returns on capital; and a passive, bamboozled membership, most of whom don't even bother to turn up to the Annual General Meeting. In legal terms, however, these members may retain democratic control over the credit union if only they have the necessary awareness, confidence and basic knowledge and skills to exercise that control. I say *may* retain—because it depends on whether the rules of the institution and/or the State laws allow the use of proxy votes, and on whether there is in fact a minority of shareholders who control sufficient voting shares to dominate the board and even the Annual General Meeting.

I wonder how many readers belong to a credit union and how many of those attend their Annual General Meeting, or are aware of the investment policies for which they share responsibility. I wonder how many know the rules and understand the meeting procedures. There is plenty of scope in some existing credit unions for educating and organising the membership so that they can exercise more direct control over investment. In New South Wales recently an Annual General Meeting of a large building society voted to convert this democratic institution into the Advance Bank, thereby allowing it to be controlled by a majority of shares of capital instead of a majority of people. What's going on? While hundreds of social activists are out sailing canoes in front of warships, yet another institution has thus been poached from the (formal) democratic control of ordinary people and put into the hands of capitalist shareholders. The Advance Bank is now at liberty to invest in the making of more weapons— or whatever its professional managers find most profitable.

I don't for a moment mean to put down the courage or value of activists who concentrate on direct action. Civil disobedience is a powerful and sometimes necessary part of a strategy for social change. However, direct action ought to be but one creative tool in a campaign—and not, as sometimes happens, a compulsive ritual which substitutes for advanced planning. The point I wish to make is that the warships are breeding because warships are in the hearts of the people who control the investment of capital. The global war machine has not yet been stopped, and it will not be stopped by putting bodies in front of it. But in the long run it might be choked off, by starving it at the source.

Considerable change in the credit union sector has already begun. Action of a quite low-key nature by a handful of people has already helped to bring their turn-around from an obsession with high-tech and the bottom line to a reawakening of their original, social goals. Maggie Niven from the Australian Federation of Credit Unions attended the Earthbank Conference in Sydney and, as a result, passed on precisely this message that others were taking up the torch of social change that had been dropped by the old credit unions. Articles on "social audits" carried out amongst Canadian credit unions have now started appearing in Australian credit union publications. The Australian Credit Union Convention in November 1986 was called *Credit Unions and Social Positioning*. Its sessions had titles like "Bringing about a better society" and "Can credit unions have a social conscience?" Considerable attention was directed to the democratic and cooperative nature of credit unions. Indeed, the Convention Workbook opens with an article by Eldon Anderson, a former editor of Canada's *Credit Union Way*, which advocates the introduction of social audits as an addition to financial audits into credit cooperative policies. And since the Credit Union Convention we have witnessed an expensive national advertising campaign promoting credit unions as organisations of social responsibility and of member control.

It remains to be seen whether this development simply represents a corporate marketing strategy, or whether it will be backed up by sincere drives for member participation — together with changes in interest rates and investment policies and practices. Raising the awareness of those members who attend Annual General Meetings, and running teams for board positions on ethical investment tickets would immediately give existing boards some indication of member response to ethical investment policies — hence of the advisability of introducing them. It is very important that any campaign for ethical investment be ethically and openly conducted.

Towards a cooperative bank:
The most powerful catalyst for building a self-managed sector is a democratically controlled cooperative bank. Such a bank can concentrate the necessary combination of skills in finance, management support and market analysis to give adequate support to new or ailing coops. It is the key to building a strong and united sector — as against a hodge-podge of small coops struggling individually in the market place.

This has been demonstrated most decisively in the Mondragon cooperative sector in Spain, where (so far) coops never fail, where workers are never made redundant and where the cooperative sector takes over capitalist companies instead of the other way around as in Australia. While I hope we can improve on Mondragon in terms of appropriateness of production, we should seriously heed the lessons to be gained from its economic success.

Our bank has to be as astute as any commercial bank in *understanding* the business world. It will be up to us and the effectiveness of our strategies as to how democratic and ethical that bank, and the coops it fosters, turn out to be.

The cooperative movement in this country has been trying for years to get a licence for a cooperative bank. Occasionally, they have been fed very positive noises by successive federal governments, but now they have temporarily moved the project to a back-burner through lack of action. The cooperative federations need help in intensifying and broadening the scope of lobbying for that bank. By getting involved in the lobbying, groups may position themselves to have some say in the structure and policies of that bank when it is set up.

In the meantime we have a Clayton's Coop Bank. A few years ago the Australian Association of Cooperatives established a Centralised Banking Scheme, which allows the Association's member-cooperatives to throw all of their surplus funds into a central pool. The Association's banker can then invest this in large whacks to get higher returns than any individual coop could. This Centralised Banking Scheme is also able to give loans to member-coops at lower rates of interest than they can get elsewhere. As well they can receive investment advice from it. Any surplus made from the investments is owned by the member-cooperatives and is used under the board's direction to finance the legal, training and consultancy services that the Association provides to members.

There may be some scope, within schemes like this one, for member coops to earmark their deposits for a sub-pool — which might then lend funds to other members using ethical criteria. A national working party of housing cooperatives is currently negotiating with the Association to establish a low-interest housing fund. However, like credit unions, these schemes have a number of legal restrictions on how they can invest funds. It goes without saying that these restrictions simply disappear if a banking licence can be obtained. Another possibility is that such centralised banking schemes might be in a position to oversee and ensure the security of investments by a member-coop that is incorporated as an investment society. This would present opportunities for *individuals* to put their money into a democratic institution — feeling all the while that their savings are secure. Effective lobbying (including a few hundred letters to local members and federal ministers) may just tip the balance in favour of a coop bank. Failing that, we can establish the necessary range of functions by coordinating other organisations.

Ethical investment of union superannuation funds:
The capital available for conscious ethical investment could be vastly increased if the multi-million-dollar superannuation funds being established by trade unions could be ethically invested. This may depend upon an increasing number of people with a commitment to resource and power-sharing and appropriate production becoming effectively active in trade unions and pressing their elected leaders to follow ethical investment policies. In this optimistic scenario the process of democratising and humanising Australian industry could be well advanced within a couple of decades.

The prospects for establishing the necessary institutions for ethical investment by unions are now very good. Whether union funds are actually used to stimulate progressive change or simply to maximise profits will depend, as in credit unions, on the policy guidelines that are democratically set by the membership. At the time of writing an announcement had just been made that the ACTU and the Colonial Mutual Life office (CML) were considering establishing a joint venture "to provide financial services, including quasi-banking facilities, for union members". [15] CML already manages ten union-sponsored superannuation schemes. The collective financial power involved is significant when we consider that the ACTU has 160 affiliated unions with a combined income of at least $300 million a year.

Over recent years the union movement has studied a number of international models for a new "union bank". The Swedish experience has been very influential. Over recent decades the Swedish trade unions have moved their emphasis from industrial democracy policies aimed at gradually increasing information-sharing and worker participation from the bottom up towards policies of economic democracy whereby controlling interests are to be purchased in Swedish industry through the combined financial power of the savings of the whole union movement. The general manager of the CML has recently been in the United States studying the Union Privileges Benefit Plan of the AFL–CIO, the American equivalent of the ACTU. They have also been looking at the Unity Trust model in Britain where 17 unions set up a 50–50 joint banking venture with the Cooperative Bank in 1985. Unity Trust's first year was very successful; its pre-tax profit was $164,000 and it increased its balance sheet from $15.9 million to $39.9 million. [16] Unity Trust began issuing a new savings vehicle called a BRIC (British Regional Investment Certificate) which allows investors to deposit funds securely at competitive interest rates while supporting economic activities in their own region.

The British alliance between the unions and the Cooperative Bank is unlikely to be repeated soon in Australia. There is still a strong adversarial attitude between the boards and management of many primary producing cooperatives which employ farm and factory workers and the unions. By this myopic attitude the rural cooperative movement deliberately puts itself in a cross-fire between union disputes and the competition and takeovers it faces with the huge agribusiness conglomerates. The best chance cooperatives have of survival in Australia is to cooperate with each other and to close ranks with the unions to extend their combined economic clout and organisational support. At least the path to higher productivity and industrial harmony in the primary sector has been lit by the progressive NSW Abalone Divers' Cooperative by sponsoring their casual factory workers in establishing a worker cooperative. The self-managing factory workers are earning more money, while productivity and product quality have risen. Production continuity is guaranteed since the conflict relationship has been *structured out* of the workplace and insecure casual jobs have been transformed into secure self-managed employment with full award conditions.

STRATEGIC ETHICAL INVESTMENT

Ultimately, the capital pooled together by ethical investors will only be transformative when it is invested in a skilfully planned and coordinated way to finance appropriate production. This will probably require forms of peak organisations which can concentrate and develop the necessary economic and technical skills to ensure that such investments are viable, mutually compatible and, where possible, mutually supportive. The strategic coordination of ethical investment may, for example, allow a large number of local institutions to combine and purchase controlling interests in corporations which are undemocratic or destructive in their practices. Foreign "ethical capital" might even be attracted for very expensive "takeovers". After restructuring production appropriately, and restructuring the organisation on a suitable democratic basis, its shares could be resold on an equal vote basis to those people or organisations which have a stake in its operations. Democratic restructuring would be, in all likelihood, on the worker cooperative structure of "one employee one vote". In some cases it may be more appropriate to institute a division of voting power amongst some combination of employees, suppliers, consumers and the community affected by operations. It may even be preferable to sub-divide the organisation into a group of interacting cooperatives. Since the capital is recovered after reselling the enterprise, a very substantial *revolving fund* might be available for strategic ethical purchase.

I think that the following principles should be considered in determining the institutional manner in which co-ordination of investment might happen: (1) The basis of coordination should be through democratic representation from individual ethical investment institutions, not by command from government even if that government is democratically elected; (2) Policy decisions about the range and nature of investments should remain subject to the democratic decision of the members and boards of individual institutions; (3) A common research and information service should be funded collectively by ethical investment bodies. There is an urgent need for reliable and up-to-date information on the practices of companies operating in Australia; (4) Strategy guidelines could be agreed on in a peak negotiating body. Information could then be shared about each relevant investment decision so that progress can be assessed. Close relations between institutions might allow quite precise industry planning by a combination of funding new enterprises and buying controlling interests in existing enterprises whose production and structure could be re-directed in appropriate directions.

Let me give some examples of what I mean by "strategic ethical investment". *Option A*: We might agree to democratise sections of the mass media by choosing the right moment and coordinating purchase of a controlling interest in a television station or newspaper. After converting the legal structure to a consumer cooperative the organisation would be resold to consumers on a "one user one vote" basis. The membership would then elect a board which would appoint editor and staff; and the recouped capital would return to a revolving fund for a future buyout. *Option B*: We might agree to develop an autonomous capacity within Australia aimed at building industrial solar energy systems within ten years. *Option C*: We might agree to coordinate investment so as to develop, by the year 2000, an indigenous capacity to build re-programmable multi-purpose industrial robots under democratic control—thus providing for the regional dispersal of manufacturing capacity, and for ownership to be vested equally in the entire population of the region in which each automated factory is established. *Option D*: We might agree to buy up several properties in a particular bio-region for resale after appropriate and coordinated development. *Option E*: We might agree to buy up forests in a threatened region, resell shares in a governing trust to conservationists, and to fund new cooperative enterprises to provide alternative employment for loggers. *Option F*: We might decide to cooperatively develop an automated factory which produces super-cheap and durable electric vehicles (with maybe a 50 kph maximum speed) for export to the Third World, while simultaneously offering low-interest loans to local governments which plan for an appropriate support structure, including battery exchange and recharge stations, public education and lowered speed limits.

To try to do all of these things in a piecemeal way as opportunities arise over a decade will change a lot a little. To consciously focus resources might ensure success in key areas of change and provide an outstanding fulcrum model for an alternative economy. The question to punt for is: what are the keys to the next millennium? Before turning to an examination of the cooperative movement for models of industrial democracy at work let's briefly look up to some grand-scale practical approaches to the democratisation of industry, approaches which can be pursued at the level of government taxation policy and at the level of large institutions. Then let's look down to an earthy barter approach, an approach which is easily accessible to grass-roots organisation.

Employee Share Ownership Schemes:
Employee Share Ownership Plans (ESOPs) in the United States now cover some ten million workers in about 7000 companies.[17] An ESOP is formed when a trust fund is established which first purchases shares in a company and then allocates them to the employees of that company. Payment for these shares may be paid out of profits over time. Legislation offers tax incentives to companies using these trusts.

ESOPs can be wide-ranging and provide complete employee control of a company; on the other hand they can also institute methods of profit-sharing which in fact give no control whatever to employees. In a review of ESOPs, Australian Mark Burford noted the dangers of tokenism with ESOP trusts which do not allow employees to vote their shares:

> *A critical problem with such trusts is that they can separate employee owned shares from the control of the employee owners and, as a result, separate share ownership by employees from control of the company by employees.* [17]

Burford indicates that workers have no voting rights at all attached to their shares in 85 per cent of ESOPs in the United States. In an age of automation, to offer a share in profits to workers without sharing control may be a way of buying temporary loyalty to the company (instead of to a union) until that job can be occupied by a machine. The machine has two advantages for the employer: a machine will not strike, nor will it consume a share in future profits. Profit-sharing is revocable, as it is the decision of the employer. Power-sharing, however, requires democratic decisions for change: if a labour-replacing machine is introduced in a democratic workplace, power-sharing means that increased profits will either be shared by *all*, or used to decrease working hours, or else to increase the number of jobs through expansion of operations. When introduced to undemocratic workplaces, machines maintain exclusive control of profits while reducing the number of jobs at existing hours and wage rates.

In a speech to the H. R. Nichols Society in September 1986 the Leader of the Opposition, John Howard, put a lot of emphasis on profit-sharing and ESOPs as a means of increasing productivity and of breaking the loyalty of workers to unions.

> *Tax incentives to facilitate employee share ownership schemes are under consideration by the Opposition—including the possibility of providing concessional tax treatment for the* purchase *of such shares.* [18]

At no time does Howard mention a need to increase worker control or to institute industrial democracy. "The aim," he says, "must be to ensure that workers have more to gain from their firm making profits than from the industrial success of their union."

It is clearly possible to pursue quite distinct aims through employee share ownership. It can be used to increase democratic control of machines if there is a complete sharing of voting power, or it can be used as a way of buying temporary loyalty and breaking trade union power and so to clear the way for unrestrained automation under elite control.

Universal Stock Ownership Plan:
A second innovative American approach to democratisation of ownership of large corporations has been devised by Stuart Speiser. [19] The Universal Stock Ownership Plan (USOP) is a form of "social capitalism". Where at present only six per cent of US citizens derive their incomes from ownership of capital, the USOP aims to distribute income from newly formed capital to the *entire* population without confiscation of property or new taxes. USOP legislation would establish a government-guaranteed long-term loan program which would finance loans for all new capital investment in any of the largest 2000 corporations (to begin with). The corporations would issue stock in the names of all eligible citizens. None of the new shareholders would have to pay out any cash. They would be in the same position as Messrs Bond and Murdoch, who are able to purchase huge shareholdings to take over companies on the basis of borrowed funds guaranteed by their existing assets. The government would hold all shares in trust until profits from the new operations had repaid the loan plus interest, after which ownership and future dividends would transfer to the citizens. Since every USOP participant would receive shares in every one of the 2000 companies, none would suffer greatly if any of the companies did poorly.

Speiser advocates retention of the shares in the USOP trust — with restrictions on individual rights to buy, sell or vote the shares. This would prevent the inexperienced being swindled or squandering their income source. Democratic participation by shareholders would be by election of the Board of Trustees of the USOP which would then be empowered to elect members onto the boards of the 2000 companies. Speiser asserts that USOP is not utopian since it "accepts human nature as it is and deals with the realities of the corporate finance system".[20] He says that the political debate over implementation of USOP began in September 1984 when Dr David Owen, Leader of the British Social Democratic Party, proposed the adoption of a USOP-like plan to the Party's annual convention.

It is urgent that debate on schemes like ESOP and USOP begin in Australia. Designing schemes that are viable in the Australian context and which bring workplace democracy will take some time. Formation of the political will to implement such schemes will be a far harder and longer task.

Experimental economies: Local Exchange Trading Systems:
A Local Exchange Trading System (LETS) has been operating successfully for over two years in the Comox Valley in British Columbia. LETS are now being established in Vancouver, Canada, in Whangarei, New Zealand and in the Lismore region of Northern NSW. The first issue of *Work Matters* described the LETS, or Green Dollar Exchange, as a form of "credit card bartering".[21] The article used the example of a baby-sitting club where each member accumulates points for the number of hours of baby-sitting they do for any other member. These points are converted into the right to equivalent hours of labour from any other member. A Green Dollar Exchange allows a more general accounting of labour and services. Labour time by gardeners, tradesmen, dentists and baby-sitters can be interconverted by medium of "Green dollars" which can be exchanged only with other members through a central accounting facility. Each member asks that their own account be debited when they receive a service from another.

The idea of a local currency is based on underwriting the "Green dollars" with local community labour and assets instead of the guarantee of a commonwealth government. Until the seventies the international gold standard used to provide gold bullion as a real asset backing to national currencies. Since then national dollars are no longer backed by any tangible assets. The community currency offers the advantage of locally assessible and accountable resources as a real value standard against which labour and other resources can be measured.

People who bank partly in local currencies are thus insuring themselves—against inflation, or even the collapse of government-issued "funny money", which is subject to the vagaries of the vast international financial markets. Rural communities or special interest groups with low mobility and high levels of trust would seem to offer the best prospects for the strong development of community currencies which need to be backed by chains of personal guarantees, that is to say, by *trust*. Use of a community currency has the added advantage of building community solidarity.

HUMANISING WORK: COMBINING ECONOMIC AND INDUSTRIAL DEMOCRACY

People are hard to manipulate or dominate when they are self-reliant and self-confident. People are not very inclined to dominate others when their most significant relations with others are ones of trust and cooperation. Cooperatives are intensive breeding grounds for self-reliance and trust. In principle, they are directly democratic and so encourage values and skills oriented towards the empowerment and participation of others as well as of self. While this commitment is most strongly developed *between* individuals within a coop or collective, it also flows naturally beyond the boundaries of the institution. Furthermore, coops are basic economic building blocks. They are sites at which production of wealth, refinement of skills and transfer of human skills and energy into machines takes place. The nature of human relations at workplaces, the most strategic sites for control in a society, has effects which are many times multiples of other sorts of human relations. In time, these workplace relations distil into all other human relationships and into the laws and customs that are ongoing cultural correlates of those particular relations.

In our threatened and threatening world surely one of the most pressing tasks before us is to strengthen such organisational forms that by their nature build trust, mutual responsibility and mutual empowerment into economic interactions. The modern cooperative movement was born out of the turmoil of the industrial revolution. It has repeatedly shown its ability to survive, and at times to grow rapidly during periods of economic crisis. The remarkable new growth in the European and Canadian cooperative movements since the early seventies only confirms the present vitality of the movement. In a recent book called *The Search for Community: From Utopia to a Cooperative Society*, the Canadian cooperator George Melnyk described four historical traditions of cooperation as (1) the Liberal Democratic Tradition, (2) the Marxist Tradition, (3) the Socialist Tradition and (4) the Communalist Tradition.[22] Only the first and last of these have been active in Australia. Australian commercial cooperatives — from retail, taxi, fishing and dairy coops to credit unions and RSL clubs — are based on the British Rochdale principles of the Liberal Democratic Tradition. In summary, the six modern international principles of this tradition are:

1. *Membership is voluntary and open to all who will use the services and accept the responsibilities of membership.*

2. *Democratic control on a "one user member one vote" basis.*

3. *Strictly limited rate of return on share capital.*

4. *Surplus distributed equitably amongst members in proportion to transactions with coop or reinvested in development of coop.*

5. *Education of members, staff and community in cooperation.*

6. *Cooperation between cooperatives at local, national and international levels.*

The Communalist Tradition has long been marginally active through monasteries and religious communities. Since the sixties secular and new spiritual communities have grown quietly around the country in what is often called the Alternative Lifestyle Movement (ALM). The Nimbin area is probably the most famous region for ALM activity but is probably not the most successful.

The Marxist Tradition of post-revolution, government-formed cooperatives has never appeared in Australia due to an extreme scarcity of revolutions. As Marxist cooperatives generally do not recognise the principle of open and voluntary membership and do not maintain independence from government, this tradition would be incompatible with contemporary Australian culture and it is unlikely that we will see it develop. The Socialist Tradition of multifunctional common ownership coops which is strong in Israel, Africa and Europe has barely survived on the fringes of the Australian trade union movement, although it has recently shown some renewed signs of life. Even in the liberal-democratic tradition the Australian cooperative movement has not developed as vigorously as it should have. A major reason for this is that it has failed to practise the fifth and sixth principles. Coops have usually been adrift in the market doing their own thing. Cut off from other coops and from their origins and spirit through lack of member education, many members have lacked commitment. Some have even lacked understanding of the nature of a coop. Many Australian coops are only now beginning to recognise the value of skill-sharing and the dramatic market advantages that cooperation between coops can bring. A strong resurgence of the movement appears to have begun at a number of levels within Australia.

On the global scale too, there are signs of growing communication and cooperation between the movements in different countries. If this continues, the international cooperative movement may have a key role to play in building a bridge across the gulf between East and West. While the country in which a cooperative movement evolves puts a very strong stamp on its style and values, the spirit of cooperation is nevertheless strong enough in each of the four traditions to allow the development of common understanding and the pursuit of mutual interests. The current development of international coop to coop trade may be the first span in the bridge across the gulf.

How not to cooperate—lessons from the past:
The early British experience of industrial cooperatives was unimpressive. The cooperative factories of the last century did not learn how to work with each other, and they also failed to learn the importance of having only active employees as members since they allowed members who were leaving to retain their share capital and voting rights. If the cooperative was successful it was easy for private investors to buy control of the coop from these "dry" shareholders

—and then convert it to a company in which the number of shares an individual owns determines their economic return and their voting power. In a coop the economic reward is in return for *effort* invested in the coop rather than in return for capital invested; and each user member has equal voting power regardless of how many shares they own. In Australia we have repeated the fatal error of the British industrial cooperative movement and allowed "dry" members who have stopped using the coop to retain their voting power; hence they can sell out the coop to corporate raiders. This happened to the partially employee-owned company NVC in 1986. NVC failed to repurchase the shareholdings of the 38 employees who left over time, so a private investor was able to buy them out and take over the business regardless of the wishes of the 20 remaining employees. It has been largely through such "dry" sellouts that, over the last decade, the Australian cooperative movement has been decimated by ravenous corporate raiders. The primary sector has suffered most—with SAFCOL, Primac, Nepean Dairies, Southern Farmers, and Farmers and Graziers Coop all being taken over. As a result farmers today are scraping to survive while private agribusiness is making record profits.

Industrial self-management: the Mondragon experience:
While cooperative structures have been developed for application to almost any sort of economic or social activity you might imagine, the current revolution in automation is making the industrial cooperative a key to the future. The most common model for industrial coops today is the worker coop. In a worker cooperative all regular employees are full voting members of the coop and all capital reinvested in the coop is owned in common. Employees who leave must have their shares repurchased so there are no "dry" shareholders to sell out.

The structure used in the Mondragon worker coops requires an initial input of capital by any new member and also an allocation of a portion of the coop's annual surplus to each member's individual capital account (50 per cent at present). This individual capital account and shareholding is withdrawn by the member on retirement or departure.

The world has one impressive working model of industrial self-management. The system of cooperatives in the Basque province of Guipozcoa in Northern Spain operates successfully on a broad institutional scale. While the Mondragon experience should not be taken as an appropriate model for Australia to follow, some very important principles can nevertheless be learned from it. At the very least, it can be said that at Mondragon self-management works in practice — thus demonstrating that such self-management can develop within the interstices of a society which operates by a contrary logic.

The Mondragon cooperatives developed within, and in spite of, a dictatorial fascist government and a capitalist economy.[23] The Mondragon cooperative sector is a coordinated network of industrial, producer and support cooperatives employing more than 19,000 people.[24] The system began modestly in 1943 with the training of unemployed youth by a Catholic priest inspired by cooperative economic principles. In 1956, four of his students opened a workshop to build paraffin stoves. This was followed by a credit cooperative in 1959. Then the sixties saw a rapid expansion to a system of interacting industrial, consumer and support coops coordinated by the credit cooperative bank. By 1986 the system had expanded to include over 90 industrial cooperatives, supported by specialist service cooperatives which provided the functions of education, research and development, social security, housing and health. Even during the recession of the seventies the Mondragon system, although it expanded more slowly, continued to generate new cooperative employment in contrast to strong falls in employment in capitalist firms.[25] The cooperatives generally performed better than private firms during this time and even took some over (four in 1979). According to an economic analysis by Thomas and Logan, "the finding is conclusive that the cooperative enterprises have made considerably better use of their available resources than have private enterprises."[26] These authors stress the importance of the "linkage between a credit cooperative and a group of cooperative factories" in the success of the system. The credit coop plays a planning role in establishing new cooperatives and coordinating their activities. And so far *not one cooperative in the Mondragon system has failed.*

Although there are no inherent constraints in this system to induce socially and environmentally appropriate choices of product or technology, the strong reinforcement of cooperative values makes such appropriate choices far more likely to occur than in capitalist enterprises. The economic success and technological innovativeness of Mondragon, when stacked up against capitalist industry, makes it worthy of close study with regard to its transferability. *Ikerlan*, the research and development cooperative, employs 36 scientists and appears to be looking well ahead in its efforts:

> *Its researchers have investigated the use of computers in process automation and control, the design and application of robots, the various solar energy products already available and their susceptibility to improve as part of programmes in the general areas of electronics, thermodynamics, mechanical engineering, and informatics. In following this path, the cooperatives are adopting the successful Japanese model of moving from copying to innovation as a means of carving out a niche in the international economy.* [27]

The British labour movement is now looking favourably towards the Mondragon model. In Australia all political parties look on the Mondragon model with varying degrees of favour. The consensus around the desirability of Mondragon-style worker cooperatives is highlighted by the strong support coming from both the Metalworkers Union *and* the National Civic Council. The process has already begun of setting up the institutions which can plan, coordinate and finance an adaptation of those principles of the Mondragon model which are suited to our conditions.

In times of economic difficulties cooperative movements tend to revitalise. This is already happening, both in Europe and in Britain. It is also undoubtedly happening in Australia, and it is happening at three different levels. There is a keen and growing interest on the part of government and opposition parties in the eastern States, and I suspect that this interest is in the main a reaction to the mobilisation of the cooperative movement itself which is happening at the level of cooperative organisations as well as from the grassroots level.

Government action on cooperation:

The federal Labor Government is responsive to representations about cooperative development in two areas where they are faced with deep structural problems. Cooperatives do not provide quick-fix employment creation, but they do offer the prospect of long-term and stable, Australian-controlled jobs. The Minister for Employment and Industrial Relations, Ralph Willis, convened a Local Employment Initiatives Conference in Canberra last year which included a special session on cooperatives with a guest representative from the Mondragon cooperatives. The Minister for Primary Industries has also been supportive of cooperative development as a means of strengthening and retaining indigenous control of Australian primary industries. The federal government has not, however, come across with a licence for a cooperative bank. Nor has it made any serious moves towards uniform federal cooperative legislation which might help to prevent the takeover of cooperatives by corporate raiders. Neither has it made any moves towards tax incentives to encourage new cooperative development or the reinvestment of capital — something which is crucial to the medium term survival of existing cooperatives. In a speech to the International Labour Organisation early in his prime ministership Bob Hawke had promised support for the development of rural cooperative communities along Israeli lines. This support has not been forthcoming except in a tokenistic way — despite recent research by David Dummerick of the Australian National University showing that well-established communities can successfully reduce demand for jobs and for welfare. Earlier research by Liz Summerland had focused on recently formed communities and reached pessimistic conclusions. More recently Scott Williams has canvassed more sustainable approaches to rural employment generation.

All of the State governments on the east coast of Australia are currently showing strong interest in cooperative development. The Victorian government established a Ministerial Advisory Committee on Cooperation in February 1984. This MACC produced a report in July 1986, entitled *The Cooperative Way: Victoria's Third Sector*, which proposes, amongst other things, government support for the formation of independent associations in each cooperative sub-sector.

If sufficient initiative were forthcoming from cooperatives, this approach may indeed give a boost to the movement in Victoria. However, to date the Victorian process seems to have remained as a rainbow in the sky without reaching the pot of gold in realising cooperative development on the ground. In Queensland the State Department of Employment and Industrial Affairs has allocated a million dollars for the development of worker cooperatives or employee ownership under the "Group Enterprise Scheme", while in New South Wales a separate Ministry of Cooperatives was created for the first time in Australia in 1986 with Bob Debus being appointed as Minister.

Debus has proved to be a very active and practical Minister and has moved quickly to establish working parties to advise him on co-operative finance, legislation, education and research and a Cooperative Trade Fair to be held in August 1987. The strategic aim of these combined initiatives is to create a favourable environment for cooperative growth and to stimulate new growth and integration in the sector. Debus also oversaw the passage into law of the most far-reaching amendments to the NSW *Cooperation Act* since it was drawn up in 1923. The main thrust of the legislation was to prevent cooperatives from being taken over against the wishes of their active members by corporate raiders who generally take control of cooperatives with the assistance of "dry" or inactive members. Non-user members frequently lack commitment to the cooperative since they are not making use of its services. The history of the cooperative movement is strewn with the stripped shells of coops that were sold out by non-user shareholders. But now the amended Act will ensure that only people who make active use of the cooperative within any two-year period will remain eligible for membership.

Organisations of cooperatives: looking to the grassroots:
In 1980 the Cooperative Federation of New South Wales introduced a Centralised Banking Scheme to allow member coops to combine their investments. The scheme financed such a rapid growth in services and staffing levels for the Cooperative Federation that in 1986 it was able to expand into a nation-wide organisation called the Australian

Association of Cooperatives. The new board of the AAC so far has actively encouraged the entry and participation of all sorts of cooperatives into the Association.

This bringing together of the great diversity of Australian cooperatives is stimulating a new energy and spirit of cooperation. Conservative farmers and fishermen and businessmen are discovering common ground and interests with people from worker coops, housing cooperatives and communes. While the Cooperative Federations in the other States have so far shown little sign of renewed life, a whole range of new initiatives has been set afoot by the AAC.

The credit union movement has thrived because it has cooperated around astute initiatives in automation and has developed the necessary sophisticated financial management skills to make its way in a world controlled by capitalist banks. One consequence of achieving technical success in this area has been the significant acculturation of credit union boards and staff into the capitalist values of image-building, of technical efficiency and of accumulation for its own sake. Many large credit unions appear to have lost their sense of social mission and their old regard for and pursuit of *active* member participation. One of the great hopes for success in the economic democratisation of this country is that the credit union movement now appears to be reconsidering its move away from the cooperative spirit of member empowerment. If the established credit union movement joins with the wider cooperative movement in making a renewed commitment to the pursuit of societal improvement and member participation, then the outlook clearly is promising.

The ideology of the community movement also emphasises sustainability of the individual community, and to a lesser degree, sustainability of the biologically defined region (bio-region) of which it is a part. The formation of the Australian Association of Sustainable Communities (AASC) in 1983 formalised a network amongst communities for the first time. AASC was intended as a body for negotiation with government after Hawke's offer of support. But it still has no substantial income and is unable to offer support services to its movement. Failure of the movement to commit itself to the development of AASC as a provider of support services or as a significant lobby group reflects, in part, a lack of resources and political skill. I think it also demonstrates a continuation of the cultural dynamic of Alternative Lifestyles Movement participants in *retreat* from mainstream culture and structured organisation. My impression is that this dynamic has come to a turning point, and that residents of self-reliant communities are now finding the confidence to exert their values on mainstream culture in more organised ways.

New-wave coops: grass-roots growing into organisation:
A new generation of cooperatives is being formed by people who have realised that they can best provide themselves with basic needs such as shelter, food and employment by joining together with others. Cooperative purchasing of fruit and vegetables and dried foods is happening in share households, in local communities and sometimes out of youth support centres. Some peter out, some grow and incorporate. Some eventually establish premises and a retail store. At this stage chances of survival increase. Indeed there are many Australian retail cooperatives from the established movement which have been in business since the turn of the century. In Victoria the traditional retail coops and the new-wave food coops began working together towards a second-tier common purchasing and distribution coop. Moves towards a food warehouse and distribution centre are now quite advanced. In Victoria too, unlike the other States, the office of the Registrar of Cooperatives has proved supportive of grass-roots cooperative development.

Worker cooperatives have been developing strongly in New South Wales during the eighties with the financial and managerial assistance of a series of government-funded support programs and the Association of Cooperatives. There are now some 20 worker cooperatives in operation. There is still a fair way to go to develop the sort of sophisticated financial and managerial support services necessary to integrate these cooperatives into a self-sustaining and mutually supporting sector—as has happened in Spain. The Worker Enterprise Corporation (WEC) has been playing the lead role in getting new worker coops off the ground and also in conversions of private firms into worker coops. The WEC has supported the setting up of worker coops in areas such as electronics, refrigeration, printing, pottery, labour supply and furniture manufacture. The success rate of worker coops in terms of survival is dramatically better than the survival rate for small private businesses which have a 50 per cent failure rate within the first three years. There have been 24 worker coops set up in New South Wales by the WEC since 1981, and only three have failed.

The Australian Association for Employee Ownership is an organisation of worker coops and of partly employee-owned companies. It has a lowest common denominator approach to industrial and economic democracy. While it favours a "one worker-member–one vote" system of control, it does not insist upon majority worker control for its member organisations. The danger of tokenism in buying off employee commitment without giving real control has already been mentioned. With the rapid rate of technological change, it is not much use for employees to share in profits and a few decisions — to then find themselves laid off by the decision of a board which is not accountable to them. Mere profit-sharing also leaves the door open for takeovers or shutdowns against the wishes of employees.

One of the most interesting recent experiments in Australian cooperation, as discussed earlier, has been the setting up of a worker cooperative by the highly successful NSW Abalone Divers Cooperative. This may prove to be a significant model for the improvement of industrial relations and for the increase in productivity for primary industries in general. Another organisation, Grafton-Ullamara Dairy Cooperative, permits and encourages its factory workers to become members of the cooperative. There is some debate over which of these two organisations is the better model; but both are steps towards resolving the "blind spot" of liberal democratic coops which allows a relationship of equals between user members — even while retaining what is still formally called the "master–servant" relationship with employees. An employment development agency is being planned for Lismore in order to assist local cooperatives.

Transition to self-management:
Self-management is a mature form of an economic system which can be realised only in a mature society, a society where the majority of adults have been able to develop their confidence and management skills. In today's society such skills are almost the *exclusive* preserve of professional managers and military officers. Self-management therefore requires the development of cooperation as a social value, so that those who currently possess an advantage in skills and confidence will try to *share* these and make others more self-reliant . . . rather than use their advantage to maintain others in a dependent relationship. If we assume that the process has begun seriously, it will still take more than one generation to develop the necessary degree of social maturity and cooperation. I don't share the view of those who believe that self-management can be successfully instituted in one fell swoop without a prior (laborious) development of public commitment.

Legislation and institutional structures should be worked for because they can *allow* or *facilitate* self-reliance and local self-management. However, if the will and the intensive skill development necessary are not active in the people living within those institutional structures, then tendencies back towards centralisation will become overwhelming. The result can be to discredit the very possibility of self-management for another generation: "It isn't practical, it's against 'human nature'." There needs to be a widespread, strong commitment and a fairly wide development of skills in self-reliance and management before *large-scale* institutionalisation of self-management can be sustainable. Any attempt to force a *general* institutionalisation of self-management onto a relatively stable society like present-day Australia, prior to the emergence of popular will and an adequately skilled popular culture, is simply doomed to failure. It represents a form of political opportunism which is in contradiction to the cultural reality of self-management itself. For self-management to emerge in a society, the practice has to lead the idea. Once the point of balance towards transformation has been reached then nothing will stop the idea or the legal structures.

CONCLUSION

Workplaces must change fundamentally, not superficially. To relax the squeeze on people in authoritarian workplaces we have to *shift control of decisions* at those workplaces. We are invited to embark on a long and determined campaign for *industrial democracy*. The deepest (and fastest) structural level at which the process of democratisation can be made to happen is at sites where investment decisions are made. This campaign is for *economic democracy* and ethical investment.

We are trying to humanise a highly competitive and efficient economic system. If investments are made according to the purest of ethical criteria but without the necessary business nous and understanding of the market then they will fail . . . and we will be back to square one. It's too late for square one. Cooperators and ethical investors have to learn to understand how business works *better* than capitalists; yet they must choose to restrain themselves from accumulating wealth for the sake of power, and from investing wealth as undemocratically and destructively as capitalists so often do. As the Mondragon experience has proved, if we can attain a critical level of capital and infrastructure then mutual cooperation will give us the edge over those who continue to slash each other's economic throats.

If we can succeed in mobilising a sufficiently disciplined network of organisations and skilled people together with public support, then we have a chance of developing a democratic and sustainable economy. In the sort of self-reliant, self-managed society that we *could* build in Australia, very few people would need or want to depend on welfare; few would depend completely on selling their labour to others to survive, and the *need* for big government and heavy taxes would diminish. Income would accrue to the great majority of people from a combination of the work they perform and the return on their capital share in automated factories. At present, significant return on capital invested accrues to a small percentage of the population who pay little tax and are able to choose to do no work at all— whereas workers work long hours and pay high taxes. If Australians make the choice soon, then we can build a just economic structure without blood. Workers will work less and share in control of capital and its investment; and a few capitalists may have their return on capital and control over investment diminished somewhat — although it is unlikely they'll need to work more.

The message our Bonds and Spalvins and Fairfaxes need to pick up is "share power today or suffer with the rest of us tomorrow". For if Australia slides into ever-increasing poverty then political instability and possibly terrorism will inevitably edge towards centre stage and *you*, the few who have most freedom to choose, will have chosen it! Let's hope a few of the powerful can recognise where survival lies and support a peaceful transition to a sustainable and civilised economy. Let's hope our new movement can skip the symptoms of problems and aim for their sources, and let's hope it averts the recklessness and division that have plagued so many old movements for change. If, however, we organise well enough and work hard enough, and bring joy to each other in the process, we'll have neither the time nor the need for so much hope.

8:
GREENING EDUCATION

Noel Gough

NOEL GOUGH *is a senior lecturer in the Department of Curriculum and Teaching at Victoria College, Clayton, Victoria. He taught biology, science and media studies in Victorian high schools before moving to the institution now known as Victoria College in 1972. Since then he has developed and taught a number of teacher education programs including a postgraduate course in curriculum administration and pre-service courses in curriculum design (with* particular reference to environmental education, science, home economics and textiles education) and futures studies. Noel also teaches Master of Education courses in curriculum study at the University of Melbourne and is Australasian Editor of *the* Journal of Curriculum Studies. *His publications and conference presentations in environmental education have focused on environmental ethics, environmental inquiry and environmental education across the curriculum. Noel is also the current Convenor of the Victorian Ministry of Education's Environmental Education Curriculum Committee.*

At the heart of Green politics is the concept of *ecology*—an understanding of how organisms, including humans, interrelate with each other and with their environments in the totality of the earth's ecosystem. Thus, many Green writers and activists are interested in education primarily as an instrument for changing human values, for fostering an holistic understanding of "the oneness of all living forms and their cyclical rhythms of birth and death, thus reflecting an attitude towards life which is profoundly ecological".[1] However, to date the attention of the Green movement in education has tended to focus on curriculum content and on the politics of educational administration. That is, on the one hand, Green educators have worked for the sorts of issues addressed elsewhere in this book to become subject matters of school curricula—issues of nature conservation, peace, social justice, sustainable futures, alternative lifestyles and so on. On the other hand, Green politics supports the devolution of authority in education from centralised state bureaucracies to local communities. In this chapter I will argue that a "profoundly ecological" understanding of education has significance for much more than relatively superficial matters of curriculum content and administrative control; rather, such an understanding suggests an underlying *ecological paradigm* for education, and it also suggests imperatives for substantial changes in educational purposes, priorities and practices.

My own practice, initially as a school teacher and later as a teacher educator, has given me first-hand experience of both the superficial and deeper implications of ecological understanding for education. Thus, for example, when I first began teaching, I dutifully taught "ecology" as a topic in biology and science (the subjects for which, in a conventional academic sense, I was qualified to teach). But, in retrospect, I believe that the way in which I designed and taught a course in media studies (for which I had no formal qualifications whatsoever) was much more in keeping with an ecological paradigm for education. Similarly, as a teacher educator with particular interests in curriculum design and evaluation, I have been involved with either developing or accrediting courses, or assessing student achievement, in such subjects as environmental science, home economics and textiles education at the senior secondary level. As I will show later in this chapter, while environmental science is superficially Green, both home economics and textiles are in some ways—at least in schools of the State of Victoria—more likely to exemplify ecological approaches to education.

SOME ASSUMPTIONS ABOUT GREEN EDUCATION

There is no easy consensus as to what it might mean to be Green in education, but a preview edition of *Green Teacher*, an "international, cross-curricular, radical and practical" journal launched in 1986, sets out some underlying assumptions that are likely to be shared by the majority of educators who align themselves with Green politics. While an ecological consciousness is pervasive in the journal, it also emphasises approaches to education which are *evolutionary, exploratory* and *participatory*. Thus, for example, its editorial policy views Green concerns and the idea of being a Green teacher as evolving concepts to be the subjects for continued exploration by its subscribers and contributors. The journal also makes the following assumptions:

Whatever topic or subject an educator is dealing with, he/she will want to help students to develop their understanding of, and their skills in helping with:

- *People's need to cooperate with, and care for, the earth.*

- *People's need to cooperate with, and care for, each other, across boundaries of all kinds.*

- *People's need to grow as independent, self-reliant, confident individuals, able to fulfil themselves.*

- *People's need to design and use technologies and lifestyles which support these aims, towards a sustainable society.*

- *People's need to work at new ways of "doing politics", in the basic sense of controlling their future.*

- *People's need to take part in the spiritual transformation whose "shifted paradigms" must underlie all other change.* [2]

In this chapter I will not be pursuing the debate as to whether or not Green politics is itself some sort of "new paradigm". [3] Rather, I will be describing and defending a paradigm shift in education which complements the personal and social changes in values and behaviours promoted by the Green movement. That is, I believe that the evidence and arguments in support of an ecological paradigm for education do not necessarily derive from Green political assumptions. Rather, there seems to have been a kind of convergent evolution of educational and social philosophies which could and should result in mutually supportive educational and social reforms.

PARADIGMS AND PARADIGM SHIFTS

The significance of paradigms in education is illustrated by Table 3 in which the foundations of physical architecture—the clay, sand or rock on which a building rests—are compared metaphorically to the paradigms of social "architecture": the understandings of reality, nature and human nature upon which we build our social institutions.[4]

Table 3

	Physical Architecture	Social Architecture
Superstructure	Buildings, streets, signs, walls, doors, windows	Language/symbols, customs, laws, constitutions, institutions
Underlying framework	Footings, substructure	Cultural, ethical, moral norms
Site/ Foundations	Clay, sand, rock, water	Understanding of reality, nature, human nature

Education is, of course, a piece of social architecture—an institution designed and built by human societies—and much educational reform begins when we notice weaknesses in existing structures and we seek to identify and remedy the frictions, failures, faults and flaws which may have caused them to appear. All too often, we merely patch up and paint over the cracks in the superstructures of education, so as to temporarily minimise the appearance of weakness, without investigating the soundness of the underlying structures and paradigms. But there is little doubt that, in recent years, our understandings of reality, nature and human nature have been changing.

As a consequence, a social institution like education, that has been built upon such understandings, is also in need of being repaired, redesigned or reconstructed.

> The social construction of reality that once provided a certain coherence to Western society has been unravelling for decades. It was a world view that valued progress, economic efficiency, science and technology—and saw a world composed of separate entities such as atoms, individuals, academic departments, corporations, cities, and nations. Causes were separate from effects, present from future, variable from variable, and "we" from "they".[5]

The nature of the paradigm shift which will supplant such a world view is far from clear. Recent survey data have documented what appears to be a significant strengthening of "inner-directed" values (ecological, humane, spiritual) in Western industrialised countries. Underlying this value shift is a deeper and more subtle shift in beliefs "away from the confident scientific materialism of the earlier part of this century, and toward some form of universal transcendentalism".[6] A parallel shift in developing countries is again partial and indistinct, but its direction is away from Western materialism and toward a reassertion of native cultural values and beliefs. "The change in both cases is fundamentally a shift in our attitude toward our inner, subjective experience, affirming its importance and its validity".[7]

The Green movement may well be riding the tide of this change but it is by no means inevitable that a new world view will contain all of the features—such as feminism, nature conservation and esoteric spirituality—which are commonly associated with Green politics. However, there is one feature of the changing world view which does seem to have some inevitability—namely, its holistic emphasis:

> The most striking feature of the postmodern world is its systemic character, its astounding proliferation of linkages among once separate cultures, governments, economies and ecosystems ... In the postmodern world everything is connected to everything so that cause and effect, present and future, we and they are utterly ensnarled;

even separating them for analytic purposes becomes far less
convincing than it was in the heady recent times when academics
talked with great confidence of factors and variables.[8]

Mainstream education in Australia is anything but holistic. Indeed,
conventional schools—especially secondary schools, with which I am
most familiar—reinforce a view of "a world composed of separate
entities" through every aspect of their design, construction and modes
of operation. Age-graded children study separate subjects with
specialist teachers in specialised classrooms according to a timetable
which both symbolises and actualises a fragmented world view.
However, during the last two decades there have been a number
of countervailing tendencies, including increased support for "interdisciplinary" and "integrated" studies, which are consistent with a
shift towards a more holistic world view.

THE RISE OF ECOLOGICAL SUBJECT MATTERS IN EDUCATION

So far in Australia the most visible manifestation of an holistic world
view in education has been the creation of new subject matters which
focus on the interconnections between what were once studied as
separate entities. Thus, for example, a subject such as Physical
Science–Technology and Society which is offered in Victoria's Higher
School Certificate course allows students to study the ways in which
the properties of matter, and the workings of machines and human
societies, are interrelated rather than studying each of them separately
in such subjects as chemistry, physics and history. It should be noted
that many of these new subject matters can be seen to be *ecological*
in their educational rationalia without necessarily being orthodox
Green concerns. For example, the seventies in Australia saw a boom
in both environmental education and media studies. Each of these
subjects involves a partial study of human ecology, ie a "study of
interaction of persons with their environment".[9] Environmental
education and media studies are similar insofar as each can be seen
as a way of increasing the learner's awareness and understanding
of some of the environments with which he/she interacts: the first

subject focuses on human interactions with the environment provided by other living systems of the earth, whereas the second focuses on the environment created by some of humankind's most pervasive inventions—the texts and technologies of the mass media.

The subject matters which *are* characteristic of Green concerns—such as environmental education, peace studies, development education and women's studies—may also contribute to the development of an holistic world view by emphasising global concerns and attempting to open up rather than to close in on global problems and issues. For example, the blossoming of peace studies in the eighties owes much to worldwide concerns about a nuclear winter, to the widespread resurgence of community action groups such as Freeze in the United States and the Campaign for Nuclear Disarmament in Britain and to the United Nations' proclamation of 1986 as the International Year of Peace. But education for peace has rapidly gone beyond the subject matters of nuclear threat and disarmament to consider the wider meanings of peace in society and culture. Similarly, development education has moved out from its initial focus on the plight of the Third World to encompass issues of over-development in Western nations and their consequences for the global economy and ecology.

However, the fate of environmental education in Australian schools suggests that the creation of ecological subject matters represents a very superficial form of educational holism. While much of the impetus for environmental education in Australia during the early seventies grew out of a concern for the global environmental crisis, there is little doubt that its proponents were engaged in a form of social reconstruction that is consistent with the ideals of Green politics:

> *They were part of a movement which sought to encourage students to anticipate a new social order and promote those values which might hasten it. At the classroom level there was a growth of composite studies, such as environmental studies, which were thought to be of more interest to students and towards more social relevance in subjects, such as increasing awareness of the problems of ecological imbalance as a result of our present economic system.* [10]

But by the end of a decade which saw a great deal of activity in the name of environmental education (including substantial support by the national Curriculum Development Centre and the formation of the Australian Association for Environmental Education) one of its central figures observed:

> ... *few programs in school that have been claimed to be environmental education actually meet all the aims of environmental education. They are more concerned with education in and about the environment than education for the environment or social action. Thus it could be argued that environmental education has been subjected to incorporation into the existing hegemony in a neutralised form—the radical "action" components having been deleted and the less controversial knowledge and skills components retained* ...[11]

Ecological subject matters are a superficial form of educational holism for two reasons. First, while preaching an holistic perspective they still tend to be presented as separate entities; and second, they have preserved the teaching practices and learning experiences that complement an atomistic world view. In my experience, learning in these new subject matters continues to be dominated by the authority of teachers, textbooks and timetables and by trivial pursuits such as memorisation of information and rote performance of skills and procedures. Thus, in terms of a shift in educational paradigms, it is important to distinguish what is superficial from that which is significant about the recent legitimation (at least in some quarters) of environmental education, peace studies, development education and women's studies. The incorporation of such archetypal Green concerns into the research agendas of universities and the teaching timetables of many educational institutions is mere tinkering with the superstructure of education. Of more significance is the fact that the existence of such studies is indicative of changes in underlying cultural norms, assumptions and values.

These transformations may have resulted from our pursuit of a deeper understanding of human ecology and from our struggle to reconstruct our world view in the light of our new understanding. For example, the feminist critique of human history and culture has undoubtedly helped us to perceive and understand the global and local destructiveness of patriarchy—whether this is manifested by industrialism, by militarism, by the exploitation of developing countries by transnational corporations, or by the gross undervaluing of women's work in maintaining families, communities and societies. But if all that is achieved by this critique is a transformation of, say, school history from a study of men and warfare to a study which also recognises the roles of women and which celebrates peace, then we will not have achieved very much. A shift towards an ecological paradigm for education does not simply mean more environmental education, peace studies, development education and women's studies on school timetables. A paradigm shift involves changes in our *total* world view. And it may be very difficult—even for self-styled Green educators—to accept that the education system in which they practise, and of which they are themselves products, provides a structured misrepresentation of reality, nature and human nature.

TOWARDS AN ECOLOGICAL PARADIGM FOR EDUCATION

My concept of an ecological paradigm for education, and my sympathy for the Green social philosophy which complements it, has arisen from several different but interrelated sources. The term "ecological paradigm" is borrowed from Fred Emery.[12] Unfortunately in my view, Emery uses terms like "new" and "emerging" to distinguish an ecological paradigm from the one he calls "old" and "traditional". My senses of chronology and geography must be different from Emery's because the educational paradigm that he rejects has dominated merely the last two centuries of Western industrial civilisation—relatively recent periods and locations of human history and culture. Terms like "old", "new", "traditional" and "emerging" are transient and reflect changing fashions in education rather than enduring positions.

I prefer to think in terms of a shift from an *epistemological* paradigm towards an ecological paradigm. There are two reasons for my choice of the term "epistemological". Firstly, as commonly used in education, "epistemology" means the study of the origins and method of knowledge; thus the core assumptions of Western industrial society's systems of education rest on an epistemology—on a particular set of theories about how humans gain knowledge of themselves and their world. Secondly, the term "epistemological" has connotations of the *kinds* of knowledge which are valued; the ancient Greek word *"episteme"* referred to *theoretic* knowledge, and the kinds of knowledge which have dominated Western education are those which have been structured by Western society's dominant form of theorising— namely, positivist empirical science.

Emery's concept of an ecological paradigm for education is based largely on his synthesis of the results of relatively recent studies in human perception. I find Emery's argument very persuasive, but it is also rather lengthy and complex. Here I will only be able to give a very brief and over-simplified account of why it is one of the sources of my own concept of an ecological paradigm.

Another source of support for an ecological paradigm comes from the longer-term history of Western education prior to the scientific revolution. In particular, it comes from the Aristotelian scholastic curriculum which dominated European scholarship until the eighteenth century. Within that tradition, no strong distinction was made between matters of fact and matters of value regardless of whether one was studying nature or human nature.[13] The ideal of scientific detachment, or of any attempt to eliminate human values from supposedly "objective" world views, was rightly regarded as absurd.

A further cornerstone of my belief in the validity of an ecological paradigm for education is the apparent success of recent innovative practices in education, practices which can be seen as being consistent with a shift towards this paradigm. I will focus in particular on Earth Education (or what was once known as "Acclimatisation"). The significance of Earth Education is not just that it exemplifies good practice in an unmistakably Green subject matter (environmental education); Earth Education also represents, in fact, a true shift towards an ecological paradigm for education—although so far as I am aware this is not really understood by its creators or supporters. I will draw briefly on my own experience to show how the principles of Earth Education can be adapted to other subject matters.

In conclusion, I will discuss some ideas about the study of futures in education which are consistent with an ecological paradigm for education and a Green social philosophy.

RECENT RESEARCH ON HUMAN PERCEPTION

For two centuries educational practice in Western industrial society has been dominated by a particular set of theories about how it is possible for humans to gain knowledge. But if we allow educational practice to be dominated by such theories we must also ask the question: what if the theories are wrong? For two hundred years much educational practice has been based on the empiricist theories of perception and knowledge espoused by Locke, Berkeley and Hume. Their arguments are, indeed, very reasonable if it is also assumed that the world is as Newton depicted it and that the transfer of information from an object to a viewer obeys Euclid's geometry. According to this view, light reflected from an object to the retina yields only a "chaotic two-dimensional representation of reality . . . any useful knowledge of a three-dimensional world (such as what stops one falling off cliffs) would have to come from some sort of intellectual inference".[14] Locke, Berkeley and Hume "proved" that in a Newtonian world, based on Euclidean space, individuals could have no sure knowledge of a world outside them—in short, that stimuli could yield no direct and immediate information about a three-dimensional world of solid, persistent objects and causal relations. Subsequently, Herbart spelt out what this implied for educational practice. The Locke–Herbart paradigm as it became known was then extended by the work of behaviourist psychologists like Pavlov, Thorndike, Hull and Skinner. Their extensions "enabled the paradigm to be preserved in the face of Darwinian challenges as to how such incompetent perceptual systems could have had survival value".[15]

It is clear that conventional practice since the onrush of positivist science has not valued an individual's perceptions as a source of knowledge. The meaning of perceptions is held to emerge from intellectual processes of analytic abstraction and logical inference (hence the conventional separation of perception from cognition) and the prime task of education is to distribute the valued knowledge which has been so gained. Learning has therefore become a process of guided induction into bodies of organised propositional knowledge, through the workings of formal logic and fluency of textual expression.

Clearly, the theoretic foundations of Western industrial society's systems of education have been under threat for some time. In the early part of this century Newton's Euclidean model of the world was displaced by Einstein's: what if human perceptual organs are geared to Einstein's time–space and not to Euclid's geometry? But an even more serious challenge came from the work of Fritz Heider. In his research Heider questioned the assumption that the *meaning* of perceptions (such as the perception of order) can only emerge from intellectual cogitation.[16] Heider's papers (written in Berlin *c*. 1926–30) were not translated into English until 1959, by which time his research had been paralleled (and was later extended) by J. J. Gibson.[17] Heider and Gibson demonstrated the plausibility of an ecological approach to perception. What they suggested is that the environment has an informational structure at the level of objects and their causal interactions, and that human perceptual systems have evolved to detect and extract that information. Other researchers in human perception have drawn similar conclusions:

> There is ample evidence that the senses are not only generally preattuned but become more sensitively calibrated to pick up those exigencies of the environment that bear directly on the survival, success and wellbeing of the perceiver—what has sometimes been called the education of the senses.[18]

Thus, in a sense, Western industrial society's dominant paradigm of education seems to have borne the seeds of its own destruction, because it is in the fruits of scientific research during the last 50 years that we find some of the most critical challenges to its assumptions about the nature of the world we inhabit and about how humans interact, through their perceptual systems, with that world.

The educational implications of an ecological approach to perception can be summarised as follows:

First: *Since limitless information is present in our environment, then any person with some intact perceptual systems can access as much or as little as he or she needs for as long as they live. Access is restricted only by habits of and lack of confidence in perception. The pretence that knowledge can be accessed only through years of schooling in certified educational institutions is a sham. The claims that the real knowledge is locked up in the storehouses of knowledge that are so jealously guarded by a priesthood of scholars and scientists is also a sham . . .*

Second: *Education is first and foremost the education of our perceptual systems to better search out the invariant characteristics and distinguishing features of our personal, social and physical environments. It is an education in* searching *with our own perceptual systems not an education in how to someday* research *in the accumulated pile of so-called social knowledge. An education in searching is an education in generative thinking.* [19]

"Generative thinking" is Edward de Bono's term. His work with learners as diverse as five-year-old children and highly literate adults leads de Bono to conclude that generative thinking about our environment and our place in it is a matter of perception, of seeing things more clearly and of seeing things in context, not a matter of puzzling over images and abstract ideas in our minds: "The teaching of thinking is not the teaching of logic but the teaching of perception." [20]

A third educational implication of an ecological approach to perception is the "recentering" of teaching from the teacher–learner relationship to the relations between learners and materials and settings. For many teachers, at present, the perceptions of the learner are a distraction from the task of instilling theoretic knowledge, and they undermine the teacher's authority and centrality. In an ecological paradigm, however, such authority and centrality are destructive of learning. If students are, as it were, looking over their shoulders at their teachers, then they will be distracted from attending to what is before their eyes. Thus in an ecological paradigm teaching will be recentred into "the complex task of guiding children, and adults who have been blinded in the old paradigm, into the multiplicity of ways in which they can enhance their capabilities for extracting information from their world."[21] Table 4 summarises these differences:

Table 4

Empiricist Theories of Perception	Ecological Theories of Perception
Suggest that human perceptual systems provide no reliable knowledge of our world, which can only come through *analytical abstraction* and *logical inference*	Suggest that human perceptual systems have evolved to detect informational structure of environment and become more sensitive through *practice in perception*
↓	↓
Socially structured knowledge (largely theoretic and technical)	Individually structured knowledge (practical, personal)
↓	↓
Education as distribution of structured knowledge	Education as searching environments
↓	↓
Teaching as guided access to the storehouses (museums?) of propositional knowledge	Teaching as creating tools, techniques and settings which sustain learners' perceptual work

I am not so blind an optimist as to think that Heider's and Gibson's conclusions will convince educators, parents and employers that the presently dominant paradigm of education is a thoroughly misleading guide to the design of educational systems and programs. The existing system of mass education is powerfully supported by entrenched social interests. On a more pragmatic level, it is difficult to imagine those of us who have been inducted into the "priesthood of scholars and scientists" willingly turning our backs on the storehouses of theoretic knowledge with which we are so familiar and encouraging our students to do likewise. Nor should we. But an ecological paradigm puts the "storehouses" into perspective: as *part* of the "personal, social and physical environments" that an "education of the senses" should help us to *search*.

A LONGER-TERM PERSPECTIVE ON AN ECOLOGICAL PARADIGM

The conceptual foundations of an ecological paradigm for education are broader, and span a longer timeframe, than its links with recent research on human perception suggest. Prior to the scientific and industrial revolutions, the disciplines of the medieval scholastic curriculum were conceived as *practical arts* rather than as theoretic "sciences". That is, the purposes of studying literature, natural history or social history were essentially the same: to help resolve the practical problems faced by humans when their desires are not matched by their circumstances. These disciplines focused on the interactions between human moral purposes and the personal, social and physical environments in which they were situated. The goal of scholarship in these disciplines was practical not theoretical, ie "to perform good works" rather than to discover or demonstrate some final good or universal truth. [22] This goal changed under the influence of "scientific method", with many of the humanities being reconstructed as social "sciences". Thus, faith in the scientific method could allow Engels to say that Marx was "the first to discover the great law which governs the march of history . . . the more or less clear expression of struggles between social classes . . . This law bears the same relationship to history as the law of conservation of energy bears towards the physical sciences." [23] By way of contrast, a medieval scholar would have been less interested in demonstrating an historical "law" than in resolving practical problems of social justice in which he (they were all "he") was — at least potentially — an active moral agent.

The distinction between the theoretic, practical and technical modes of human thinking goes back to Aristotle's writing. As I have argued elsewhere, a revival of interest in a neo-Aristotelean view of a *practical* curriculum strengthens the case for an ecological paradigm by putting it into a longer term historical perspective. [24] By comparison with a scholarly tradition which spans more than 2000 years, a paradigm which has dominated education for a mere two centuries seems to be a relatively recent aberration.

A curriculum which is focused on practical problems is intrinsically more ecological and holistic than one in which learning is focused on theoretic or technical concerns. Practical problems can only be resolved in the light of complex human–environment interactions — whereas theoretical and technical problems can, relatively speaking, be solved in isolation. Table 5 provides criteria for distinguishing between theoretical, practical and technical problems and provides examples in each category of questions addressing Green concerns.

It will be apparent from Table 5 that many, perhaps most, of the problems used as foci for learning in such subjects as environmental studies are theoretic and technical. I would argue that shifting the emphasis to practical problems is more consistent with an ecological paradigm. Theoretic and technical questions will still arise, but they are more likely to be self-motivated and more likely to be seen in relation to the complex interactions between humans and their environments from which practical questions, issues and problems emerge. In Victoria, an explicit focus on the resolution of practical problems is now part of the design of Year 12 curricula in Home Economics–Human Development and Society, and in Textiles.[25] Practical problem-solving, as I have described it here, is also a major emphasis in the Ministry of Education's P–12 curriculum guidelines for the group of subjects known as "personal development", which includes Home Economics, Health and Human Relations, Physical Education, Outdoor Education and Textiles.[26] These subjects are doing more for the Greening of education than many other areas of learning because they are deliberately countering the myth that practical problems can be solved, as some educators would have it, by "applying scientific knowledge, methods and skills".[27] In subjects like Home Economics and Health Education it is being recognised more widely that practical problems (if they *are* practical and not merely technical) *necessarily* involve subjectivity. Their resolution requires personal knowledge, critical skills and value judgments, not just the "objective" methods of science and technology.

Table 5

Theoretical problems	Practical problems	Technical problems
	Subject matter	
Concern matters of universal, general, abstract truth	Concern matters of choice, action and judgment in particular times, places and circumstances	Concern matters of skill and technique in producing an embodiment of an idea, image or pattern
	Form of solution	
Propositional knowledge ("knowing that..."); warranted conclusions and generalisations, usually in the form of a description or explanation	Practical judgment ("knowing I/we should ..."); defensible decisions which can be justified as probably better or worse than alternatives in the circumstances	Skill ("know-how"); productive procedures—effective means to achieving given or desired ends
	Source of problem	
States of mind; areas of the "not known" marked out by what is "known"	States of affairs in relation to ourselves — conditions which we may wish to change	"States of the art" in relation to products or goals; skills, techniques, tools and procedures we wish to be more productive or effective
	Method of solving or resolving problem	
Controlled by the guiding principle of logical inference (induction and deduction), eg the experiment and other forms of planned "scientific" inquiry	Deliberation leading to a change in the state of affairs or in our desires, eg discussion or debate about alternatives	Controlled by the guiding principle of production, eg trial-and-error

Table 5 continued

Theoretical problems	Practical problems	Technical problems
	Examples of questions	
• Why do Australians have a relatively high intake of animal protein?	• Should Australians reduce their animal protein intake?	• How could Australians reduce their animal protein intake?
• How is sunlight energy transformed into chemical energy?	• What sort of heating system should I choose for my house?	• How can household energy consumption be decreased?
• What factors affect people's perception of environmental qualities?	• Would native trees look better here?	• How can we propagate native trees?
• Why is Australia's population increasing?	• Should I have children?	• What techniques are available for population control?
• What is nuclear energy?	• Should Australia export uranium?	• How can I make my views known?
• How is social power distributed between men and women in Australian society?	• Is affirmative action for women unjust to men?	• What are some strategies for affirmative action?

INNOVATIVE PRACTICES: BUILDING BRIDGES TOWARDS AN ECOLOGICAL PARADIGM

There are several examples of well-developed educational practices which are consistent with an ecological paradigm but which seem to have arisen more or less independently of each other and of the recent research on human perception. In addition to de Bono's approaches to the teaching of thinking, referred to above, examples include "structural arithmetic"[28] and several approaches to learning to read and write.[29] Earth Education is an approach to environmental education which illustrates how the learning of theoretic knowledge can be incorporated into educational programs which in most other respects exemplify an ecological paradigm. Earth Education originated in camp nature programs in the United States but has spread worldwide as a voluntary, cooperative, participatory and non-profit movement. In the words of one of its key figures, Steve Van Matre, Earth Education was "created partially out of frustration with the usual identifying–collecting–dissecting–testing approaches to nature" and to help learners "build a sense of relationship—through both feeling and understandings—with the natural world".[30] Its consistency with an ecological paradigm is most clearly demonstrated in its commitment to sharpening learners' perceptions of their environments: "Our aim is to help young people interact more directly with the fascinating array of living things around them."[31]

I have incorporated approaches modelled on Earth Education into pre-service and in-service teacher education programs for such courses as Environmental Education, Studies in Teaching Home Economics, Textiles, Educating for the Future, Curriculum Studies, Assessment Practices and so on. In so doing, I have found ample evidence to satisfy me of their success in developing perceptual skills and conceptual understandings in learners. However, most explanations of the *reasons* for Earth Education's successes (including Van Matre's own description of the "mechanics of learning" as he understands them) betray the neutralising effect of the now dominant paradigm. For example, many of the techniques used in Earth Education are rationalised as though they exemplified the principles of Skinnerian behaviourism. But I would argue that the effectiveness of Earth Education is better explained by its similarities with other exemplars of an ecological paradigm such as de Bono's courses in "generative thinking". Both programs frequently depend on the imaginative use of *tools*:

> de Bono . . . *found it necessary to provide tools that would block, or at least hinder, the established perceptual practices of taking a quick sampling of the perceptual offering, making a snap judgement about what was offered and retreating into further abstraction and logical inference . . .*
>
> *The tools are contrived to help the learner by blocking his* [sic]

easy slide into perceptual error or making snap judgements. In effect they are reminders to look again . . . that there is information to be gained from perceptual work that cannot be gained by the mental processes of abstraction, classification and generalising. The blocks make them conscious of processes that are normally habitual. [32]

The "tools" used to sharpen sensory awareness in Earth Education programs range from such simple devices as blindfolds and mirrors to more elaborate props and gimmicks (as well as mental "tools" such as role play); but in each instance of their use they function in much the same way to sustain "perceptual work" as distinct from "retreating into . . . abstraction". Earth Education also encourages concept building, but the key concepts which presently summarise our theoretic knowledge of ecology (energy flow, cycles, adaptation, etc.) are treated less as products of analytic abstraction and logical inference and more as further tools for perceiving and searching the natural environment.

Conventional schooling differentiates and fragments conceptual understanding and generalises sensory awareness. Learners study their world by examining smaller and smaller "bits" of it in the form of facts, propositions, definitions, generalisations and abstractions:

The senses, however, are lumped together in one homogenised mass. Kids are encouraged to believe that they should not trust their own perception and thus should do little to sharpen their senses. They are told to be objective, to disregard emotions and feelings, and to experiment to find the truth. Even when they "take a look" at a problem, they rarely see anything; they merely talk it to death in the classroom. [33]

In Earth Education, this approach is reversed (see Table 6): "We differentiate in our sensory awareness and generalise in our conceptual understanding. We strive to strengthen individual senses, but opt for the big picture in understanding life." [34] Earth Education provides many examples of how learning settings can be created so as to encourage the simultaneous development of an holistic conceptual understanding of ecology and differentiated sensory awareness of environments. Also, teaching in Earth Education is very much the "recentred" activity referred to earlier in this chapter: its main aspect being the setting up of the materials and settings and to provide the tools with which learners can search environments. Earth Education may, therefore, be a useful model of how practical "bridges" can be built between conventional educational practices and those more characteristic of an ecological paradigm.

Table 6

	Conventional Schooling (Epistemological)	Earth Education (Ecological)
Concepts	Differentiated (focus on smaller and smaller bits of material)	Undifferentiated (emphasise the "big" or overall picture)
Senses	Undifferentiated (emphasise thinking more than perceiving)	Differentiated (focus on sharpening individual senses)

The simple framework provided in this Table is useful in determining the extent to which various educational programs and practices are informed by an ecological perspective.

A CASE STUDY: AN ECOLOGICAL APPROACH TO TEXTILES EDUCATION

Being an examiner of both Textiles and Environmental Science subjects in Victoria's Higher School Certificate course, I have been able to observe that while Environmental Science is the subject which most people would associate with ecology, in fact it is Textiles that is examined (and, therefore, very likely taught) in an ecological way.

Both textiles and environmental science are quite explicitly studies of interactions between humans and certain environments. In terms of the Earth Education model, the minutiae of the environment being studied should not be of foremost importance in an ecological study.

For example, in Environmental Science there is little point in the student dissecting a frog so that he or she can make a labelled drawing of its digestive system: the important conceptual understandings of the subject should be concerned more with frogs in relation to ponds or streams, and ponds and streams in relation to water cycles. Similarly, in Textiles there is little point in the student memorising minutiae about the properties or structures of various fibres, since the important conceptual understandings of the subject should be concerned more with fibres in relation to textile products, and textile products in relation to human experiences and activities (eg as consumers or designers).

None of the above should be interpreted as meaning that detail is unimportant in an ecological study. But its investigation should be purposeful rather than arbitrary and should *follow* rather than precede the learner's grasp of the overall picture. Thus, concern about the effects of industrial waste discharged into inland waterways might well lead to dissecting a frog to look for evidence of the biological magnification of toxic chemicals. Similarly, the need to make certain textiles purchasing decisions might lead to seeking detailed information about a particular fibre's structure or properties. If one is attempting to assess the learner's understanding of the overall picture, then it follows that an external examination of an ecological study should not require students to recall trivia, minutiae or isolated "facts"; rather, it should provide them with opportunities to demonstrate their perceptual discrimination and conceptual understanding.

As already noted, I believe that Textiles is achieving a better approximation to this ideal than Environmental Science, possibly because Textiles at the senior secondary level in Victoria is more free from the dead hand of the past. The course description for Environmental Science is written in conventional terms, with numerous specific objectives to be mastered and specific items of content to be remembered and understood. The course description for Textiles, on the other hand, has broad learning goals; and it presents content in terms of key concepts and generalisations, which are foci for exploration rather than objects of mastery. Indeed, the Textiles course description is written in such a way that it is wellnigh impossible for an examiner to write a trivial question requiring nothing more than the recall of factual information.

In helping teachers of Textiles see their subject in ecological terms, I have found Garth Boomer's notion of teaching as "bushcraft" to be an appropriately Green metaphor:

> *In the ecology of the school "bush" there is a bewildering array of texts, tests, assignments and artefacts. The teacher should be used to finding interesting and pertinent specimens and talking about their characteristics, habits and habitats. Students should be encouraged to familiarise themselves with funny creatures like science textbooks, learning how to tame them, remembering where dangers lurk and noting little peculiarities.*
>
> *Teachers should not drive students in a tourist bus through the school curriculum, encouraging the bland recital of tourist blurbs. Students should be obliged to savour the texture of life, wild and rich.* [35]

The similarities between this view of the school "bush" and a subject such as Textiles should be apparent. In the ecology of the Textiles "bush" there is a bewildering array of artefacts, experiences, symbols, materials, methods, media, processes, products and problems. But the textiles environment does not only include tangible "specimens" like fibres, yarns and fabrics; it also includes a great deal of territory that exists only in human minds—ideas, designs, motivations and interests. The Textiles course description in Victoria can be seen as a guide to this complex environment. It represents one way of conceptualising the "big picture" of the textiles world—by providing a word map of the territory and a scheme for identifying and (more importantly) exploring the interactions among the "interesting specimens" that can be found in it. An explicit goal of the Textiles course is that students will be able to "read" that map and use the scheme: they will be able to use the subject's key concepts and generalisations as tools in their own explorations of the Textiles "bush".

As Boomer's statement suggests, a student's "bushcraft" might be learned by apprenticeship to a teacher who models it. This is so especially if the teacher can communicate the perceptual discriminations and conceptual understandings that underlie his or her craft with genuine enthusiasm and flair. For the key concepts and generalisations of a course such as Textiles do not occur "naturally" in examination papers and textbooks, and learners may need assistance in seeing them in the real world of textiles. The natural "habitats" of such concepts and generalisations are in various forms of print, visual and electronic media, as well as in everyday discourse. Students should be encouraged to become more adept as connoisseurs and critics of the textiles-related meanings that abound in popular culture and media. Television programs and commercials, fashion columns of daily newspapers, magazines and so on regularly provide numerous examples and illustrations of textiles-related concepts and generalisations. Indeed, the profusion of textiles-related concepts, generalisations and problems that can be found in the real world of trade and popular media makes conventional school textbooks for the subject almost redundant.

The majority of school textbooks are products of an approach to learning which fragments and compartmentalises conceptual understanding in a way which is anything but ecological. Being virtual museums of ideas and information, textbooks encourage "the bland recital of tourist blurbs" (a typical example: "The cultivation of the silkworm is called sericulture . . . In order to produce 1 kg of silk, 104 kg of mulberry leaves need to have been eaten by about 3000 silkworms"). Textbooks are, indeed, "funny creatures"; and apart from their occasional use for reference purposes, they may do more harm than good if relied on to excess. Certainly, teachers should familiarise themselves and their students with the little peculiarities of school texts and point out where dangers lurk in their use. For example, many textbooks seriously distort their subject matter in some way. One textiles textbook which claims to be "scientifically correct" and to encourage "scientific techniques of analysis and understanding" persistently misuses and distorts the meaning of the term "experiment" throughout its pages. Experiments are among the most fundamental "scientific techniques", and the book's distortion of the concept therefore erodes the uncritical reader's understanding of the very methods the text purports to encourage.

I have deliberately focused this section of the chapter on Textiles to demonstrate that an ecological approach to teaching and learning, as encapsulated in the Earth Education model and the "bushcraft" metaphor, is not restricted to those subject matters which represent more orthodox Green concerns. Indeed, I am convinced that the directions currently encouraged in Victoria's Year 12 Textiles course (namely, heightened perception of environments, holistic conceptual understanding, reality-centred projects, practical problem-solving and so on) underlie most of what I would regard as good — and Green — practice in all areas of education.

EDUCATIONAL PRACTICE IN AN ECOLOGICAL PARADIGM

A summary of the major differences between the educational practices and experiences which are characteristic of epistemological and ecological paradigms of education is provided in Table 7.[36] Many of the practices and experiences listed as "ecological" are supported by the rhetoric of educational reform in Australia during the past two decades. Thus moves towards more school-based curriculum development, greater community involvement in school decision-making, increasingly non-competitive and cooperative assessment practices, more issues-based and inquiry-based learning and so on all seem to be consistent with an ecological paradigm for education. However, this apparent consistency may be deceptive because each of these reforms may affect *practices* (or, more correctly, *procedures*) in education without altering *purposes*.

As already noted, the core of Western industrial society's educational world view lies in assumptions about how people gain *theoretic* knowledge. Many educators who pay lip-service to the practices and experiences which exemplify an ecological paradigm, and many of those who attempt to make such practices and experiences a reality in schools, have not abandoned these assumptions. Thus they fail to achieve any real change in the objects of learning and the disposition of the learner: they are still orienting the learner towards the "storehouses" of theoretic knowledge. That is, the practices consistent with an ecological paradigm may often be used

Table 7

	Epistemological	*Ecological*
A: The Practice		
Object of learning	Transmission of existing knowledge; abstraction of generic concepts	Perception of invariants; discovery of serial concepts; discovery of universals in particulars in learners' environments
Control of learning	Asymmetrical dependence teacher–pupil; competition between learners	Symmetrical dependence; co-learners; cooperation between learners
Coordination of learning: (a) *behaviour settings;* (b) *timing*	Schools/classrooms age-grading; school calendar and class timetable	Community settings; synchronised to and negotiated with community settings
Learning materials	Textbooks, standardised procedures (eg laboratory exercises)	Reality-centred projects
Learning activity	Paying attention; rote activities; memorising	Discrimination; differentiation; searching; creating
Teaching activity	Lecturing; demonstrating	Creating and recreating; learning settings
System principle	Pedagoguery	Discovery
B: The Experience		
Cultural mode	Work/religion; "serious drudgery"	Active leisure; "exciting, frustrating"
Dominant group emotions	Dependency; fight-flight	Pairing

Table 7 continued

	Epistemological	Ecological
Personal development	Conformity-bullying; divorce of means and ends; cheating self-centredness (autonomy) hatred of learning (and swots)	Tolerance of individuality; depth and integration Equal consideration for self and others (homonomy) Learning as living

simply to provide a more attractive route to achieving the objects of the dominant paradigm. The incorporation of "reality-centred projects", "community settings" and the "cooperation of learners" into many educational programs does not necessarily serve an "education of the senses" but may rather merely make the transmission of existing theoretic knowledge more palatable.

Yet it is also worth noting that the programs cited here as examples of an ecological approach to education seem to arise as independent outcomes of *practical* deliberation and judgment rather than applications of the theoretic foundations of the paradigm. For example, neither de Bono nor Van Matre appears to be aware of Heider (or, for that matter, of each other) and each appears to have created their programs out of their own perceptions and subjective responses to their experiences of alternative practices. Thus Van Matre states that Earth Education was created partly out of frustration with conventional approaches to environmental education. Also, and more importantly, "it was moulded by people who were excited about kids and learning and life itself, who like to laugh, but who took their work seriously, who wanted to open up new doors of perception for their learners."[37]

Such observations contain implicit challenges for Green educators. How, for example, do we open up new doors of perception for *our* learners and, more importantly, for ourselves? Redesigning the whole of education (not just those subject matters that address orthodox Green concerns) in accordance with an ecological paradigm may seem to be idealistic, but the struggle towards the Greening of education begins with small yet significant steps: first, to trust our personal subjective experiences rather than to defer habitually to the entrenched status of accumulated propositional knowledge; and second, to begin to educate our own senses rather than to stand on the laurels of our proven capacities for mental abstraction.

FUTURES THINKING AND GREEN EDUCATION

The failure of many educational reforms on all but the most superficial levels — such as the political neutralisation of environmental education referred to earlier in this chapter — can be attributed, at least in part, to a failure to adequately conceptualise possible futures in education. The concepts and methods of futures study are, therefore, strategically important for the Greening of education.

Any curriculum can be seen as a kind of "collective story we tell our children about our past, our present and our future".[38] The stories we compose — whether we title them "environmental education", "peace studies" or whatever — almost inevitably bear the imprint of our own educational experiences; and thus many curricula are little more than reinforcements of the taken-for-granted, the stereotypical and the status quo (hence the regression of environmental education programs during the seventies from their ideals of social action and education *for* the environment to the more conventional education *in* and *about* the environment). If we are to transcend our own histories we must attempt to design curricula which reflect, in a critical and creative way, our anticipations of alternative futures. It is particularly important to note that imagining and inventing the widest possible array of alternative futures is not just a matter of forecasting or of being forewarned about what lies ahead. Rather, images of alternative futures serve also to inform our understanding of the past and reveal our choices within the present. Our lives are suffused with hopes, fears, expectations and intentions which arise from our interpretations of the past and present but which also determine what we try to recover from the past and perceive in the present.

Education in Australia has long been shaped by an uncritical acceptance of what has been inherited from the past. And recent attempts to reform education have tended to emphasise the present, as is evident in the almost obsessive contemporaneity of those who champion "relevance" in education. The future is a missing dimension of Australian education, despite lip-service to the contrary. It is all too easy to find the stereotypical jargon of futures-thinking in the language and literature of schooling. The reports and recommendations of educational authorities and the proceedings of professional conferences bristle with references to "technological change", "post-industrial society", "the information revolution", "economic scenarios", and the like. But beneath the new buzz words we are telling the same old stories of scientific, technological and economic determinism which have pervaded and persisted in Western industrial society's systems of mass education for two centuries. These are the stories of prediction, trend extrapolation, modelling, simulation, and of economic and technical forecasting. In these stories, the future is invested with a spurious objectivity. Times to come are seen as the metaphorical equivalents of places to visit, as though they had a tangible presence "out there".

But the future exists largely in human minds and, thus, in an objective sense it is never "out there". In a subjective sense too the future is clearly part of the "here and now". It is this subjective sense of futures that is of most significance for the Green movement, and Green educators may therefore need to be cautious of suggesting that the future can be controlled objectively. This is sometimes implied by typical Green rhetoric, such as assertions about "people's need to work at new ways of 'doing politics', in the basic sense of controlling their future". [39] The cultural transformation which Green politics seeks to lead or to catalyse is one in which the importance and validity of our inner, subjective experiences are affirmed. Futures-thinking, for Green educators, should therefore be located firmly in our present consciousness, in critical reflection on the concepts, values, meanings, images and metaphors which we use to negotiate the cultural transformation in which we are engaged. Recognising that futures are intrinsic to present action and existence liberates the critical and creative imagination. It allows us to explore longer timeframes than those who are concerned with prediction and control usually dare to imagine, and it allows us to explore possible futures without colonising them. [40] Above all, Green educators must ensure that debates about human futures focus on human potentials, on the creative possibilities and forces of the human spirit which are not necessarily determined by the developments in science, technology and the macro-economy that conventionally frame such debates.

Confidence in human potentials is what an ecological paradigm for education, as described in this chapter, is all about. Conventional schooling teaches us to distrust the very things that education should celebrate and enhance—namely, human perception, reason and intuition. I have suggested that the purposes and practices of education that emerge from an ecological paradigm are consistent with the core values of Green social philosophy. Moreover, they are warranted by research on human perception, by the longer-term history of education, and by the practical experiences of myself and others. However, an ecological paradigm for education cannot be defended by reference to any predicted outcomes of learning. Like Green politics itself, the processes of an ecological paradigm are evolutionary and its goals are emergent. Greening education should, therefore, give us all a pleasant surprise.

9:
CHRISTIANITY
AND GREEN POLITICS

John Cribb

JOHN CRIBB *was born in 1927. He spent his first seven years on a sheep-station near Longreach. His family was driven back to his birthplace, Ipswich, by drought and depression. Then he spent the next ten years hating school. During a plodding Commerce degree John was grabbed and radicalised by the Student Christian Movement. After two equally plodding years of business experience, he departed for Congregational theological studies and then to the Papuan Gulf for 13 years. In 1968 he swapped Papuan jungle for inner London, where he stayed for the next 14 years: first in a schizophrenia-inducing parish (made up of lively midweek ecumenical and community involvement as well as a Sunday congregation of elderly commuters pining for past glory), then eight fulfilled years of industrial chaplaincy at the Elephant and Castle and of community development round Waterloo. John made a cautious return to Queensland in 1983 to make a brief unsatisfactory sortie into a parish followed by 18 months of locums, unemployment and other peace and justice activities. He presently functions as QIT chaplain, liaison worker with unions, and church irritant.*

Christianity owes its existence to a man who left no writings and no blueprints for an organisation, yet a host of differing and often conflicting institutions claim his authority.

Jesus of Nazareth was a layman who strongly challenged the professional priesthood, yet the Church developed an exclusive caste of priests with authority over laity. Jesus was a peasant artisan who chose manual workers as disciples, but the churches' leadership has been mostly from the middle and upper classes. He owned no property, identified with the poor and sternly warned against the dangers of riches. Yet the Church has accumulated vast wealth, and most Western Christians live comfortably with the mores of an acquisitive society. Jesus refused to exercise temporal power and urged his followers to be servants, yet the Church acquired enormous power and wielded it ruthlessly. He was an associate of outcasts and riff-raff, yet respectability is the hallmark of most present-day followers.

Those who hold to the Greens' philosophy, and who look for vindication in Christianity, should not be too disheartened if they find little supportive evidence in the Church. It is necessary to look not only at the Nazarene carpenter himself but also at the many attempts in history to rediscover and exemplify that remarkable life in community.

The early Christians were mainly simple people, sharing in participative community and refusing the emperor's demands for worship and the bearing of arms. Despite scorn and persecution, their values penetrated society. But as the Church grew, its structures began to reflect those of its host society. The emperor Constantine greatly accelerated that process by adopting Christianity as the official imperial religion. Since then the Church has usually existed in uneasy partnership with the state. It has reflected its hierarchies and power structures and has baptised many of its assumptions.

There were, of course, many attempts to reassert the claims of simple, non-hierarchical, participative community. Some were crushed; some, like the Albigensians, survived in semi-secrecy in remote areas; some found a measure of acceptance in the orders of the Catholic Church. Francis of Assisi's adventurous new model for a simple band of brothers was distorted and corrupted even in his lifetime, but something of the vision survived to nourish future generations. This simple, uncomplicated reverence for the natural world and its essential goodness runs counter to the conventional understanding of Adam's charge to "subdue the earth", interpreted as giving a licence to exploit it for our ever-increasing appetite. Moreover, Francis of Assisi's embracing of all life forms, as brothers and sisters to be loved and to whom we have responsibility, is a special Christian legacy to the Green movement.

It was a fourteenth-century English cleric who asked the prophetic but reasonable question, "When Adam delvt and Eve span who was then the gentleman?" The Reformation churches, product of the political ferment two centuries later, took their hard-won freedom only so far, and were soon persecuting the more radical egalitarian experimenters in their own ranks. Luther stamped hard on peasant demands for a more thoroughgoing social reformation, while Cromwell, that early defender of Christian democracy, had no patience with Diggers and Levellers wanting to apply New Testament models to English society.

One group that emerged from the Reformation retained its egalitarian structure and radical stance on war through to the present day. This was the Society of Friends. Their belief in every person's inner light blurs the boundary between insider and outsider; while their freedom from credal constraint offers a base on the edge of the Church for those who can no longer subscribe to traditional theological statements. Their faithful witness to non-violence in times of war and peace alike and their contribution to the struggle for justice is quite disproportionate to their small numbers. It is appropriate that the Green Party should gather regularly in the Quakers' meeting houses.

There is a fundamental difference in theological understanding which determines whether or not one is likely to become a "Christian Green". Throughout history and within Scripture itself there are two strands — one which is world-affirming, the other world-denying. The first tendency makes one perceive the world in positive terms — incomplete and distorted perhaps, but capable of being transformed by co-workers with the Creator. The Church is called by God to that struggle—called not only to summon individuals to holiness, but to love the world and its structures into the shape intended by its maker.

The other strand sees the world in the thraldom of evil. The Church is like a lifeboat rescuing and nurturing souls, and protecting them through the turbulence till they are safely landed in their eternal home. The world benefits by spinoff from transformed individuals. Structures will come right only when enough individuals within them are converted, but the ultimate purpose of the Church is to populate heaven, not renew earth. It is to build the redeemed community, not reform earthly structures.

If these positions are the poles on a Left–Right spectrum, then most Christians, I suspect, would cluster somewhere between centre and mid-right. There has, however, been vigorous activity at both the poles. A great resurgence of evangelical fundamentalism stemming from North America has been matched by an increasingly vigorous growth of liberation theology spreading from its cradle in South America. This latter has been a contribution mainly of Catholic theologians living close to impoverished Third World communities, but it has now seeded Protestant thinking round the world and been the springboard for considerable ecumenical action. As products of liberation theology, the "Basic Christian Communities" in South America and Asia have released people from former attitudes of dependence and lethargy; and "conscientised" peasants have discovered from this regular meeting of equals their powers to think, plan and act corporately and decisively in the cause of justice. This cellular movement has been actively fostered by clergy, but is feared by some of the hierarchy as threatening obedience to clerical authority and polluting Christianity with Marxist ideology.

Brian Gore's experience in the Philippines is a striking example of his pioneering Basic Christian Communities in an area where 1.5 per cent own 80 per cent of the land. He says, "We tried to give the people a sense of self-worth and dignity. For the first time in their lives these poor mountain people realised they were not the shit of the earth."[1] Basic Christian Communities (BCCs) are simply a network of self-motivating socio-political prayer groups, but they are proving that change comes from below. Evidence of this is the comment in a national security report that BCCs are "infiltrated by subversives, anti-institutional and anti-establishment and are building an infrastructure of political power in the entire country."[2]

While liberation theology owes something to Marxist analysis and insights, it is essentially a rereading of the Gospel through the eyes of the poor. What emerges is the picture of Jesus the peasant crafts-man befriending the marginalised; warning the wealthy; challenging the legal and religious establishment; and, not surprisingly, being then condemned as a revolutionary. When the powerless discover this and refuse any longer to leave the interpreting of the Gospel in the hands of the powerful, then the revolution is born. An "ideological suspicion" grows which increasingly reveals that the Bible, although actually written from the standpoint of the oppressed, has, since Constantine, been interpreted by the powerful. At this point traditional Christians may enter a stage of aggressive questioning of all the Church's understandings of the human condition. Some discard Bible and Christian ethos altogether, because their past presentation seems impossible to reconcile with the insights born of the new critical analysis. Others, however, begin exploring the Bible that lies behind the conventional understanding and discover, with joy, that it supports the aspirations of the oppressed. Mary's song, the *Magnificat*, is no longer an advent chorale sung by a robed choir, but is seen to be God's revolutionary intention for the one who is about to be born:

> *He scattered the proud with all their plans. He brought down mighty beings from their thrones, and lifted up the lowly. He filled the hungry with good things and sent the rich away with empty hands.*[3]

In the Old Testament we find a small nation, Israel, struggling for its existence against the great powers. God is on the side of the weak, enabling them to hold their heads high. The New Testament describes not a nation, but a covenant family drawing into it mostly the poor and marginalised. God chose one of the weak ones, a village carpenter, just as he had chosen a weak nation. The cross is the inevitable end of that life pitted against the powers of Church and state. The resurrection is a victory that does not bring temporal power to his followers, but confidence to face death and persist in the face of enormous odds. Thus frightened, dispirited fishermen become courageous, articulate leaders. Paul is an exception, one of the repentant powerful who brings his gifts to the ranks of the despised, becoming their most formidable defender and suffering their fate.

Inevitably we all bring our own presuppositions to the reading of the Bible. Defenders of the status quo emphasise its eternal truths and moral certainties—"the faith once for all delivered to the saints". Obedience, order, peace are the qualities writ large. But those who read the Bible through oppressed eyes see action, struggle, change, growth. James Cone says, "Faith is the community's response to God's act of liberation. It is saying yes to God and no to oppressors."[4] God is involved in human struggle on the side of the poor—a hard concept for those of us who live comfortably with the fruit of our colonial past and our contemporary stranglehold on the world's wealth and resources.

The sins most mentioned in the Bible are not the privatised sins of pulpit moralising, but the sins of injustice and exploitation. The proclamation of salvation is at least as much about corporate liberation as it is about personal immortality. The "Kingdom" is of today—it is a new order in the world, signs of which can be discerned by the perceptive. Those who respond to the announcement of that kingdom are called to struggle for its fulfilment. The kingdom is to be sought first, before the satisfaction of individual needs. It is bound up with the corporate reign of justice, not simply individual faith and obedience.

Ideological suspicion must extend not only to commentators on the Bible, but to its translators, who also bring their cultural and political assumptions to the task. For instance, the choice of the word "righteousness" rather than "justice" has enabled the Church to read the concept as "moral uprightness" instead of the more usual meaning of "just dealing". Moral uprightness is the virtue of the pharisee—

conventional goodness and moral achievement measured against the yardstick of the law. It is characterised by dispensing charity to the poor. Kim Chi Ha, a Korean Christian poet, declares

> *The chief priests and pharisees defuse the people's bitter resentments and moral indignation with sentimental charity. The people are emasculated by mercy. The god of philanthropy serves the oppressor by turning people into a mob of beggars. That is why I cannot admire Albert Schweitzer.* [5]

It is not for us, in our Western comforts, to sneer at the Schweitzers and Mother Teresas of the Christian story, but they are venerated by the world precisely because they follow the Church's traditional response of treating symptom and relieving crisis suffering. Dom Helda Camara's famous remark highlights this: "When I feed the poor they call me a saint. When I ask why the poor have no food they call me a communist."

Ian Frazer, from his experience in the Third World with the World Council of Churches, writes:

> *It is part of the sickness of this church that it has so often acted through history as patron rather than servant. It has used power positions to make Christ's disciples into the church's dependants . . . The poor are rising in revolt. It is a time when fresh opportunity is given to the church to turn again to servanthood—to release from the lowly a sure touch for essentials; to regain wholeness in some of the world's dirty Jordans.* [6]

Liberation theology not only helps free the poor from bondage, but offers rich and powerful Christians the opportunity of learning from the poor. Like Saul of Tarsus, the majority of Western Christians are in no way marginalised—they are "at home with the system". Many of us feel guilty about our privileges: aware that we are part of the regime that sustains injustice and gross inequality, both nationally and globally. The task is to turn those feelings of guilt and dissatisfaction from murmurings of penitence to energies for change.

THEORY AND PRACTICE

I came across liberation theology in the context of two inner-London ecumenical teams. One was a group of industrial chaplains trying to analyse complex industrial structures and find ways of enabling them to become more human. Two things were clear from our "loitering with intent" round workshop benches and carpeted offices. Management needed to adopt a more participative style and to communicate better with the shop floor, while unions needed to recover an earlier vision of broad-based justice. We felt equally sure that, given confidence, "small people" can accept responsibility and wield power. We were also committed to "praxis", believing that change happens only when action and reflection are combined. Praxis meant analysing a situation; making an assessment; testing this in action; reflecting on the outcome of the action; then modifying the assessment before embarking on further action. The Young Christian Workers, a mainly Catholic working-class organisation within industry, embody praxis in their slogan "see, judge, act".

While we could not, on the whole, initiate action within industry, we found a good deal of openness to ideas and challenge. There appears to be still a measure of goodwill towards the Church amongst those who long ago discarded religious practice. Being paid mainly from Church sources, there were no pipers within industry calling our tune; we were fairly free agents and, being outside the power structures, we would be non-threatening within the hierarchy. Thus it was sometimes possible to draw people together from widely different strata for dialogue and for the informal bouncing of ideas. Hopeful and enjoyable as many of these were, we nevertheless learned to our frustration how wide a gap there is between talk and decisive action—how little flexibility and option for change there is in large organisations with tight budgets and traditional management/union relationships.

We participated as closely as possible in the debate stimulated by that courageous experiment in industrial democracy, the Lucas Aerospace Combine. In order to avert further closure of plants, a coalition of union representatives had taken a bold initiative to management. They recommended a diversion of resources away from armaments to a range of 100 socially useful products which the Combine Committee had already researched. Here was a positive initiative concerned not merely with the health of their own community, but with global issues. It came from people normally expected to have only reactive power and normally tunnel-visioned for wages and conditions. It produced leaders of high competence and broad outlook, but it failed because the momentum of traditional capitalist structures was strong and because the assumptions of power-sharing in its proposals were rightly seen to be revolutionary. I spent a week with chaplains and unionists from round the country engaged in theological reflection on the experiment, and discovering the resonance with that other bold social alternative of the first century.

In the other area of my experience, radical ideas and action were more effectively married. "Settlements" in South and East London were turn-of-the-century Christian experiments in social action. They were set up in areas of intense deprivation and were supported mainly by Oxford and Cambridge Colleges as well as by public schools. Volunteers from these sources provided much of the staffing. Blackfriars Settlement is a modified survivor on the boundary of Lambeth and North Southwark. A Christian community worker from there in the late sixties began to engage a small group of professionals with local issues. An elderly Anglican sister and I were unofficial representatives from the churches. Gradually local groups emerged: tenants associations, pensioner groups, a housing coop, a children's playground. A victory was won against the Imperial War Museum's planned extension on to a precious bit of local green space. People began to gain confidence—badgering Council officers, lobbying politicians, marching on County Hall, speaking in public inquiries. There was nothing specifically Christian about the enterprise, though local Christians were involved. A lively young Anglican priest arrived and became one of the leaders in the Battle for Waterloo—the fight for low-cost housing and open space on a semi-derelict industrial area of the South Bank near Waterloo Bridge. The battle was waged with big city developers planning high-rise offices and hotels. It extended through three long and costly public inquiries, and was finally settled by the House of Lords in favour of the local community in 1983.

This victory of David over Goliath; this alliance between local Cockneys with a few concerned professionals and supportive councillors was not so much the considered application of Christian principles as a conscientising process for the Christians involved. A great deal that was happening in that awakening community resonated with aspects of the Gospel, which was much talked about but seldom practised. Every person was assumed to be gifted; nothing was done *for* people that they could do for themselves; and responsibility was shared as widely as possible. (The empowerment of first-century fisher-men is largely lost sight of by the inner-city Church which relies on professional clergy and imported middle class leadership.) Hierarchies were avoided. ("The kings of the pagans lord it over their people," said Jesus, "Not so among you . . . the leader must be a servant."[7]) Around every issue a small group formed to research, plan and organise for change. (The Kingdom is like "leaven in the lump" — the ferment of small groups putting love into action.)

Sometimes action emerges from a combination of exploring ideas and perceiving needs. Fritz Schumacher was something of a guru to our chaplains teams, so "Small is beautiful" and "appropriate technology" became two of our basic tools of trade. Because at St Thomas' Hospital I was engaged in the industry of high-technology medicine, I began gathering groups to examine the possible application of appropriate technology to health care. We began by exploring the notion of barefoot doctoring in the inner city. The groups comprised health professionals from hospital and community, and a variety of lay people. Some of the professionals were tolerantly dismissive; some incensed; one suspected a communist conspiracy; but the ideas gained currency and were tested out at the community centre by other people. In due course an Education trust offered a year's funding for a worker and, from that appointment, a number of results began to emerge. People started to ask more questions of professionals and to take more responsibility for their own bodies. There was a growing awareness that health is more than a privatised function of experts dispensing care to patients; that community groups can have a say in the style and quality of health services offered; that health is a corporate, political issue in which everyone should have a say.

We made a survey of local general practitioners and informed them of our findings. We gathered groups to learn about and discuss depression, menopause, cancer, and so on. We lobbied council and health authority for better local facilities. Other funding was found and we appointed a second worker. A free drop-in counselling centre was begun and the authorities, who had patronised or ignored this brash amateur venture, took more notice. Because the project had become part of a lively established community centre, it was able to plug in to the existing networks and activities that overlapped—the struggle for green space, better housing, safer crossings, a local chemist shop and so on. Moreover, the umbrella group under which we sheltered had become a "local government council" (a grass-roots local authority) enabling us to better capture the attention of wider authorities. It was also a training ground for the art of politics.

The project was strengthened by some astute professionals—a child psychologist, a medical sociologist, a general practitioner, the secretary of the Community Health Council—but they did not dominate the community workers. By keeping a low profile and leading from behind, they enabled local leadership to emerge and exercise power. Michael Wilson, both doctor and priest, writing in *Health is for People* summarised our vision by defining health as a public creation, not a private specialism:

> *Community development is nearer to a model of health care because it is concerned not only with the basic necessities of life but also with the people's struggle to obtain them and enjoy them together... They are making value choices about what they think makes good community life together. They share decisions. They work together to put their plans into effect, and this cooperation in itself is part of what [it] is to be a healthy community. Health is the milieu (human and environmental) which enables people, individually and socially, to grow towards fullness of life.*[8]

CHURCH AMBIVALENCE TOWARDS SOCIAL EXPERIMENT

Quite a lot of social experiment springs out of the Church, but tends to be disowned when it becomes radical. The French worker–priest experiment was discontinued when, instead of winning converts to the Church from the shop floor, the blue-collar priests instead became active in radical political causes. Nearer at hand a nun from a Catholic teaching order became increasingly restive teaching middle-class children in a prestigious girls' school — a far cry from the vision of the order's founder, whose aim had been the provision of illegal schooling for poor Irish. With the permission of her superiors, she moved to a deprived working-class community near Brisbane with a high incidence of social alienation, crime and unemployment. Her home became the centre of meeting for women, many of them unsupported mothers caught in the poverty trap and the crippling self-image that the area imposed. With growing awareness and confidence, they were able to plan events, learn skills, and speak out, supporting one another as they tackled bureaucracies. While the sister felt tolerated by her order, she was also aware of pressure to return to a normal vocation, and of embarrassment over her forthright presentation of the injustices uncovered in the system. Her successor has met resistance and lack of understanding from both her order and the local parish.

A similar experiment began in an inner suburb suffering from the process of development and "gentrification". Blocks of offices and luxury units were replacing low-cost housing; demolition sites became carparks; and expensively restored colonial homes for sale or rental attracted new affluent residents. An ecumenical group, with the cautious blessing of their churches, appointed a worker to explore the community's agenda and generate action. Gradually results emerged — a Community Centre, housing and food coops, and various activity groups. After five years of quiet growth and precarious year-to-year funding, the rug was finally pulled out by the Uniting Church on the grounds of needing to support a wider, higher-profile operation called Metro Mission. Over a year later Metro Mission shows no sign of emerging.

Radical Christian communities that do not rely on church funding and recognition have proved more sustainable. Members of the House of Freedom in Brisbane come from a variety of church backgrounds and some retain a secondary loyalty to their former denominations. Their shared community is dedicated to the working-out of the Gospel in the corporate areas of life—extended family, residential community and political issues, from local to global. The community owns no property and is impatient with the churches' absorbing concern with buildings, bureaucracy and the maintenance of a professional ministry. Worship and Bible study are close to the centre of their life, sustaining and directing their energies towards peace, justice and the breaking down of hierarchies and stereotypes. While they have, as yet, failed to break out of the middle-class captivity of their churches of origin, they at least share the radical vision of the World Council of Churches—"a just, participatory, sustainable society". It is interesting that the House of Freedom, with that other notable radical community in the ghettos of Washington, "The Sojourners", has its roots in the evangelical tradition. The list of Sojourner concerns would, however, make many traditional evangelicals' blood run cold. They are: serving the needs of the inner-city community; non-violent protest against nuclear weapons; women's rights; supporting the people of Nicaragua threatened by US-backed Contras; offering refuge to those who flee oppression in Central America; supporting the "Free South Africa Movement"; supporting persecuted churches in the Soviet Union. Another high priority in the community's life is the search for the relationship between spirituality and politics, worship and action, evangelism and social justice.

CHARISMATIC RENEWAL

It would surprise many to find echoes of a Green ethos in that very different Christian base—the charismatic movement. Its origins lie in the Pentecostal revival at the beginning of the century in both the United Kingdom and North America, but it has spread with rapidity through all continents in the last 30 years. Sometimes it is contained within the historic churches; sometimes it breaks out into new entities, usually of fundamentalist mould. While there is often a highly authoritarian element in these fellowships, they also develop a remarkable degree of lay involvement and they travel light to traditional hierarchical patterns and constraints. As they believe that all the gifts of the Spirit exercised in the first-century Christian community are still available to the Church, there is a high degree of lay confidence and participation in both worship and ministry. There are many experiments in community living, with small groups providing education, mutual support, impetus to outreach and, sometimes, social concern. In the event of illness, they tend to turn first to prayer, laying on of hands and counselling. In some communities, resort to professional, curative medicine is seen as a symptom of doubt.

In the West the charismatic movement has not broken out significantly from the middle-class mould of conventional churches, but in the developing world it has had a major impact in peasant and working-class cultures. As a new model of cooperative living, effective networking and the release of confidence and human resource it tallies with many aspirations of the Green movement. There are, however, some serious limitations. It tends to be strong on evangelism and free-wheeling worship, but weak on the claims of justice, though there are some exceptions to this in South America. A strong emphasis on the closeness of the end, and the unimportance of the physical world, often weakens its witness for peace and the nurturing of earth's resources. Its fairly rigid application of traditional Christian mores limits its usefulness as a pattern for the secular world, while a somewhat simplistic piety often makes it remote from the complexities of the real world. However, something of its warmth, effervescence and spontaneity is penetrating most of the mainline churches, and is contributing to the ferment of change from below.

CONCLUSION

There is no doubt that Christianity is one of the important seedbeds for the growth of Green philosophy. The fact that many within the Green movement who seek an appropriate spirituality are turning to Eastern sources is a comment not so much on the paucity of

Christian spirituality itself as on the shallow, dull, formalised worship seen to be offered by most churches. It reflects also the failure of so many to match words and piety with action for the world.

With so much in common, it is important for both Church and Green movement that there be more cross-fertilising of ideas, sharing of experience and mutual challenge of blindspots. That may be possible only with the radical and liberal wings of the Church. The others are likely to equate Green with Marxist, occult, humanist, or some other convenient epithet which safely isolates. It is my hope, however, that as our present human collision course with catastrophe becomes more obvious, there will be a great rallying to a broad Green coalition to bring about a radical change of course towards what one writer calls "a sane, humane, ecological (SHE) alternative".

10:
BUILDING COMMUNITIES: THE GREEN ALTERNATIVE

Dudley Leggett

DUDLEY LEGGETT *moved to northern NSW with his wife and child in 1972 to establish a rural "alternative" lifestyle community and whilst continuing to share in the development of that farming community he has been involved in establishing two community schools, the local People for Peace group, and the local Homebuilders Association, and also the Australian Association for Sustainable Communities, a national network. Dudley has coordinated a "sustainable lifestyles" education course for the unemployed, funded by the Federal Government to evaluate potential support programmes for people interested in cooperatives. Dudley also was involved in non-violent action demonstrations for rainforests at Terania Creek in 1979, for beach-dune protection at Middle Head near Coffs Harbour in 1980, for the Franklin River protection and in various anti-nuclear and Aboriginal land rights issues. In 1981 he organised a Green election campaign by standing as one of a team of independents for the NSW Upper House; he organised a similar campaign in 1983 for the Federal Senate. Also in 1983, Dudley attended the United Nations Special Session on Disarmament in New York as a member of the Australian delegation of non-governmental peace organisations. For the International Year of Peace, Dudley initiated and coordinated an unfunded "Peace Train" which toured Australia for nine months, covering 24,000 km, promoting education and training in peace-making skills. Currently he is Chairman of the Sustainable Lifestyles Education Collective and the Rural Resettlement Task Force, and as a consultant to the NSW Department of Housing he is developing the first or "pilot" rural cooperative community settlement for low income earners which is supported by the NSW Government.*

It was probably inevitable that the rural-based "alternative lifestyle" movement would become involved in—indeed grow to be an integral part of—the so-called Green Politics. Perhaps one way to trace the many paths that have led to this integration might be to introduce a personal history. It is not, I hope, atypical.

My interest in the Green movement, with which I now identify, began at a very early age when I became aware of a poverty of spirit and directionlessness in society about me. I determined then to seek a practical way to meaningful life and unity with the spiritual force of life, a way that I might share with others. Interest in the sciences and the need for financial security led me to study Chemical Engineering at the Royal Melbourne Institute of Technology, whilst my special interest in people and mind caused me to pursue studies in psychology at Melbourne University during the same period. Following graduation I joined the Esso-operated, first Australian petro-chemical plant at Altona, Victoria, then in its early days.

Four years as an engineer in the Technical Department gave me experience in understanding the flow and exchange of matter (chemicals) and energy, the focus of the chemical engineering science. This early materialistic knowledge was to prove later of exceptional value in unexpected ways, when coming to understand (1) the problems of an advanced industrial society, and (2) the flows and exchange of social and cultural energies. It now also helps me envisage a future balance between high technology and small-scale, ecologically safe technologies. During these years I participated actively in my local Christian church which, being close to Melbourne University, provided an opportunity for fairly intense debate on the relevance of Christianity to the world of today.

The next four years were spent working and travelling throughout Asia, the Middle East, Europe, the United States and Mexico, 46 countries in all—including three years in Eastern countries, where for one school year I taught mathematics and social studies. This provided me with the opportunity to study the development of Asian cultures and the history of ancient civilisations. Primarily I sought to experience how cultures, living standards and lifestyles compared with my own in bringing happiness and fulfilment to the various peoples. I also gained insight into the influences and realities of world affairs and how first-hand experience differed from mass media reporting.

Soon after reaching South East Asia early in 1966, I met people from the "Flower Power" culture of California and immediately identified with them in their search for a simple way of life which more closely related to human needs for self-knowledge, social relationships and spiritual ways. By the time I reached the west coast of the United States by way of Mexico, I felt strongly bonded to the brothers and sisters of the "alternative lifestyle" culture. They were strongly opposed to militarism, exploitation, oppression and excessive materialism. They sought a way of life sensitive to the needs of others and the natural world, and focused on the development of love and harmony through a society primarily concerned with the growth of "higher consciousness" rather than of Gross National Product.

I knew then that my purpose was to return to Australia to begin a real-life experiment in social organisation and in life support systems. In the next decade, this might be of value in understanding how Australian society as a whole might be transformed into a viable society capable of nurturing the growth of its people towards fulfilling their highest potential.

The need to develop a model in some degree of isolation from the impact of mainstream thinking seemed obvious, as did the ability to produce our own essentials of food and shelter. Similarly it seemed that we would need to provide for the educational needs of our children.

So whilst teaching secondary level science and mathematics I did part-time teacher training and my wife full-time teacher training. We then sought, and found, property in a warm and moist climate to minimise our food and shelter.

The approach to building the community has been to expand at a comfortable pace while sharing the co-responsibility for providing our group's life support needs and giving attention to personal growth and interpersonal relationships. Trial and error, taking guidance from the experience of others, and keeping a spiritual focus have been accepted as fundamental. Minimising disturbance of nature and its processes, and avoiding where possible manufactured chemicals and fossil-fuel-based energy use, were also given high priority. A non-hierarchical group ownership and management structure was established and a commitment to consensus decision-making was enshrined in legal documents so as to minimise any tendency to over-ride minority opinions or desires. We sought wholeness while encouraging diversity of individual growth and expression.

Basically, the premise underlying this experiment was that if the aspiration for an ecologically sound, socially just and physically and spiritually fulfilling social lifestyle was to become a reality—and if it was to do so in the context of a technologically empowered humanity rapidly outgrowing its niche in the solar system—then neither a theory nor even a detailed blueprint would be sufficient. If the crunch came and rapid change was seen to be inevitable, only tried models and personal experience could be sufficiently convincing to act as guidance for an adequate response.

Since 1972, when we began our experiment, many other approaches, each with variations on the same theme, have been and are being pursued. Evidence of the need for such exploration has continued to accumulate and numerous unforeseen obstacles have been encountered. Many of these obstacles have been overcome or strategies devised to deal with them. Concurrently many closely related Green causes rose to prominence on the Australian and world scene, and those involved in the alternative lifestyle or sustainable community movement found themselves part of what has become known as the Green political movement.

My first move back into the larger social context came in 1979 when conservative reaction in our local community moved the local council to threaten to demolish homes of neighbouring community settlers because they did not conform with state planning and building codes. Participating in our quickly formed Home Builder's Association led me and others to share Green views with local and State government bureaucrats and politicians. An immediate gain for the wider society was the adoption statewide of a revised attitude to planning for rural resettlement, with policies still evolving under the title of "Multiple Occupancy". This represents a new approach to community settlement patterns and opens the way for more ecologically sensitive land use and a rural decentralisation.

The next interaction culminated later in 1979 when alternative land use settlers gathered together to insist on a halt to local rain-forest logging. Those with our aspirations had logically been drawn to settle close to the most natural (untouched or wild) environments that we could manage, so as not to lose touch with what we perceived as vital to the resurrection of human spirit and in keeping with our understanding of wholeness in creation as it once was. This vital rainforest resource was therefore fiercely defended, as if it were life itself—which it virtually was, especially for those of us who had committed themselves to the rigors and demands of starting from scratch in the task of coming to terms with nature without overpowering it.

This experience, and the politically successful outcome, resulted in political know-how and insight for many. It also powerfully reinforced belief in the power of the individual in cooperative company; the growth of the individual through caring and sharing; and the rightness of the cause of preserving nature. The month-long direct action could be sustained by so many for so long simply because most were resident in the area—a lesson in the inherent power of local people over local decision-making. This action had broader outcomes by contributing through the media to public awareness of the plight of rainforests generally throughout the State and the nation.

Further Green actions followed, with a three-month defence of a nearby coastal dune system and forest which were being destroyed by sand-mining for minerals related to, as we discovered, nuclear weapons, nuclear power plants and the aerospace industries. Then followed participation with others in forming a local "People for Peace" organisation; getting our city declared a Nuclear-Free Peace Zone; establishing a local Environment Centre; initiating a nationwide network for sharing information on sustainable settlement, named the "Australian Association for Sustainable Communities"; conducting public awareness election campaigns by standing a team for the NSW

Upper House in 1981 on Green issues, gaining more than 20,000 votes, and standing in 1983 for the federal Senate elections; and campaigning against the Franklin dam, uranium mining and for Aboriginal land rights. In 1986 I initiated an International Year of Peace "Peace Train" which travelled for nine months around Australia promoting personal empowerment, networking and positive grassroots action.

A strong, regional "alternative" community base, capable of providing adequate social interaction and information support, has been important in sustaining these actions. For me personally, it has been vital, enabling me to have a home-base community capable of carrying on with land development and family commitments as well as to participate for long periods in direct action for change.

I have endeavoured so far to sketch the history of one person's path to exploring and initiating changes and ventures aimed at wholesome authentic living for self, family and society within the confines of Australia's current social order. Elements of a personal philosophy have been made evident. Also evident is the inevitable interweaving of efforts to develop an appropriate community for rural settlement, with action for change in the greater Australian society.

Aspirations and commitments of others in the alternative lifestyle movement vary in emphasis and kind. Recently surveys have been carried out, both in Australia and overseas. I suggest that readers refer to *Communes in Rural Australia, The Movement since 1970* by Margaret Munro-Clark for a broader understanding. However I will summarise the common thrusts of Munro-Clark's argument and its relevance to the Green movement as I see it.

Clearly an underlying motivation is to seek a personally more fulfilling and less externally controlled lifestyle — one which allows for growth in self-awareness and "self-actualisation" — and to recognise that time was too often sacrificed in the attaining and the retaining of material things and career or social status rather than in experiencing being. Also prominent are aspirations to eat and live more wholesomely for oneself and one's family; to experience the self-respect of growing food and providing shelter for one's self and family; to establish a buffer against dependence on and the influence of a socio–economic process seen in varying degrees to be unsustainable, destructive, exploitative, oppressive or unauthentic.

Throughout the settlement movement there is strong identification with the peace movement since non-violence is probably the most commonly held value — including not oppressing others and not needlessly disturbing other life forms. Seeking non-violent approaches to conflict resolution, taking action to minimise the causes of conflict and eliminating current national defence techniques which are extremely damaging to the environment and to our reserves of energy and minerals are some of the elements seen as vital for world peace. Another common feature of the settlement movement is the belief that we should focus on the process rather than on the goal, and that the qualities of the goal must be present in the way of achieving it. Hence peace can only be sought by peaceful, non-oppressive methods.

Living out one's beliefs can be important in developing realistic views. Within the settlement movement a more balanced view of the "new paradigm" has been evolving. This is based on personal experiences and constitutes an idealism moderated with a healthy dose of pragmatism. For instance: for a time order can be dispensed with for the sake of freedom, and this can lead to a preference for flexible and changeable order; the "exploit nature" versus "valuing nature for its own sake" tension can be resolved with an approach based on interaction; the "material" versus "non-material" debate can entail recognition that the "good" life requires a balance in developing both. The maturation which has produced these resolutions also reflects the common aspirations — that is, the striving for a "both winners" rather than the anticipating of a "win/lose" outcome in resolving conflict.

Perhaps only a minority of us sought initially to develop models capable of influencing society as a whole. Nevertheless, being part of an alternative *within* society and not an alternative to it resulted in many of us becoming involved one way or another in responding to, or participating in, the control mechanisms of society at large. Most settlers originated in the cities, which many experienced as unsatisfying if not unwholesome. Many in fact perceive cities as equivalent to a cancer which if not treated as such will ultimately destroy the body of the nation or the earth itself. Contributing factors such as isolation from the means and effects of agribusiness in producing their food, the inevitable concentration of pollutants, their need for centralised energy sources (fossil fuels and nuclear), and the dehumanising effects of crowding are well recognised. And the response of establishing cooperative community rural settlements deals directly and positively with these endangering factors.

Many settlers who at present depend on social security benefits would probably justify their position on the cost benefits to society of establishing themselves in this alternative way, and because they are pioneering agricultural and social options which might well pay handsome dividends for society in the future. Certainly this lifestyle as it stands, and according to the current economic criteria, does not offer a viable alternative economic order for Australian society. Nor is it commonly perceived, in its current form, to be capable of providing cultural and social rewards available within the urban context.

However, no serious commitment by society as a whole has been taken in establishing the necessary infrastructure, and adapting industries, so as to suit a decentralised and renewable-energy sourced economy. If this were done and its high-technology developments (adequately scrutinised for their global resource as well as for their polluting and exploitative effects) were designed to provide for communication and culture sharing between dispersed, intimate, interdependent rural communities, then the need for cities would largely disappear. The inhabitants of such communities, through self-interest and the opportunity to be directly aware of their effects, would care for their local environment—visibly the source of their nourishment and pleasure.

A major tension has existed during the movement's growth: the question is whether to focus effort on direct social action, or to focus effort on self-growth, on raising personal consciousness and hence on altering behaviour. The experience of the past decade or so has brought an awareness that both are essential. Significantly the notion of "personal politics" has arisen, according to which our most fundamental political act is the way we live. Many community settlers would feel that they have taken the first important steps towards self-reliance and self-management and that their sense of self and of a strong community base is fundamental to their participation in determining their future and the directions of society at large. Furthermore they have gained considerable experience in determining their real needs and how they prefer to satisfy them.

Margaret Munro-Clark believes that, if one is to follow the analysis of the New Left, then "consciousness-raising is the beginning of effective resistance to economic and political forms of oppression"[1] and Jerry Rubin has declared, "Awareness of self is the final step to awareness of cultural oppression. In fact, true self-awareness leads to the realisation that full self-growth is impossible in a corrupt, repressed and polluted society. The final therapy is a social revolution."[2]

Furthermore, although mainstream society is generally unaware of it, there is a high degree of employment (unpaid of course) in many "alternative" communities and considerable acquisition of skills of all kinds taking place, eg in building, horticulture, mechanics, healing, social work, stonemasonry, forestry, animal husbandry and so on.

Commonly these communities seek individual autonomy together with community solidarity—both essential to the sustainability of social groups. Many rural communities serve the Green movement as places used by countless visitors from urban centres for respite, regeneration, and inspiration. Many thereby become more aware of the changes they want and of what is possible.

Some of the greatest concerns of the Green movement arise out of what is perceived as gross overconsumption. The growing sense of frustration and meaninglessness experienced by many in urban life is all too often suppressed by resorting to excesses of consumption in one form or another. The emphasis placed by alternative communities on personal satisfaction through creative activity or non-materialistic aspirations can help to address this growing problem. Margaret Munro-Clark, writing on the relevance of rural "alternative" communities to the wider society, states:

Nevertheless, if we suppose some marked and sudden change in our fortunes as a society, it may not perhaps be too romantic to suggest that cultural patterns evolving among today's rural communards could prove to be the forerunners of more radically cooperative forms of social and economic organisation. One necessary condition, at least, many of them have already achieved: that of a relative detachment from consumerism and from materialistic definitions of the good life. [3]

It would seem that for equality of access to essential resources, for sustainable resource usage and for minimum ecological disturbance, it will be necessary for basic values to change such that personal worth is not judged on the accumulation of material wealth; and it will also be necessary for people to cease to be employed in many of the current work options.

In referring to the "alternative" society of northern NSW, Munro-Clark declares:

It has the rare character of being an Australian cultural niche in which a low cash-income and a materially simple standard of living are acceptable for adults of good education and middle-class background, and in which personal identity is not based in some career-structure. [4]

Probably the major contribution that "alternative" communities can make to mainstream society will be to offer insights or proven approaches and to warn against mistakes in the event of a catastrophe such as war, or social, economic or ecological collapse; or more optimistically, in the event that sufficient awareness, intelligence and courage lead to efforts for change so as to preempt such a catastrophe. It seems, however, that this will require a change in our society's power structures and decision-making processes.

The priority for the Green political movement now is not so much to enunciate the crises but rather to present clear policies, proposals and strategies for restructuring our socio-economic processes. The new processes must satisfy the real needs of the people—which we must all come to understand—and must be psychically, socially and ecologically sustainable.

For myself, I cannot conceive of more satisfactory substitutes for living out one's ideas for change, for learning-by-doing and for confronting oneself directly with one's growth needs than close community living. And I believe that it is only by being close to relatively natural surroundings that we can hope to understand our place in an evolving planetary system.

From this point of view the sustainable community settlement movement is playing, I believe, an important part in the ever strengthening Green political movement.

EDITOR'S AFTERWORD

For the most part, the contributors to this book have voluntarily limited their scope to the nature of Green philosophy and politics. An equally important question, however, is how we are going to make the transition to a socially caring, democratic and ecologically responsible society. This is obviously the stuff of future publications but, before ending this book, I would like to make some observations on how this process might occur. This is especially important today when, more and more it seems, the world we know is becoming less and less sustainable. In the words of W. B. Yeats,

> *Things fall apart; the centre cannot hold;*
> *Mere anarchy is loosed upon the world . . . .*

One of my favourite authors, the ever-optimistic Theodore Roszak, reacts to these lines by Yeats by saying:

> *But sometimes societies fall apart in ways that release life-affirming energies. And what may look like anarchy from the viewpoint of the established cultural centre may be the troubled birth of a new, more humanly becoming social order. There are creative, as well as destructive, forms of disintegration . . . My purpose is to suggest that the environmental anguish of the Earth has entered our lives as a radical transformation of human identity. The needs of the planet and the needs of the person have become one, and together they have begun to act upon the central institutions of our society with a force that is profoundly subversive, but which carries within it the promise of cultural renewal.*

Unfortunately, Roszak is only half right. When things fall apart, many people react in positive, creative ways but others are fearful, lost and even terror-filled. When things fall apart in society as a whole, this fearful reaction can take the form of political authoritarianism and the suppression of scapegoated groups in the community.

Australia is approaching such a point. As the traditional realities of Australian life—the family, the local community, the welfare state, full employment, the arbitration system and industrial protection, white racial supremacy and the dependability of a "great and powerful friend" — begin to disappear under the pressure of economic crises, then the appeal of someone like Joh Bjelke-Petersen increases.

However, other possibilities also appear. Many people in Australia are repelled by the New Right's attacks on the democratic process and its single-minded quest for profits at the expense of the things that many people value — nature, wilderness, viable community life, even people's basic humanity. At the same time, they are disgusted by the way in which the Labor Party has prepared the way for the New Right with its policies of economic deregulation, its acceptance of the goal of "development" as a far higher priority than conservation, and its rejection of an independent foreign policy.

The time is right for a new, reforming initiative in Australian politics — one that goes beyond the dull pragmatism of social democracy, the sterility and undemocratic nature of the traditional Left, and the limited scope of liberalism. This new initiative will have to develop a strategy for social change which is both visionary and achievable. I would suggest that such a strategy would have the following elements.

Firstly, it is necessary to maintain certain issues on the political agenda despite the attempts of everyone in mainstream politics, from Hawke to Bjelke-Petersen, to remove them. These concerns include the environment, opposition to the nuclear industry, affirmative action for the disadvantaged, economic self-reliance, independent non-nuclear defence and foreign policies, and Aboriginal land rights. At present, this is being done by the social movements operating on a single-issue basis and the Australian Democrats in the Senate. Perhaps, in the near future, more holistic campaigns (which stress the *connections* between issues) can be waged; Democrats in the Senate can be joined by some radical Greens.

Secondly, we need to formulate a vision for Australia. At present, we have only two political alternatives before us — the conservativism of the ALP and sections of the Liberals, and the fascism of the New Right. Our vision should be of a caring, democratic, ecologically responsible society which is expressed in a clear, precise form — such as a Charter of Principles — and which is presented to the people of

Australia at conferences, seminars, discussion groups, through the independent media (whatever is left after the takeovers) and, of course, in elections. It is important to point out that this vision does not exist only in the sky or in some people's heads but is also embodied in the things that people are doing and building all around Australia.

For me, the best summation of a Green strategy is: "Flatten *alpha* (hierarchical, centralised, competitive) structures and reinforce *beta* (community based, egalitarian, cooperative) structures". To do this we need to accept that some functions (like national defence and, probably, a workable social welfare system) are best carried out in *alpha* structures. However, it should also be obvious that such structures are far too strong and far too numerous and, therefore, we should work to make them more democratic and responsive. Merv Partridge dealt with how this might be done in the areas of investment and the workplace. Jack Mundey's chapter showed graphically how Green principles can be introduced into trade unions. And the same could be true for all institutions which have the potential for democratic involvement. The "flattening of *alpha* structures" approach also means involvement in elections and, hopefully the formation of governments. Here, the example of the Greater London Council provides some inspiration. Its policies of providing support for community groups, for anti-discrimination programs and for locally based, socially responsible and environmentally sound industry have mapped out a path which Green governments might fruitfully pursue. Certainly, Greens have to be seen to be interested in job creation or they will earn only the hostility of workers. However, they will have to show workers that high technology along with the destruction of nature does not necessarily constitute the most productive method of job creation.

The heart of Green politics, though, is communitarian. The Green movement needs to support the extension of "new wave" cooperatives and ethical investment projects, community based cultural programs, urban organic farms and gardens, sustainable agriculture, alternative newspapers and magazines, holistic educational programs for children, and appropriate technology enterprises. These will become the cultural and economic bases on which the Green movement can present, to fearful people caught in a crisis-ridden world, the prospect of a peaceful, sustainable and achievable future.

DREW HUTTON
Brisbane, 1987

ENDNOTES

1: WHAT IS GREEN POLITICS?

1. Jack Mundey, *Green Bans and Beyond*, Angus & Robertson, Sydney, 1981.

2. W. J. Weston, *Transport and Trade*, Nisbet, London, 1929.

3. Quoted in Bill Devall and George Sessions, *Deep Ecology*, Peregrine Smith Books, Salt Lake City, 1985.

4. B. Maranta, *Grade 8 History*, Brooks, Brisbane, 1964, p. 68.

5. Quoted in Noam Chomsky, *For Reasons of State*, Fontana, Bungay, Suffolk, 1970, pp. 94–5.

6. E. P. Thompson, "Notes on Exterminism: The Last Stage of Civilization", in E. P. Thompson (ed.), *Exterminism and Cold War*, Verso, London, 1982, p. 9.

7. ibid., pp. 4–5.

8. Jonathon Porritt, *Seeing Green: The Politics of Ecology Explained*, Basil Blackwell, Oxford, 1984, p. 38.

9. Christopher Plant, "From Red to Green", *New Internationalist*, November 1985, p. 19.

10. Jonathon Porritt, "Economic Growth and Mother Nature", *New Internationalist*, no. 157, March 1986, p. 13.

11. Robert Birrell, Doug Hill and John Stanley, *Quarry Australia? Social and Environmental Perspectives on Managing the Nation's Resources*, Oxford University Press, Melbourne, 1982, p. 262.

12. Charles Birch, *Confronting the Future: Australia and the World, the Next Hundred Years*, Penguin, Harmondsworth, 1975.

13. Porritt, op. cit., pp. 10–11.

14. Fritjof Capra, *The Turning Point: Science, Society and the Rising Culture*, Fontana, Bungay, Suffolk, 1982.

15. ibid., p. 38.

16. Quoted in Noam Chomsky, *American Power and the New Mandarins*, Pelican, Harmondsworth, 1969, p. 28.

17. Capra, op. cit., (note 14), p. 66.

18. ibid., p. 77.

19. Stephen Cotgrove, *Catastrophe or Cornucopia: The Environment, Politics and the Future*, John Wiley and Sons, Chichester, 1982, p. 27.

20. Theodore Roszak, *Person/Planet: The Creative Disintegration of Industrial Society*, Victor Gollancz Ltd, London, 1979, p. xix.

21. ibid., pp. 196–7.

22. Chief Seattle's testimony, *United Society for the Propagation of the Gospel*, London.

3: A GREEN PEACE: BEYOND DISARMAMENT

1. Jonathon Porritt and British Campaign for Nuclear Disarmament, *Embrace the Earth*, CND Publishing, London, 1983, p. 42.

2. Community Aid Abroad, *The Arms Trade and the Third World*, discussion sheet no. 4.

3. ibid.

4. *Economic Notes*, New York, February 1975, p. 6.

5. United Nations, *Study on the Relationship Between Disarmament and Development*, October 1981, p. 164.

6. Petra Kelly, *Fighting For Hope*, Chatto and Windus, London, 1984, p. 17.

7. Des Ball, as quoted in an interview in *The Australian* by Jane Ford on 9 June 1984.

8. Brian Toohey, *The National Times*, 4–10 July 1986.

9. International Metalworkers Federation, "Metal Workers Unions and the Armament Industry", *Small Business*, 24 September 1981, p. 268.

10. Marion Anderson, "Impact of Military Spending on the

Machinists Union (IAM)", *Small Business*, 24 September 1981, p. 238.

11. Robert W. De Grasse Jr, *Studies on Military Conversion*, published by the Council on Economic Priorities, 1983.

12. Inga Thorsson, *In Pursuit of Disarmament: Conversion from Military to Civil Production in Sweden*, Stockholm, 1984, p. 48.

4: A GREEN PARTY: CAN THE BOYS DO WITHOUT ONE?

1. For a more detailed account of the campaign, see "Whither the Green Machine?", *Australian Society*, no. 5, 1984, and my Green protest against the old-paradigm editing job on the article in no. 7.

2. Permaculture is a theory of organic farming with maximum use of ecological patterns and minimum energy: Bill Mollison, *Permaculture II*, Stanley, Tas., 1978.

3. The feminist critique "Deeper than Deep Ecology" was published in the journal *Environmental Ethics* (USA), no. 4, 1984.

4. *The Sydney Morning Herald*, 30 November 1985, contains a run-down on this episode in party-political engineering. Ramona Koval's "The Sale of IVF Technology", *Search*, no. 7–8, 1985, outlines some recent Australian feminist concerns and there is a growing international literature: see Rita Arditti et. al., *Test-Tube Women*, Pandora Press, London, 1984, for starters.

5. One Canberra man told me that the press gallery refused to cover the women's action because the position of their camp upset the routine lunch touch-football game on the grass.

6. Theo Adorno and Max Horkheimer, *Dialectic of Enlightenment*, Penguin, Harmondsworth, 1972 and Herbert Marcuse, *One Dimensional Man*, Abacus, London, 1964.

7. Dorothy Dinnerstein, *The Mermaid and the Minotaur*, Harper & Row, New York, 1977 and Nancy Chodorow, *The Reproduction of Mothering*, University of California Press, Berkeley, 1978.

8. Erich Fromm, "Sex and Character", in Ruth Anshen's *The*

Family, Harper, New York, 1949 and Mary O'Brien, *The Politics of Reproduction*, Routledge and Kegan Paul, London, 1981.

9. This fundamental paradigm shift at the level of epistemology is described in Sandra Harding's recent book, *The Science Question in Feminism*, Cornell University Press, 1986. Work on difference by deconstructionists is also relevant; see Toril Moi, *Sexual/Textual Politics*, Methuen, London, 1986. I have written about these things in *Thesis Eleven*.

10. Virginia Coover and others' *Resource Manual for Living Revolution*, Movement for a New Society, Philadelphia, 1977, is a useful introduction to alternative ways of doing politics, including non-violent direct action techniques. Even the cop who trained in our affinity group at the blockade was impressed.

11. Australian Lynne Segal and British feminist Sheila Rowbotham give a moving account of their experiences with socialism in the UK in *Beyond the Fragments*, Merlin, London, 1979. Heidi Hartmann's classic essay, "The Unhappy Marriage of Marxism and Feminism" in Lydia Sargent (ed.), *Women and Revolution*, South End Press, Boston, 1981, suggests the flavour of the debate. At home, a special number of *Intervention* magazine called "Beyond Marxism?", 1983, zeroed in on the problem.

12. See Mary Daly, *Gyn/ecology*, Women's Press, London, 1979; Adrienne Rich, *Of Woman Born*, Bantam, New York, 1977, and Charlene Spretnak, *The Politics of Women's Spirituality*, Anchor, New York, 1982.

13. Just by the by, Val Plumwood was the original Crocodile Dundee. She was attacked while exploring a river in Kakadu, NT, in January 1985 and dragged under water three times by the croc, before finally escaping to run some 10 km in search of help, using strips of clothing to tourniquet her wounds. Later, in Darwin Hospital, Plumwood implored rangers not to take the crocodile's life: "It was her territory, not mine." Plans for the bumper money-spinning film followed not long after press reports of Val's adventure. Its hero was to go down in the Australian legend—as yer Aussie mate, of course.

7: BUILDING A SUSTAINABLE GREEN ECONOMY: ETHICAL INVESTMENT, ETHICAL WORK

1. Herodotus, *The Histories*, Penguin, Ringwood, 1972, p. 369.

2. "Factory of the Future", *Australian Computing*, March 1986.

3. ibid.

4. Norbert Weiner, *The Human Use of Human Beings: Cybernetics and Society*, Anchor Press, Boston, 1954, p. 220.

5. E. F. Schumacher, *Good Work*, Anchor Press Ltd, London, 1979, p. 3.

6. Santa was later convicted and gaoled, but the fact that Queensland had imprisoned a dissident wasn't reported by the mainstream media; Murdoch and Fairfax TV editors seem more comfortable with political prisoners in other countries. Not only did Santa, alias Brian Law break the Queensland law by claiming a right to free expression in the street, he did it again in the court. He asked the judge if he might make a statement about the immorality of nuclear weapons in explanation of his behaviour. Denied leave, Mr Law said, "Then I have no option but to non-cooperate with this court," whereupon he rose to his feet and walked from the court. The judge and police watched him go, flabbergasted. Only hours later did the police arrest him again. Brought back before the same magistrate and again refused leave to speak, Law once more stepped over the law and walked from the court. He was *never* charged with contempt. The state did not have the courage to publicly test its political law prohibiting free speech against Law's moral law. These court appearances were at the height of the SEQEB electricity workers' strike and the last thing the Queensland government wanted was to stir the peace and civil rights movements onto the streets shoulder to shoulder with trade unionists. They waited several months till the strike was defeated before sentencing and gaoling him. Refusing to salute the flag or to otherwise acknowledge the authority of the state to remove his freedom, Law was confined to solitary.

The media and the Left maintained their silence. Special Branch is reserving a second political warrant on Law for its convenience.

7. This is called "job blackmail" by Richard Kazis and Richard L. Grossman. See their book, *Fear at Work: Job Blackmail, Labour and the Environment*, Pilgrim Press, New York, 1982.

8. From J. S. Mill, *Principles of Political Economy*, 1871, quoted in "Workers' Cooperatives as an Alternative Organisational Form: Incorporation or Transformation?" in David Dunkerley and Graeme Salaman (eds), *The International Yearbook of Organisational Studies*, Routledge and Kegan Paul, London, 1980.

9. A. Toynbee, *Mankind and Mother Earth*, Oxford University Press, Oxford, 1976, p. 562–3.

10. ibid., p. 562.

11. See Stuart M. Speiser, "Universal Stock Ownership: A Way to Redistribute Income Without Welfare or Taxes", *Whole Earth Review*, Winter 1986.

12. *Good Money Newsletter*, June 1986.

13. Towards the end of 1986 Geoff passed the Earthbank Secretaryship over to Robert Rosen when he moved to the Maleny region to help design and populate a new cooperative community based on permaculture principles at Crystal Waters. A sort of phoenix rising from the ashes of the Mebbin Springs "alternative city" plan, Crystal Waters aims to be a very active and productive post-industrial community.

14. Figures quoted in "For Love and Money" by Robert Rosen in *Work Matters*, no. 1. The Earthbank Society's address is Box 93, Bowraville, NSW 2449.

15. *Australian Financial Review*, 3.3.87.

16. *News From Unity Trust: The Trade Union Financial Institution*.

17. Mark Burford, "Worker Cooperatives, Employee Ownership and Other Options", Working Paper, September 1986.

18. John Howard, address to the H. R. Nichols Society, 30 September 1986.

19. Stuart M. Speiser, op. cit. (note 10).

20. ibid.

21. Jean Norman, "Credit Card Bartering", *Work Matters*, Summer 1986.

22. George Melynck, *The Search for Community: From Utopia to a Cooperative Society*, Black Rose Books, Montreal, 1985.

23. This principle seems also to apply to the gradual movement of the Yugoslav national economy towards democratic self-management. Since 1974 Yugoslavia has been decentralising economic decision-making and experimenting with a system of enterprise-level planning and worker control. This system has developed out of, and remains surrounded by, centrally planned state socialist economies. See C. Ardalan, "Workers' Self-management and Planning: The Yugoslav Case", *World Development*, vol. 8, 1980, pp. 623–38.

24. Maria Zabaleta, public lecture, Sydney, July 1986.

25. Henk Thomas and Chris Logan, *Mondragon: An Economic Analysis*, George Allen & Unwin, London, 1982.

26. ibid.

27. ibid.

8: GREENING EDUCATION

1. F. Capra, *The Turning Point*, Fontana, London, 1983, p. 462.

2. D. Randle, editorial comment, *Green Teacher*, Preview edition, 1986, p. 1.

3. For supporting arguments see M. Ash, *Green Politics: The New Paradigm*, The Green Alliance, London, 1980, also C. Spretnak and F. Capra, *Green Politics: The Global Promise*, Hutchinson, London, 1984. For opposing arguments see J. Weston (ed.), *Red and Green: A New Politics of the Environment*, Pluto Press, London, 1986, esp. ch. 1.

4. R. Mochelle, "Future Choice—An Environment Design Approach", *Curriculum Perspectives*, vol. 6, no. 2, 1986.

5. D. N. Michael and W. T. Anderson, "Norms in Conflict and Confusion", in H. Didsbury (ed.), *Challenges and Opportunities: From Now to 2001*, World Future Society, Washington, 1986, p. 114.

6. W. W. Harman, "Colour the Future Green? The Uncertain Significance of Global Green Politics", *Futures*, vol. 17, no. 4, 1985, p. 325.

7. ibid.

8. Michael and Anderson, op. cit. (note 5).

9. *Oxford English Dictionary*.

10. A. E. Greenall, "Environmental Education: A Case Study in National Curriculum Action", *Environmental Education and Information*, vol. 1, no. 4, 1981, p. 286.

11. A. E. Greenall, *Environmental Education in Australia: Phenomenon of the Seventies*, Curriculum Development Centre (Occasional Paper no. 7), Canberra, 1981, p. 257.

12. F. Emery, "Educational Paradigms", *Human Futures*, Spring 1981.

13. W. A. Reid, "The Deliberative Approach to the Study of the Curriculum and its Relation to Critical Pluralism", in M. Lawn and L. Barton (eds), *Rethinking Curriculum Studies*, Croom Helm, London, 1982.

14. Emery, op. cit. (note 12), p. 2.

15. ibid., p. 3.

16. F. Heider, *On Perception and Event Structure and the Psychological Environment: Selected Papers*, International Universities Press, New York, 1959.

17. J. J. Gibson, "Visually Controlled Locomotion and Visual Orientation in Animals", *British Journal of Psychology*, vol. 49, 1958; *The Senses Considered as Perceptual Systems*, Houghton Mifflin, Boston, 1966, and *The Ecological Approach to Visual Perception*, Houghton Mifflin, Boston, 1979.

18. R. Shaw and J. Pittenger, "Perceiving the Face of Change in Changing Faces", in R. Shaw and J. Bransford, *Perceiving Action and Knowing: Toward an Ecological Psychology*, Wiley, New York, 1977, ch. 5.

19. Emery, op. cit. (note 12), pp. 6–7.

20. E. de Bono, *Learning to Think*, Penguin, Harmondsworth, 1979, p. 77.

21. Emery, op. cit. (note 12), p. 15.

22. R. McKeon, "Person and Community: Metaphysical and Political", *Ethics*, vol. 88, 1977, p. 208.

23. Quoted in Reid, op. cit. (note 13), pp. 173–4.

24. N. Gough, *Curriculum Programs for Practical Learning*, Education Department of Victoria, Melbourne, 1985.

25. *Home Economics—Human Development and Society* (1985) and *Textiles* (1983), Higher School Certificate Course Descriptions, Victorian Institute of Secondary Education, Melbourne.

26. Personal Development Centre, Curriculum Branch, Education Department of Victoria, *Curriculum Newsletter*, vol. 3, no. 2, 1986.

27. Victoria, Minister of Education, "Ministerial Paper No. 6: Curriculum Development and Planning in Victoria", Government Printer, Melbourne, 1984.

28. C. Stern and M. Stern, *Children Discover Arithmetic*, Harper & Row, New York, 1971.

29. E. Gibson, *Principles of Perceptual Learning and Development*, Prentice-Hall, New York, 1969; E. Gibson and H. Levin, *The Psychology of Reading*, M.I.T. Press, Cambridge, Mass., 1975; F. Hughes, *Reading in Writing Before School*, Pan, London, 1971.

30. S. Van Matre, *Sunship Earth*, American Camping Association, Martinsville, Ind., 1979, p. 5.

31. ibid., pp. 6–7.

32. Emery, op. cit. (note 12), p. 7.

33. Van Matre, op. cit. (note 30), p. 8.

34. ibid.

35. G. Boomer (ed.), *Negotiating the Curriculum*, Ashton Scholastic, Sydney, p. 119.

36. Adapted from Emery, op. cit. (note 12), p. 15.

37. Van Matre, op. cit. (note 30), p. 5.

38. M. Grumet, "Restitution and Reconstruction of Educational Experience: An Autobiographical Method for Curriculum Theory", in Lawn and Barton, op. cit. (note 13), p. 115.

39. Randle, op. cit. (note 2).

40. For an outline of such a "critical futures study" see R. Slaughter, "Towards a Critical Futurism", *World Future Society Bulletin*, vol. 18, no. 4, 1984 and "Critical Futures Study — A Dimension of Curriculum Work", *Curriculum Perspectives*, vol. 6, no. 2, 1986.

9: CHRISTIANITY AND GREEN POLITICS

1. *The National Times*, 25 June 1986.

2. ibid.

3. Luke 1: 51–53.

4. James Cone, *A Black Theology of Liberation*, J. B. Lippincott, Philadelphia, 1970, p. 95.

5. Kim Chi Ha, "The Dream of Revolutionary Religion" in John C. England (ed.), *Living Theology in Asia*, S.C.M. Press, London, 1981, p. 21.

6. Ian M. Frazer, *The Fire Runs*, S.C.M. Press, London, 1975, p. 5.

7. Matthew 20: 25.

8. Michael Wilson, *Health Is for People*, S.C.M. Press, London, 1976, p. 108.

9. James Robertson, *A Sane Alternative*, Villiers Publications, London, 1978.

10: BUILDING COMMUNITIES: THE GREEN ALTERNATIVE

1. Margaret Munro-Clark, *Communes in Rural Australia, the Movement Since 1970*, Hale & Iremonger, Sydney, 1986.

2. Jerry Rubin, quoted in Munro-Clark, op. cit., p. 86.

3. Munro-Clark, op. cit.

4. ibid.